TRAINING
CREATIVE THINKING

TRAINING CREATIVE THINKING

Gary A. Davis
University of Wisconsin

Joseph A. Scott
Chico State College
Chico, California

ROBERT E. KRIEGER PUBLISHING COMPANY
HUNTINGTON, NEW YORK
1978

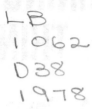
Original edition 1971
Reprint 1978

Printed and Published by
ROBERT E. KRIEGER PUBLISHING COMPANY, INC.
645 NEW YORK AVENUE
HUNTINGTON, NEW YORK 11743

Printed in the United States of America

Library of Congress Cataloging in Publication Data

Davis, Gary A., 1938-   comp.
  Training creative thinking.

  Reprint of the ed. published by Holt, Rinehart and Winston,
New York.
  Includes bibliographies.
  1. Creative thinking (Education)   I.   Scott, Joseph A.
II.   Title.
[LB1062.D38   1978]   153.3'5'07   78-8376
ISBN 0-88275-688-5

*To Pearl and Von Davis
and Eileen Scott*

Preface to the 1978 Edition

A funny thing has been happening in the world of creativity. Since the original publication of *Training Creative Thinking* in 1971, interest has grown steadily in exactly the sorts of concepts, creative thinking techniques, and training programs summarized in these chapters. For example, we initially liked Bill Bordon's *synectics* ideas well enough to devote our first three chapters to the topic. Today, synectics is virtaully a household word, and Gordon's genius is recognized not only in regard to professional creative problem solving, but for the very imaginative workbooks (for example, *Making It Strange*) developed for elementary and junior high students. Robert Crawford's attribute listing strategy (Chapter 5) is still taught in every creative thinking course and workbook, and the technique remains as elegant and effective as when he developed the concept in the 1930's. Of course, such abilities and the creative personality (Chapters 6 and 14), creativity testing (Chapter 23), and obstacles to creativity (Chapter 9) are timeless.

More and more, educators are coming to recognize the significance of deliberate training in creative and problem solving skills. As Paul Torrance often noted, what is rewarded in a culture will flourish. At present, "rewards" are funneled into programs which challenge the creative and intellectual wits of both "average" and "gifted" children. The many chapters on strengthening creative thinking in the schools (Chapter 15 through 22) furnish suggestions and guidelines for stimulating creative development in all students.

We naturally are delighted *Training Creative Thinking* has been reprinted, and we wish to thank Bob Krieger for his cooperation, effort and faith.

GAD
JAS

Preface

The purpose of this book is to examine various strategies for increasing creative productivity, particularly in industry and the schools. Intelligent consideration of these programs and procedures, however, would be impossible without a working knowledge of some important characteristics of creativity and creative individuals. Consequently, in addition to the emphasis on training imagination, the articles analyze such critical variables as the physical and psychological atmosphere which encourages or stifles imagination, intellectual and nonintellectual characteristics of creative individuals, testing for creativity, personal and social barriers to creative imagination, "selling" one's ideas, plus other important facets of creative behavior. Combined with the main strategies presented in this volume, these topics should present a comprehensive picture of *what* to teach when teaching creativity, *how* to teach it, and *why* it should be taught.

While intended primarily as a college text for business, engineering, psychology, and education students, this volume should interest persons in other fields concerned with understanding and developing creative imagination. Also, regardless of his main field of interest, the reader will find that the articles complement each other to a considerable degree: the "business" articles (Chapters 1–13) have much to say to educators, psychologists, and others; similarly, management and engineering personnel undoubtedly can benefit from psychological research (Chapters 14–15) and from educational training and testing programs (Chapters 16–23). There is no doubt that many components of creative behavior may be strengthened, and it is to this end that the present volume is directed.

The critical role of creative innovation in our rapidly changing society cannot be overstated. Since our cave-dwelling ancestors discovered fire and chiseled their first tools, the study of civilization has been a panorama of the effects of new ideas upon the health, safety, comfort, convenience, education, and entertainment of man. But even in view of such astounding advances in science and medicine as our huge Saturn rockets, heart transplants, atomic reactors, and color television, there is no reason to believe that the development of such extraordinary creations will decrease. In fact, with such modern tools as computers, electron microscopes, and solid-state electronic devices, the rate of innovation should continue to accelerate.

It also is important to note that the scientists, industrialists, politicians, artists, writers, and medical researchers of the future are currently in our schools. Yet present educational practices typically fail to foster creative growth; they perhaps even stifle the imaginations of our students. We might reasonably ask if there are not some means of improving the potential of both our present and future creative talent. Our own conclusion is a definite "yes."

During the past twenty years, interest in the deliberate training of creative thinking has skyrocketed. Attempting primarily to improve the imaginations of business and engineering students, many universities offer courses in creative problem solving. Also, influenced directly or indirectly by the Creative Education Foundation, an increasing number of "blue chip" corporations—IBM, RCA, Sylvania, Xerox, General Motors, Dow Chemical, and General Electric, to name a few—have initiated creative-problem-solving programs primarily for engineers and management personnel.

In elementary and secondary education, the teaching of creative-problem-solving skills has long been proclaimed an important goal. Unfortunately, teachers rarely have been advised of precisely what they should teach and how they should teach it. This is changing. Several theory-based creativity programs have emerged which structure the training of imagination—the *Productive Thinking Program* of Covington, Crutchfield, and Davies (Chapter 20), the *Idea Books* of Myers and Torrance (described in Chapter 21), *Thinking Creatively* by Davis and Houtman (Chapter 21), and the *Creative Behavior Guidebook* by Parnes (1967).[1] In addition to providing a creative atmosphere, these programs foster appropriate attitudes, strengthen innate abilities, and teach systematic, creative-problem-solving techniques.

The roots of the current surge of interest in developing creativity reach back to the 1930s. As a professor of journalism at the University of Nebraska, Robert P. Crawford in 1931 initiated the very first creative-thinking course which evolved from his *attribute-listing* interpretation of creative behavior (see Chapter 5). A few years later in 1937, A. R. Stevenson helped General Electric launch its creativity-training program. The next year the late Alex F. Osborn—of the New York advertising agency Batten, Barton, Dursten, and Osborn and author of *Applied Imagination* —began conducting his famed brainstorming sessions.

While there is no doubt that the earliest and still most "solid" contributions to training imagination originated in the business world, psychologists have not been idle. More interested in understanding creativity than trying to train it, psychologists sought to identify the unique characteristics and abilities of creative individuals. Such notable research as that of Barron (Chapter 14), MacKinnon (Chapter 15), Guilford (1962),[2] and Torrance (1962,[3] 1965[4]) has shed much light on the nature of creative talent, with an added impetus to the development of tests for creativity and, in Torrance's case, materials intended to strengthen many specific traits and abilities (see Chapter 23).

Although representatives of the business world have drawn freely from creativity research and theory in psychology, this line of communication has been astonishingly one-way. Apart from a passing acquaintance with brainstorming, an exceedingly small number of psychologists are aware of the existence of either the well-established training programs in industry or such professional problem-solving organizations as Synectics,

---

[1] S. J. Parnes, *Creative Behavior Guidebook* (New York: Scribner, 1967).

[2] J. P. Guilford, "Creativity: Its Measurement and Development," in S. J. Parnes and H. F. Harding, eds., *A Source Book for Creative Thinking* (New York: Scribner, 1962).

[3] E. P. Torrance, *Guiding Creative Talent* (Englewood Cliffs, N.J.: Prentice-Hall, 1962).

[4] E. P. Torrance, *Rewarding Creative Behavior* (Englewood Cliffs, N.J.: Prentice-Hall, 1965).

Inc., and Harbridge House. The Creative Education Foundation, established in 1954, is markedly improving communication among those in psychology, industry, science, education, and the arts. This communication took a giant step forward with the 1967 inauguration of the *Journal of Creative Behavior*.

We are grateful to Susan E. Houtman for her valuable assistance in the writing of this preface and most chapter headnotes and to Thomas F. Warren, Terence L. Belcher, and William E. Roweton for their generous aid in preparing the final manuscript.

January 1970   Gary A. Davis
                                                                          Joseph A. Scott

Contents

TRAINING
CREATIVE THINKING

1 | Synectics: inventing by the madness method

TOM. ALEXANDER
Fortune *magazine*

Reproduced by permission © 1965, Time, Inc., from Fortune, 1965, 72 (2), 165–168, 190, 193–194. Cartoon "Bill Gordon" is reproduced by permission of Al Capp.

The impact of *synectics* upon the field of creativity easily justifies devoting three chapters to this important concept. Taken from the Greek *syneticos,* meaning the joining together of unrelated elements, synectics is many things: an organization, a set of methods for generating creative ideas, a group problem-solving strategy, and perhaps above all, a flexible state of mind. The metaphor-based synectics, originated by William J. J. Gordon, is indeed an exciting example of how creativity may be deliberate and systematic, yet productive. In this chapter headed by an Al Capp portrayal of a typical synectics session, Tom Alexander, Associate Editor of *Fortune* magazine, sketches the background of Gordon which, along with the transcript of a problem-solving group, should give the reader a feel for the synectics atmosphere and procedures.

By listening to the faint urgings of the nonrational parts of their minds, says Synectics, Inc., corporate problem solvers can tap creativity that evades cool logic. Some big industrial clients are learning to exploit their own daydreams.

JACK: O.K., the date is March 4, 1965, the PAG is "How to make a finished gear round," the PAU is "How to grind gear without rounding" . . . O.K., start off with rounding as the key word. We need a direct analogy first.

ALEX: How about pregnancy? Swelling abdomen—rounding?

BILL: When I think of rounding, I think about the universe.

Al Capp, the creator of Li'l Abner, is also a close friend of William J. J. Gordon, founder and chairman of Synectics, Inc. Accordingly, *Fortune* asked Capp to try to evoke the spirit of a Synectics invention session with the hand that applied free association in a Dogpatch setting. Delighted by the assignment, Capp caricatured a session tackling the problem of designing a wheelchair that could climb stairs.

The leader was Gordon himself, who appears as the black-sweatered character in the drawings. Gordon began by asking the group for some "direct analogies," i.e., some

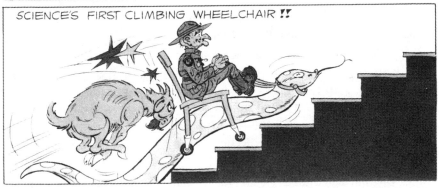

strange examples, of "climbing." From the suggestions, he picked "mountain goat" for further discussion. For a deeper look at the way a mountain goat operates, Gordon asked for "personal analogies"—how the participants would feel if they were mountain goats.

Some thought they would be nervous, some thought confident, but from one came this typical Synectics response: "I think I'll just be one of the hind legs. In fact, I'll be the muscles of one hind leg. As the goat flexes for his jump, I tighten. I get small . . . Then, wham! I get the signal and shoot out."

Gordon next asked them to sum up the essence of goats' leg muscles into a "symbolic analogy"—an abstract two- or three-word statement. After some discussion, they finally agreed that "blind direction" was an acceptable symbolic analogy.
Next Gordon asked for a direct analogy for "blind direction." One man suggested a snake pit, where snakes strike at things "blindly but with unthinking direction."

A discussion about snakes ensued, during which someone said that "in the jungle movies it always looks as if the snake is screwing himself up the outside of the tree." The group came noisily alive at this last remark—typical of the apparently irrelevant but actually highly suggestive observations Synectics teaches people to look for. The eventual result was not quite what Capp envisions above, but rather a design for a wheelchair that propels itself upstairs on long rotating screws.

HORACE: Marble.

JACK: Let's take a symbolic analogy of marble.

JIM: Ah—aged hardness.

BILL: Rainbowed constancy.

ALEX: Infinite inconsistencies.

GORDON: Might have been fun to ask him what was on his mind on that "rainbowed constancy"—unless you knew.

BILL: The glass marble has many colors . . . they're all in different patterns, very brilliant . . . yet it's a very uniform overall thing.

HORACE: You know you said something that gives me one . . . before we lose it I'll say it: watered reflections.

JACK: Let's expand on "watered reflection."

JIM: I'd be inclined to do a PA on that one.

JACK: O.K. . . . You start one since you like it.

JIM: Well, let's see, I'm a very still lake—and I get tremendous enjoyment from reflecting all the objects that come over me—and I'm terribly upset when the wind blows and the ripples form so that the reflections can't be transmitted.

HORACE: Ripples destroy the reflections.

JIM: Yeah, ripples ruin me.

BILL: On that same lake, let me get in here. I have enjoyment from the knowledge . . . that the waters from me give birth to little streams but I'm especially proud when I realize that some of the waters which come from me leave me in evaporation . . . I see this beautiful colored rainbow. I realize this is a child of mine . . .

JIM: Mother of the rainbow.

ALEX: How about this—I'm a memory way, way back. It's very indistinct, hazy and far away . . . The memory is watered down, diluted—diluted memory.

JACK: Well, we've got enough words here . . . Do any of these words suggest anything that we can bring back and close the loop?

JIM: I like "diluted memory."

HORACE: You want something that's pliable! You want to put in something that will hold the gears and that will be pliable enough not to round them up.

BILL: If you had rubber—some kind of rubber compound you could put over the arbor . . . Of course, you could have your steel center—I assume you grind these on a center.

JIM: Yeah.

BILL: You shove the gear on this arbor and of course the rubber seat takes the shape of the inside of the gear, yet the steel center would remain intact.

JIM: If you're going to go to a rubber or a spongy type of material, one of the ways you could get additional friction or grappling power is to have on the outside of that a brake-band type of material . . .

JACK: Say, that's a real good thought. It's always steel and tends to turn. You'd add friction to the O.D. of the arbor . . .

The tape recorded dialogue above is the birth of an invention—a rubber-covered machine-tool arbor for holding ring gears while they are being ground to final specifications. It solves a problem that has plagued the precision gear industry for years: how to prevent the gears from becoming distorted in manufacture. The arbor has been put into use at Steel Products Engineering, of Springfield, Ohio, a division of the Kelsey-Hayes Co., and according to division President James S. Wilkerson, it will save the company many thousands of dollars in rejected gears every year. Wilkerson, a gruff and down-to-earth forty-five-year-old mechanical engineer, was the Jim in the recorded session who said he was the "very still lake" that got "terribly upset" when the wind formed ripples on his surface. Alex was William R. Alexander, the company's engineering vice president, and Jack was John Copeland, manufacturing vice president.

Earlier this year the three men had presented themselves at the white painted door of a remodeled warehouse near Harvard Square, Cambridge. Thumbtacked to the door was a strip of cardboard with the words "Synectics, Inc." Inside, the three officers had made their way up a skeletal spiral iron staircase and thence into a large room resembling the loft studio of a Greenwich Village artist. The room was furnished with three sofas, twenty director-type canvas chairs, a few rough tables made of sawed-off blocks of wood, a nude wooden statue, many books, a worn Oriental rug, some crude working models of mechanical devices, and a couple of large professional-model tape recorders with earphones.

This is the headquarters of a company whose business is being "consultants on the creative process"; it claims expertise in the "psychology of invention" and the "sociology of innovation," and for a fee of between $20,000 and $200,000—depending on the size of the training group—it proposes to teach executives of a client firm how to tap their inventive potential. The men who run Synectics, Inc., say the methods they teach are a conscious imitation of the largely unconscious mental processes of gifted inventors.

Jim Wilkerson well remembers his reaction on arriving at Synectics: "I wondered what I had gotten into now. I was expecting a bunch of nuts in beards and sandals." He did find some startling personalities in paint-stained khakis and sneakers, but in other respects the week that followed was surprising. "By the end of the week," says Wilkerson, "I was thoroughly enjoying myself." Furthermore, when he and his two vice presidents got back to Springfield, they enthusiastically began dragging startled engineers and master mechanics into sessions just as dreamlike as the one at Synectics. Within a month and a half after their return they were pointing to solutions to several nagging old mechanical problems.

Harnessing with metaphors

The word Synectics is a neologism, based on the Greek, and meaning "the fitting together of diverse elements." The little company in Cambridge sees itself as fitting together the diverse thoughts and insights that stem from many different fields of science, technology, and business practice. Among Synectics' working hypotheses are these: (1) that creativity is latent in almost everyone to a greater degree than is usually suspected; (2) that when it comes to creativity and invention, the emotional and nonrational are as important as the intellectual and rational; and (3) that these emotional, nonrational elements can be methodically harnessed through training and practice—especially in metaphorical thinking. Using these hypotheses, the four staff members at Synectics have devised a formalized ritual for summoning creativity's elfin presence.

In many industrial and academic quarters the still evolving attempt is generating enthusiasm; in a few others, disparagement. The Synectics technique has won the attention and blessing of numerous psychologists. There have been attempts to apply the technique in the educational process at several places, including Harvard and elementary schools in the Boston area.

But what counts more, Synectics has had a welcoming response from industry, which well appreciates the price of a good idea and what a generally messy business thinking is. Pupils have flocked to Harvard Square from, among others, the Army Management School, Chicopee Manufacturing Division of Johnson & Johnson, Colgate-Palmolive, Fuller & Smith & Ross, General Electric, I.B.M., Johns Manville, Kimberly-Clark, Monsanto, Pillsbury, Remington Arms, Singer Manufacturing, Esso Research & Engineering, Union Carbide, Western Electric, and Whirlpool. A number of other organizations have sent groups to Synectics for help in solving specific problems; these include the Department of Defense, U.S. Steel, General Motors, and Oneida Silversmiths Ltd. Besides teaching the art of inventing, Synectics also spends a great deal of time with its clients on what it calls "the sociology of innovation." This has to do with the astonishingly difficult chore of getting a good idea through the viscosity of the average company and into the marketplace.

The fastest pigs in the East

Synectics had its origins twenty years ago in the observations and theories of William J. J. Gordon, now forty-five, who is chairman and half owner of the corporation. A few outsiders who were familiar with Gordon's early work, in fact, assert that Synectics *is* Bill Gordon and that without him around it probably wouldn't work for long. This is vigorously denied at Synectics. A complicated and infectiously energetic personality, quite often described as "brilliant" (though sometimes as "brilliant nut"), Gordon has attracted coveys of fervent admirers and a few equally fervent detractors. One acquaintance—who is no disciple—says, "Bill, out of the fullness of his personality, has developed, I think, a new religious order of which he's the principal prophet and for which he has a catechism . . . He's ribald, demanding, egotistical, and also the greatest clown. I've never had so much fun with anybody."

During his formal education Gordon dipped into history, biochemistry, physics, psychology, and philosophy at the universities of Pennsylvania and California, Harvard (A.B. in philosophy), and Boston University. At one point, newly steeped in biochemistry, he retired to a farm in New Hampshire to raise pigs. "I thought I would build a pig that would have only bacon, using vitamins and hormones. What I ended up with was a lot of bone and not much bacon, but they were the fastest pigs in the East. They could jump four feet."

At other times he has worked as the master of a sailing schooner, as a schoolteacher, horse handler, ski instructor, inventor, author, and college lecturer. In World War II he was an ambulance driver and combat salvage diver in North Africa. Later in the war he wound up as a research associate with the Harvard Underwater Sound Laboratory, the wartime group assigned to develop an acoustic torpedo.

It was then he noticed that one of the several teams of men set up to explore aspects of the torpedo problem seemed more productive than the others. Suspecting that its "style" of operation had something to do with it, Gordon wangled his way onto this team and began observing the members at work and recording their discussions on wire recorders. He also recorded his own flitting thoughts and feelings when he was trying to devise inventions of his own; he holds nearly fifty patents. Meanwhile, he read everything he could find on creativity, including the biographies of many inventors and whatever psychological theorizings on the subject he could find.

In-house zanies

In 1952, Gordon was hired by Arthur D. Little, Inc., the seventy-eight-year-old consulting firm in Cambridge, to set up an "Invention Design Group" to turn out inventions for client companies. Deliberately avoiding purely technical men, he assembled a group made up of a biologist, an architect who had been an aeronautical engineer, a chemist who sculpted, a psychologist who was also a jazz clarinetist, and an engineer who was a painter on the side. This strange aggregation invented several devices, though not too many have yet found their way to the marketplace.

Some contend that the group really served a more important function at Little, that of showpiece zanies, to be trotted out to impress clients with their sheer unconventionality. Gordon at this time sported a substantial paunch and a full-blown flaming red beard (both since vanished) and had a theory (also vanished) that the use of swearing helped free up the mind for creative work. (A colleague described the Bill Gordon of that day as a "blasphemous Santa Claus.")

In 1955 the management of Kimberly-Clark Corp. commissioned one of its staff, a Canadian chemical engineer named William Wilson, to spend a year or so looking around the country's universities and corporations for approaches to creativity that might be suitable for the company. Eventually, Wilson ran across the Arthur D. Little Invention Design Group and enlisted its help. Several Kimberly-Clark men were installed in a corner of the invention group's laboratory to learn how to be creative. Gordon began by telling them about his creativity hypotheses, which had by then become multisyllabic and, by and large, incomprehensible; he eventually ended up telling them to "watch what we do and then you do the same."

After a year of spending several days a month watching the Gordon crew at work, the Kimberly-Clark team went into operation and quickly scored with several ideas—including the idea of compressing Kleenex to save space. Kimberly-Clark's management was intrigued enough to send a large second group out to be trained.

In 1960, Gordon and five other members of the invention group left Little and formed Synectics, Inc. By this time Gordon had written a book, *Synectics,* that attempted to theorize about the attitudes and psychological tricks that would spur invention. It was hailed by several top-notch academics in the field of creativity, who thought it was on the right track. But the book made little headway in telling anybody just what he ought to do to be creative; furthermore, the Synectics staff now agrees, it incorporated some dogma that was wrongheaded. For instance, it advocated careful selection of people to take the training, specifying that no one over forty should be allowed. Since then Synectics has found that plenty of people over forty are more flexible and productive than younger men.

The man in the brick-red trousers

The man who turned Gordon's theories into "operational mechanisms" was George Prince, who came over from Little with Gordon as a cofounder of Synectics, Inc. Despite a liking for brick-red trousers and bright yellow sport shirts during office hours, Prince is a quiet and earnest man, quite opposite in nature to the flamboyant Gordon. He was formerly an executive vice president of Rumrill Co. Inc., the advertising agency, and was one of the early proponents of motivational research. Like others, he fell under Gordon's substantial personal spell and went to work for the Arthur D. Little Invention Design Group. "Gordon was interested in some ideas I had been having about creativity and I was interested in his. But not long after I joined up I found out that he didn't know as much as I thought he did, and I didn't know as much as he thought I did," comments Prince, a man of disarming frankness.

One observation that alarmed Prince was that Synectics group discussions seemed to work best only when Gordon was there to lead them, and even then only when he was feeling right. So Prince began a careful study of what the group did on the days when Gordon was feeling good. From these observations, he evolved a kind of "flow chart" by which Synectics could be taught whether Gordon was there or not. Most of these techniques and mechanisms have been evolved within the past two years, but by now appear to be so well articulated that a training group can learn as much Synectics in one week as former groups learned in a year.

A little like an LSD party

At the heart of Synectics are a number of insights into the psychological nature of creativity. For one thing, many people's best ideas come when they are not consciously thinking about the problem at hand. Inspiration arises during a period of "incubation," such as when a man is driving to work or standing before his shaving mirror. At times like these, the theory goes, the preconscious mind is at work, daydreaming and dredging up weird analogies from the unconscious that are normally repressed by the hidebound and logical conscious mind. There is evidence that a lot of the clues for productive thinking come from the analogies brought up by the preconscious from the unconsciously stored raw materials out of past experience. According to Synectics theory, it's not necessary to wait for the conscious mind to be caught off guard before the preconscious mind can work productively. Instead, Synectics tries to invoke the preconscious and watch it at work.

The techniques encourage problem solvers to oscillate between a rational consideration of the real problem and a search for nonrational analogies. In this way, they widen the scope of the search for solutions instead of beating up and down through the same unproductive ruts. The more farfetched the analogies the better, for a farfetched analogy increases the likelihood that the solution will not have been thought of before. Synectics counts upon an intuitive feeling of "rightness"—familiar to creative people and called, in Gordon's jargon, the "hedonic response"—to serve as a guide when a solution to the problem is being approached.

An additional rationale for the analogical approach is that it permits people of diverse backgrounds to communicate in a common language—that of everyman's experience. Such communication is essential for many of the more complex modern problems that overlap into diverse areas.

To the uninitiated, a full-blown Synectics session is a startling affair —like an LSD party, maybe, or an experiment in group psychotherapy.

One man calls it an "occult means of reducing repression." Most participants swear to a powerful exhilaration. "You come out of a Synectics session feeling as though you'd had five pots of coffee," says the research director of one large manufacturing firm.

A typical session usually includes an expert on the problem at hand. He starts things off by familiarizing the participants with the characteristics of the "problem as given" (called the PAG). The group converts the PAG into the "problem as understood" (the PAU), a limited approach to the problem that is picked temporarily for discussion. At this point the member of the group who acts as leader usually begins posing "evocative questions"; he might ask for a "direct analogy" (DA), an object or phenomenon brought to mind by some key phrase in the PAU. Part of the skill in using Synectics is learning to avoid analogies that are too exact or too obvious—not "strange" enough. To generate the required "strangeness," Synectics, for instance, searches biological fields for direct analogies to mechanical problems, or mechanical fields for analogies to personnel problems.

The leader might then ask the group for "personal analogies"—i.e., to pretend that they are the object picked as a direct analogy ("I'm a very still lake") and to express how they feel in such a situation. The idea behind the personal analogy is to help free the problem solvers from viewing the problem merely in terms of previously analyzed elements. It is a little like the "Method" school of acting. After a few members have suggested their personal-analogy reactions, the leader will ask them to put together these PA's into a "symbolic analogy" or "SA." The ideal symbolic analogy is a short phrase that describes the problem abstractly but has within itself some built-in surprise or "strain." It may be implicitly paradoxical or it may make associations between things that are not normally thought of in connection with one another. A symbolic analogy for a grinding wheel might be "precise roughness," for example.

At this point the leader will ask for another DA—a strange example of the symbolic analogy. A DA for "precise roughness" might be "the law of averages," because it is precise when dealing with very large numbers but crude when dealing with few. Having selected this analogy, the group would then analyze it for what suggestive light it might throw on the original problem, which is by now far removed. This whole chain of analogies constitutes what Synectics terms an "excursion." During the excursion the original problem is all but forgotten—and deliberately so. "If you know where you're going, you're not going anywhere," says George Prince.

Unlike most conventional problem solving, there doesn't appear to be anything "logical" about such excursions. But apparently there is some kind of hard-to-fathom intuitive perception that Synectics exploits, and it helps the group snatch out of the air just the idea—from all those floating around—that may be useful. Synectics buffs say, furthermore, that in case one approach fails, their techniques always furnish a way of launching another attack on the problem: you take one of the unused analogies or make up some more and start the "ladder" of DA's, PA's, and SA's all over again. Thus there is always material to keep the discussion going— something that's missing in the conventional corporate conference on the typical ancient problem.

"Fear, hostility, resentment, and sabotage"

Gordon and his associates are careful to point out that their doctrine is still imperfectly formed and that they are constantly experimenting. For example, Synectics formerly advocated that when trained groups go back to their company they should be provided with their own working quarters, shops, and labs, and be given an almost total freedom from routine corporate control. Dean Gitter, vice president of Synectics, looked into how this worked at the first five client companies—Kimberly-Clark, Whirlpool, Johns Manville, Pillsbury, and Singer. He discovered that in nearly every case the freewheeling "elite" status of the Synectics groups had so infuriated other people in the company that the groups encountered, in Gitter's words, "fear, hostility, resentment, and sabotage." This became so bad that some of the companies had dissolved their Synectics groups. Gitter's observations led to recommendations that the groups not be given any special status when they get back to their company, and that they make every attempt to include any outsider who wants to sit in on problem-solving sessions.

Only thirty years old, Gitter has a background almost as diverse as Gordon's. He took his B.A. from Harvard in drama, ran a talent-management business for folk singers, recorded folk songs himself, founded and acted in the Repertory Theatre of Boston, and then graduated with distinction from Harvard Business School in 1962. The fourth staff member, Cavas Gobhai, twenty-eight, is a native of India with an M.S. degree in mechanical engineering from M.I.T. He was a consulting engineer before joining Synectics.

After a client's group has been trained for a week and returned to its home base, Gobhai or another Synectics staffer pays several follow-up visits to be sure that the group is becoming comfortable with the system and also to help it develop a "style" in pushing ideas through the development and testing stage in the face of the ever present corporate inertia. If, for example, the group has found that an idea it liked got bogged down in "normal channels," it is encouraged to devise ways of maneuvering outside these channels—for example, to go outside the company for needed materials.

"Three heads are better than one"

Opinions of client companies about the worth of Synectics are generally favorable. Although a few have decided reservations, many are wildly enthusiastic. The firm with the greatest exposure to Synectics is Colgate-Palmolive, which over the past years has sent some fifty men to training courses of various lengths. Ted LaPier, Colgate's director of research administration, estimates that of the fifty, "80 percent are pretty well sold it's a good thing. About 10 percent are disciples—enough to be completely nuts about it. Two or three are violently opposed, to the point where you can't use them in Synectics. They don't, for example, understand how a mechanical engineer can contribute to a chemical engineer's problem."

LaPier cannot point to any new products on the market that have come solely out of Synectics procedures, but some are making their way through the slow development and testing grind. "Synectics has mostly been valuable in providing words for advertisements, and suggesting certain technical wrinkles that are, for example, being exploited in a new shampoo," he says. Colgate has been running a series of experiments in conjunction with Synectics, Inc., in which small "commando teams" are given sole responsibility for developing a new product idea and carrying it all alone through the development, testing, pilot-production, and marketing stages.

Summing up, LaPier says, "I look at Synectics as an excuse to get together and isolate the problem. The group members can excite each other and become emotionally involved in the situation. In the Synectics game, you can say silly things and it doesn't cast reflection on your ability."

David Graesser, vice president of research for Singer Manufacturing, says that he has a Synectics team working in a promising area, from which he thinks something will emerge. But he doesn't believe that Synectics is for everyone. Of twenty people selected at random from a corporation, only two or three are likely to find the techniques compatible, he says.

John Maddox, a senior vice president for marketing service with Fuller & Smith & Ross, Inc., the New York advertising firm, says that Synectics has been "an exploder for my mental energies," which has "tripled my effectiveness." He and four others from the company trained in Synectics four years ago, and since then he himself has trained five-man teams for each of the agency's five offices in other cities.

One of Synectics' latest clients is the Sandia Corp., Western Electric's nuclear R and D subsidiary. Dr. Sherwood Peres, an industrial psychologist at Sandia, calls Synectics "a shot in the arm. Our business is ideas and Synectics is a powerful technique to get the brains going." According to Peres, what Synectics shows is that you can work in committee, "that three heads are better than one if they are on the same frequency. This gives you a climate where it's OK to let your mind down, where you can fly a bit. The social dynamics is unlike anything I've ever seen. You are giving real-time verbal feedback of what you are thinking."

Dr. Albert Muller, vice president of science and engineering at Air Reduction, Inc., took some of his men up to Cambridge with a sticky problem in chemical engineering. It was never solved but, Muller feels, "The time wasn't wasted. We got a feel for the controlled approach to creative thinking."

2 | Synectics

WILLIAM J. J. GORDON
Synectics, Inc.

William J. J. Gordon's 1961 book *Synectics*, from which this article is adapted, already is a classic in the area of training creative thinking. Gordon describes the history and evolution of the synectics methods— his strategy for studying the creative process, the history of synectics research, his working hypotheses and assumptions, and, particularly, the synectics methods or mechanisms themselves. While giving emphasis to the use of Direct and Symbolic Analogies (especially those drawn from nature), Gordon also summarizes his Personal Analogy method, in which members achieve new perspectives on a problem by imagining themselves to be one of the problem objects, and his Fantasy Analogy, in which ideal but perhaps far-fetched solutions are proposed. Finally, "playing" or free-associating with word meanings and "pushing laws out of phase" (for example, repealing gravity) also are suggested as devices for stimulating new ideas. In simplified forms, these synectics methods may be used for stimulating the imaginations of elementary and secondary school students. Even very young pupils, working as individuals or as a class, can acquire ideas by examining similarities between the problem at hand and solutions metaphorically provided by other people, animals, birds, insects, or plants. For example, a transportation problem could be attacked by having students think of how lower animals "move things from here to there," or an air or water pollution problem could be solved by thinking of ideas associated with "cleaning things." Students also can learn to look for "perfect" or "ideal" solutions, such as having the problem solve itself (for example, the Westinghouse oven cleans itself, some tires seal their own leaks, and a new shaving cream heats itself). Recently, Gordon and his colleagues at Synectics, Inc., have created metaphor-based materials for use in inner city schools. The *High School Social Studies Text* and *Making It Strange,* an elementary-level, creative writing workbook, both evolve around the creative thinking principles and strategies described in the present selection. Gordon summarizes the specific content and rationale of the two inner-city texts in his recent volume, *The Metaphorical Way of Learning and Knowing.*[1]

Introduction

The word *Synectics,* from the Greek, means the joining together of different and apparently irrelevant elements. Synectics theory applies to the integration of diverse individuals into a problem-stating, problem-solving group. It is an operational theory for the conscious use of the preconscious psychological mechanisms present in man's creative activity. The purpose of developing such a theory is to increase the probability of success in problem-stating, problem-solving situations. This increase depends on awareness of the mechanisms which must be worked through to arrive at solutions of fundamental novelty. (Novelty is fundamental to the degree that it is general. A special cam may be a new way to make a particular apparatus function better, but this cam is not applicable to any other piece of apparatus. A transistor, on the other hand, is applicable to a wide range of uses.)

The study of creative process is encumbered by the fact that, being a process, it is in motion. Traditionally, creative process has been considered after the fact—halted for observation. But when the process is stopped, what is there to observe? The Synectics study has attempted to research creative process in vivo, while it is going on. To understand the digestion process of a cow it is possible to put a picture window in the cow's stomach(s). However, a window opening onto the brain of a man who is acting creatively would be useless because not enough is understood about the brain to know what we would be seeing. Therefore, the only way to learn about creative process is to try to gain insight into the underlying, nonrational, free-associative concepts which flow under the articulated surface phenomena. To do this, Synectics research has required problems to be solved and people to be observed.

The Cambridge Synectics group, which was the first and is a continuing source of the data and hypotheses examined in this book, enjoys a symbiotic relationship with industry. In spite of substantial assistance of many kinds from personnel at the Department of Defense, the Institute of Contemporary Art, the Rockefeller Foundation, Harvard University, and Massachusetts Institute of Technology, American industry has become the most prominent laboratory element in Synectics research. The Cambridge

[1] These three documents are available from Synectics, Inc., 28 Church Street, Cambridge, Massachusetts.

Synectics group needs problems to solve and groups with which to work in order to continue its research. Industry needs problems solved and must have creative groups within it to continue producing basic novelty. In the course of this work the Cambridge Synectics group has developed increasing experimental insight into the conception and reduction to practice of radically novel ideas—from observing its own process as well as the process of groups in training.

The present Cambridge Synectics group consists of six men of varied background (physics, mechanics, biology, geology, marketing, and chemistry). Part of their time is spent in sessions attacking invention problems. Tape recordings of successful sessions (where a concept promising enough to test is developed) are analyzed to learn how the concept originated. Another part of their time is devoted to implementation—building working models, conducting experiments, and investigating market potentials. There are frequent discussions of progress which serve two purposes. First, they keep the group in touch with how a project is going. Second, by hearing about how individuals overcome specific problems, more is learned about the invention process. The other activity of the group is teaching. Certain members select candidates and train selectees from client companies in the use of the Synectics method.

The group functions under two leaders. One handles administrative matters; the other guides the sessions themselves. However, there is a high degree of democracy. For example, any member can call together other members of the group for a session, and administrative decisions of any moment are decided by the whole group.

This book is an interim report on research which will continue for years to come. The objective of the research to date has been to develop an operational concept of human creativity and to test this concept. The conclusions stated and implied in this book form the basis on which other successful Synectics groups have been founded; when a scientific experiment repeatedly yields similar results, such confirmation is held to be a demonstration of the validity of the underlying hypothesis. However, not all the conclusions (although based on experimental evidence) are to be taken as fixed and final, but as hypotheses in transition, suitable for further research and study. Synectics research hinges on the following assumptions:

1. that the creative process in human beings can be concretely described and, further, that sound description should be usable in teaching methodology to increase the creative output of both individuals and groups. This assumption places Synectics theory in direct conflict with the theory that any attempt to analyze and train imagination and those aspects of the human psyche associated directly with the creative process threatens the process with destruction. In other words, true analysis

of the creative process is considered impossible since if the individual attempts to examine himself in process, the process ceases immediately, and his examination is bankrupt. This theory implies that illumination is destructive. At present this prejudice seems groundless. Synectics' attempts to illuminate the creative process have resulted in several working hypotheses which are useful in practice and have increased markedly the creative output of both individuals and groups;

2. that the cultural phenomena of invention in the arts and in science are analogous and are characterized by the same fundamental psychic processes;

3. that individual process in the creative enterprise enjoys a direct analogy in group process.

The purpose of the book is to describe the evolution of Synectics' theory of creative process, the hypotheses that underlie the theory, and the actual implementation of the theory in specific cases.

Research

The aim of Synectics research, since 1944, has been to uncover the psychological mechanisms basic to creative activity. The recurrent problem has been how to discover these mechanisms when they were buried within the subjective responses of individuals. The main body of this research consisted of oscillating between gaining concrete insight about the psychological mechanisms and testing the validity of these mechanisms in problem-stating, problem-solving situations. The latest part of Synectics research has been directed toward exploring the use of problem-solving groups trained in the Synectics mechanisms. Test groups are presently operating in a number of American companies with considerable—and increasing—success. This success results from the Synectics mechanisms becoming defined more and more functionally as the research develops along increasingly concrete lines. Growing interest has been shown in the implications of Synectics at all levels of education. Up to now the methodology had to be tested in a practical climate where experiments could be judged on the basis of pragmatic criteria. However, Synectics research is about to be applied experimentally to educational processes as known today in our schools and colleges.

Hypotheses

Synectics theory holds that:

1. creative efficiency in people can be markedly increased if they understand the psychological process by which they operate;

2. in creative process the emotional component is more important than the intellectual, the irrational more important than the rational;

3. it is these emotional, irrational elements which can and must be understood in order to increase the probability of success in a problem-solving situation.

History of Synectics researches

Throughout our research into the creative process, observation of Synectics groups at work in seminars and as individuals building models has revealed the insights. The psychological states and mechanisms that occur when an individual creates are normally underground. The Synectics group situation, which forces each participant to verbalize his thoughts and feelings about the problem at hand, can bring elements of the process out in the open where they can be identified and analyzed.

We have found that for problem solving, as well as for the purpose of research into creative process, a properly operating group has advantages over an individual. Indeed, a Synectics group can compress into a few hours the kind of semiconscious mental activity which might take months of incubation for a single person. This "efficient" use of the subconscious leads to our insights. This phenomenon, which happens repeatedly when a well trained group is operating smoothly, depends on members of Synectics groups being willing to function on a more or less nonrational basis. In other words, they must avoid trying always to express rational completed concepts. The seamless sphericity of a "closed loop" thought presents an idea association in the impregnable form of a perfectly smooth surface. When an idea is expressed after being completely worked out it is either acceptable as true or unacceptable as untrue. It resists modification. It lives or dies as uttered. No one else can find his way in and build on it; the author of the thought finds himself adorned with a conceptual jewel which is isolated and untouchable. Nonrational communication, on the other hand, produces evocative metaphors, images with rough surfaces, and fissures on which others can get a grip and participate. Of course, this kind of nonrational interplay is only part of a process which spirals up toward increasing coherence. Ultimate solutions to problems are rational; the process of finding them is not.

Another advantage of the group situation is its effect upon individual daring. To achieve radical new approaches to old problems it is essential to take "psychological chances," to abandon familiar ways of looking at things, even to transcend one's image of oneself. A can say, "I feel like defying the law of gravity now." Taken literally, this is a hair-raising announcement. But A has confidence that the group will interpret him figuratively, sensitive to his sudden vague desire to fly in the face of accepted physics. It does not attend so much to the exact implication of his statement as to its motivation. It wants to help him. His predicament arouses it. The risk he has taken has psychological prestige for the group, as though he had launched himself on a dangerous mission.

The backgrounds of the individuals who have made up the central Synectics group in Cambridge during the last few years have been enormously varied. Before there was any attempt to establish other Synectics groups, membership in the central organization shifted to include various combinations of painters, sculptors, mathematicians, advertising men, physicists, philosophers, chemists, actors, mechanical engineers, architects, electrical engineers, marketing men, chemical engineers, sociologists, biologists, physiologists, musicians, anthropologists, and zoologists. These changes in personnel were part of the experiment; they were not planned to meet particular invention requirements. The purpose was to integrate into a Synectics group people of opposing personality and differing academic background. The most elegant solution to a given problem is one where the solution is the simplest in proportion to the complexity of the variables involved. In other words, the following equation holds:

$$elegance\ of\ solution\ =\ \frac{multiplicity\ of\ variables}{simplicity\ of\ solution}$$

The multiplicity factor is represented by the number and diversity of members of a Synectics group. The simplicity factor, hopefully, would result from the application of Synectics theory toward unifying participants and concepts. Our hypothesis was that a general level of novelty (as opposed to marginal improvements) depends on the widest variety of skill, knowledge, and interest being brought to bear. Obviously the problem was to draw interaction and constructive communication from people whose difficulty in understanding each other could lead to mistrust. This interaction was brought about by the mechanisms which make up a methodology common to all areas of creative thought and which can be used to unify the most widely diverse groups.

The most important (and most underrated) single aspect of a Synectics project is the implementation (in the form of working models) of those concepts developed as solutions. Such model building is vital to the success of a new product or invention program. Moreover, we have observed that unless a teaching program includes the experience of "getting the hands dirty" by actively implementing conceptions, the program is threatened with incompletion and impotence precisely because it is limited to over-abstract discussion.[2] Abstraction breeds more abstraction and more generality instead of leading to tough yes-no tests. Without the pragmatic "does-it-work?" criterion which can be demanded of something reduced to

---

[2] Actual laboratory implementation involves working out solutions to the specific problems which arise in reduction to practice. These solutions are as important as the original concept, but concepts have more prestige in our culture because conceptualizers usually attain the status of administrators, and administrators keep their suitcoats on; they don't build working models.

practice, it is impossible to get the specificity and concreteness necessary to the evolution and proof of principle.

A corollary to the experience of implementation is the pragmatic criterion derived. How better judge the *effectiveness* of Synectics theory than by the value of the "hardware" it produces? When we discover what we think is another insight into creative process, we define it operationally. If, in use, it leads to repeated breakthroughs, we call our operational definition a mechanism. As a mechanism we test it with other Synectics groups to make certain it isn't merely a superficial accidental aspect of our own operation. If it continues to lead to new concepts and these concepts lead to successful working models, then we accept the mechanism's validity as being proved.

During 1957 reviews of tapes, together with closer observations and questions of individuals, suggested to us several psychological conditions necessary for successful inventive effort. We noticed that the ability to tolerate and use the irrelevant was of fundamental importance for a solution. By the irrelevant we understand attitudes, information, and observations which, from a common-sensical and (more often) from a technical point of view, do not seem relevant to the problem under consideration. As a companion state, the ability to play, to sustain a childlike willingness to suspend adult disbelief, emerged as a psychological condition of making the familiar strange. However, words like "play" and "irrelevant" are operationally meaningless, and in 1958–59 we turned our attention from a study of recurrent psychological states and the conditions which support them to a further study of those mechanisms which would help us to make the familiar strange. We reviewed and analyzed tapes of sessions which had contributed to successful invention projects; and then those mechanisms which we could isolate and partially define we used and observed in both invention and teaching sessions. Three general types of mechanisms for play have emerged from these studies: (1) play with words, with meanings and definitions; (2) play in pushing a fundamental law or a basic scientific concept "out of phase"; and (3) play with metaphor.

Play with words, meanings, and definitions involves transposing a specific invention problem into a general word or a general statement. Thus, in one Synectics group an assignment to invent a radically new can opener began with a three-hour session which was sustained play with the word "open." We also included "inversion" in this mechanism as another method of play with accepted meanings. Thus, while we usually assume that a large magnet draws to it a piece of iron we can invert and say that the piece of iron has hunted for and found a place to go. In a small way we have made the familiar strange because we have shifted our concentration from the persuasive female lodestone to the aggressive little piece of male iron.

The effort to push a law or a concept out of phase can range from postulating a universe in which water does run uphill (in order to approach a problem in hydrodynamics) to asking: "How can we really deny or repeal the second and third laws of thermodynamics?" Or: "How can we *apparently* deny entropy?" Recently we have used this mechanism with invention success by simply concentrating on the question: "What law shall we choose to push out of phase?" or, granted a given invention problem: "What law would it be most appropriate or advantageous to upset?"

Play with metaphor is one of the most fruitful of the mechanisms which can be used to make the familiar strange. We have experimented with metaphors which involve expressed or implied comparisons between relatively "like" things or states: "Wiring a building should be like plumbing," as well as with metaphors which have the shock value of comparing unlike things or unlike states: "For humans 'absence makes the heart grow fonder.' Essentially, this is in conflict with the inverse square law." As a special extension of metaphor we make considerable conscious use of analogy, i.e., comparisons between things with like functions and different forms. Personification and anthropomorphization fit here with the question: "How would it feel if it were human and could feel?" "How would I feel if I were it?" As a further special case of feeling as an inanimate object would feel, we have experimented successfully with attempts to empathize, to feel, kinesthetically, in interrelation of the muscles themselves, the state of an inanimate object, a motion, or a relationship.

The operational mechanisms

Synectics defines creative process as the mental activity in problem-stating, problem-solving situations where artistic or technical inventions are the result. I use the expression "problem-stating, problem-solving" rather than merely "problem-solving" in order to include the definition and understanding of the problem. The operational mechanisms of Synectics are the concrete psychological factors which support and press forward creative process. The mechanisms do not pertain to the motivations for creative activity, nor are they intended to be used to judge the ultimate product of an esthetic or technical invention. Psychological states such as empathy, involvement, play, detachment, and use of irrelevance are (as we have seen) basic to creative process but they are not operational. The Synectics mechanisms are intended to induce appropriate psychological states and thus promote creative activity.

Words like intuition, empathy, and play are merely names put to complex activities in the hope that the naming of the activity will in fact describe it. Experience has shown it to be most difficult to feed back into a problem-stating, problem-solving situation such nominalistic abstractions. When dealing with an individual or a group faced with problem stating and problem solving, it is ineffectual to attempt to persuade the individual to be intuitive, to empathize, to become involved, to be detached, to play, or to tolerate apparent irrelevance. However, in our research experience the Synectics mechanisms effectively increase the probability of success when creativity is called for. They draw the individual into the psychological states.

The Synectic process involves:

1. making the strange familiar
2. making the familiar strange

Making the strange familiar

In any problem-stating, problem-solving situation, the first responsibility of individuals involved is to understand the problem. This is essentially an analytical phase where the ramifications and the fundamentals of the problem must be plumbed.

Making the familiar strange

To make the familiar strange is to distort, invert, or transpose the everyday ways of looking and responding which render the world a secure and familiar place. This pursuit of strangeness is not a blasé's search for the bizarre and out-of-the-way. It is the conscious attempt to achieve a new look at the same old world, people, ideas, feelings, and things. In the "familiar world" objects are always right-side-up; the child who bends and peers at the world from between his legs is experimenting with the familiar made strange.

The attempt to make the familiar strange involves several different methods of achieving an intentionally naive or apparently "out of focus" look at some aspect of the known world. And this look can transpose both our usual ways of perceiving and our usual expectations about how we or the world will behave. The experience of sustaining this condition can provoke anxiety and insecurity. But maintaining the familiar as strange is fundamental to disciplined creativity. All problems present themselves to the mind as threats of failure. For someone striving to win in terms of a successful solution, this threat evokes a mass response in which the most immediate superficial solution is clutched frantically as a balm to anxiety. This is consistent with the natural impulse to master the strange by making it familiar. Yet if we are to perceive all the implications and possibilities of the new we must risk at least temporary ambiguity and disorder. Human beings are heir to a legacy of frozen words and ways of perceiving which wrap their world in comfortable familiarity. This protective legacy must be disowned. A new viewpoint depends on the capacity to risk and to understand the mechanisms by which the mind can make tolerable the temporary ambiguity implicit in risking.

Synectics has identified four mechanisms for making the familiar strange, each metaphorical in character:

1. Personal Analogy
2. Direct Analogy
3. Symbolic Analogy
4. Fantasy Analogy

According to our observations, without the presence of these mechanisms no problem-stating, problem-solving attempt will be successful. The mechanisms are to be regarded as specific and reproducible mental processes, tools to initiate the motion of creative process and to sustain and renew that motion. There are romantic and popular prejudices against any such mechanization of human creativity. However, Synectics consciously intends this very mechanization. The mechanisms are thus by definition subject to conscious and deliberate use as primary *means*. In addition, through practice they become habitual as ways of seeing and acting. Even those individuals who by habit unconsciously make use of them have been observed to intensify and heighten their creative effectiveness as a result of the conscious effort to establish and expand the application of these tools.

Personal Analogy

Personal identification with the elements of a problem releases the individual from viewing the problem in terms of its previously analyzed elements. A chemist makes a problem familiar to himself through equations combining molecules and the mathematics of phenomenological order. On the other hand, to make a problem strange the chemist may personally identify with the molecules in action. Faraday "looked . . . into the very heart of the electrolyte endeavoring to render the play of its atom visible to his mental eyes" (Tyndall, 1868, pp. 66–67). The creative technical person can think himself to be a dancing molecule, discarding the detachment of the expert and throwing himself into the activity of the elements involved. He becomes one of the molecules. He permits himself to be pushed and pulled by the molecular forces. He remains a human being but acts as though he were a molecule. For the moment the rigid formulae don't govern, and he feels what happens to a molecule.

Einstein recognized the role of empathic personalized identification: "The psychical entities which seem to serve as elements in thought are certain signs and more or less clear images which can be 'voluntarily' reproduced and combined . . . this combinatory play seems to be the essential feature in productive thought. . . . The above mentioned elements are, in my case, of visual and some of muscular type" (Hadamard, 1945, pp. 142–143). Here a great man of science working in the most abstract area of thought admits "muscular" identifications even with the *a priori* constructs of mathematics. Kekule, by identifying himself with a snake swallowing its tail, developed an insight into the benzene molecule in terms of a ring rather than a chain of carbon atoms (Libby, 1922). Keats describes his writing of *Endymion:* "I leaped headlong into the sea, and thereby have become better acquainted with the sounds, the quicksands, and the rocks, than if I had stayed upon the green shore and piped a silly pipe, and took tea and comfortable advice" (Keats [Forman, ed.], 1935, p. 223). Thus, in both science and art, detached observations and analysis are abandoned in favor of Personal Analogy.

Direct Analogy

This mechanism describes the actual comparison of parallel facts, knowledge, or technology. Sir March Isumbard Brunel solved the problem of underwater construction by watching a shipworm tunnelling into a timber. The worm constructed a tube for itself as it moved forward, and the classical notion of caissons came to Brunel by Direct Analogy. Hadamard (1945, p. 9) points out, "Especially, biology, as Hamite used to observe, may be a most useful study even for mathematicians, as hidden but eventually fruitful analogies may appear between processes in both kinds of study." Albert Einstein observed that "combinatory play seems to be the essential feature in productive thought" (Reiser, 1931, p. 116). And Alexander Graham Bell recalled, "it struck me that the bones of the human ear were very massive, indeed, as compared with the delicate thin membrane that operated them, and the thought occurred that if a membrane so delicate could move bones relatively so massive, why should not a thicker and stouter piece of membrane move my piece of steel. And the telephone was conceived" (MacKenzie, 1928, pp. 72–73).

Readings of classical scientific discovery as well as seventeen years of practical invention indicate that a biological perception of physical phenomena produces generative viewpoints. Helmholtz, in discussing the invention of the ophthalmoscope, is clear about the influence of various different scientific fields coming together. "I attribute my subsequent success to the fact that circumstances had fortunately planted me with some knowledge of geometry and training in physics among the doctors, where physiology presented a virgin soil of the utmost fertility, while on the other hand I was led by my acquaintance with the phenomena of life to problems and points of view that are beyond the scope of pure mathematics and physics" (Koenigsberger, 1906, p. 77). The strained comparison of a scientific observation in one field with that of another field tends to force an expression of a problem in a new way.

The area of analogy and symbolism has been adopted by Synectics almost out of whole cloth. Mechanisms of metaphor employing Symbolic Analogy and Personal Analogy as well as Direct Analogy are implemented in our day to day experimental work. Synectics theory agrees with the conviction that a man does not know even his own science if he knows *only* it (Whitehead, 1929).

Symbolic Analogy

This mechanism differs from the identification aspect of Personal Analogy in that Symbolic Analogy uses objective and impersonal images to describe the problem. The individual effectively uses this analogy in terms of poetic response. He summons up an image which, though technologically inaccurate, is esthetically satisfying. It is a compressed description of the function or elements of the problem as he views it. In the course of making the problem familiar to himself, the chemist employs extensive quantitative tools. When using the mechanism of Symbolic Analogy he views the problem qualitatively with the condensed suddenness of a poetic phrase. The major difference between Symbolic Analogy and the other mechanisms is quantitative. In Personal Analogy the process of identification takes a long while for all the nuances to be expressed. A Direct Analogy may be quite straightforward but uncovering the comparison of its conceptual ramifications requires substantial time. A Symbolic Analogy is immediate. Once made, in a blurt of association, it is there, complete!

The cultural bifurcation of art and science in our society, and the prevalence of advanced trade schools where limited experts are ground out of the curriculum, tend to make it difficult for technical graduates to understand or use the esthetic qualitative mechanisms. However, as we have observed in the case of the other mechanisms, their use can be learned, not abstractly, but through practice. They are used apprehensively at first, but when the student sees them work, producing rich viewpoints which lead to a basic solution, even the apprehensive individual is willing to use such mechanisms to an increasing degree.

Fantasy Analogy

For Sigmund Freud, creative work in general, and art in particular, is the fulfillment of a wish, although he does not say, as he has been accused of saying, that it is nothing but a wish. The artist must know how to transform, to depersonalize, to hide the source of his wish. When he is successful in so doing, and his work is accepted, then he has accomplished through fantasy what he could have won in no other way. The wish-fulfillment theory reveals the connection between the artist's motives as a human being and his chosen method of gratifying them. Success depends upon his ability to defer consummation of the wish in fantasy and to make real the wish by embodying it in a work of art (Freud, 1949, ch. 5).

Example of Fantasy Analogy

Synectics accepts Freud's wish-fulfillment theory of art, but turns it onto technical invention as well and uses it operationally. For instance, when faced with the problem of inventing a vaporproof closure for space suits, a part of the Synectics approach was to ask the question, "How do we in our wildest fantasies desire the closure to operate?"

G: Okay. That's over. Now what we need here is a crazy way to look at this mess. A real insane viewpoint . . . a whole new room with a view-point!

T: Let's imagine you could will the suit closed . . . and it would do just as you wanted by wishing . . . (Fantasy Analogy mechanism)

G: "Wishing will make it so . . ."

F: Shh, okay. Wish fulfillment. Childhood dream . . . you wish it closed, and invisible microbes, working for you, cross hands across the opening and *pull* it tight. . . .

B: A zipper is kind of a mechanical bug (Direct Analogy mechanism). But not air tight . . . or strong enough. . . .

G: How do we build a psychological model of "will-it-to-be-closed"?

R: What are you talking about?

B: He means if we could conceive of how "willing-it-to-be-closed" might happen in an actual model—then we. . . .

R: There are two days left to produce a working model—and you guys are talking about childhood dreams! Let's make a list of all the ways there are of closing things.

F: I hate lists. It goes back to my childhood and buying groceries. . . .

R: F, I can understand your oblique approach when we have time, but now, with this deadline . . . and you still talking about wish fulfillment.

G: All the crappy solutions in the world have been rationalized by dead-lines.

T: Trained insects?

D: What?

B: You mean, train insects to close and open on orders? 1–2–3 Open! Hup! 1–2–3 Close!

F: Have two lines of insects, one on each side of the closure—on the order to close they all clasp hands . . . or fingers . . . or claws . . . whatever they have . . . and then closure closes tight. . . .

G: I feel like a kind of Coast Guard Insect (Personal Analogy mechanism).

D: Don't mind me. Keep talking. . . .

G: You know the story . . . worst storm of the winter—vessel on the rocks . . . can't use lifeboats . . . some impatient hero grabs the line in his teeth and swims out . . .

B: I get you. You've got an insect running up and down the closure, manipulating the little latches . . .

G: And I'm looking for a demon to do the closing for me. When I will it to be closed (Fantasy Analogy mechanism), Presto! It's closed!

B: Find the insect—he'd do the closing for you!

R: If you used a spider . . . he could spin a thread . . . and sew it up (Direct Analogy).

T: Spider makes thread . . . gives it to a flea. . . . Little holes in the closure . . . flea runs in and out of the holes closing as he goes. . . .

G: Okay. But those insects reflect a low order of power. . . . When the Army tests this thing, they'll grab each lip in a vise one inch wide and they'll pull 150 pounds on it. . . . Those idiot insects of yours will have to pull steel wires behind them in order. . . . They'd have to stitch with steel. *Steel* (Symbolic Analogy mechanism).

B: I can see one way of doing that. Take the example of that insect pulling a thread up through the holes. . . . You could do it mechanically. . . . Same insect . . . put holes in like so . . . and twist a spring like this . . . through the holes all the way up to the damn closure . . . twist, twist, twist, . . . Oh, crap! It would take hours! And twist your damn arm off!

G: Don't give up yet. Maybe there's another way of stitching with steel. . . .

B: Listen . . . I have a picture of another type of stitching. . . . That spring of yours . . . take two of them . . . let's say you had a long demon that forced its way up . . . like this. . . .

R: I see what he's driving at. . . .

B: If that skinny demon were a wire, I could poke it up to where, if it got a start, it could pull the whole thing together . . . the springs would be pulled together closing the mouth. . . . Just push it up . . . push—and it will pull the rubber lips together. . . . Imbed the springs in rubber . . . and then you've got it stitched with steel! (See Figure 1.)

In the above transcription I have taken the liberty of pointing out symptoms of various mechanisms in action, but the real purpose of the transcription is to give an example of the mechanism of Fantasy Analogy.

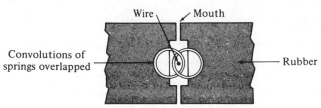

Figure 1   Cross-sectional diagram.

Conscious self-deceit appears in all the mechanisms to a greater or lesser degree but in the mechanism of Fantasy Analogy it is paramount. When a problem is presented to the mind it is most useful to imagine the best of all possible worlds, a helpful universe permitting the most satisfying possible viewpoint leading to the most elegant of all possible solutions.

A world where insects perform as required is this kind of universe. Common sense outlaws such fabrication which "foolishly" flies in the face of established law: How would our problem change if gravity didn't hold? What would happen to our viewpoint if entropy could be ignored? To tolerate these naive inconsistencies is irrational. It is irrational and like the other mechanisms, Fantasy Analogy has operated usually underground in the subconscious because the rational character of man denies himself and the world the vision of that part of himself which is other than proudly coherent.

Over a period of seventeen years Synectics research has observed that the richest source of Direct Analogy is biology. This is because the language of biology lacks a mystifying terminology, and the organic aspect of biology brings out analogies which breathe life into problems that are stiff and rigidly quantitative.

Although the mechanisms are simple in concept, their application requires great energy output. In fact, Synectics does not in any way make creative activity easier but rather is a technique by which people can work harder. At the end of sessions we have observed complete fatigue on the part of the participants. This fatigue comes less from the concentration involved in working through the constructive mechanism, and more from the variable balance which is so necessary. The mere stringing together of metaphors is nonproductive. Synectics participants must keep in the back of their minds the problem as understood so that they can identify those mechanisms which illuminate the problem. This oscillation between, on the one hand, apparently irrelevant analogy formation and, on the other, comparing the analogy with the elements of the problem is enormously tiring. Individuals who can learn (or who already know how) to entertain a great variety of variables without becoming confused are much more apt to be effective in a creative situation. However, the price they pay is exhaustion which is physical.

Conclusions

Abstractions such as intuition, deferment, empathy, play, use of irrelevance, involvement, detachment—these abstractions are almost impossible to teach because of their lack of concreteness; i.e., they are nonoperational. However, the mechanisms (Direct Analogy, Personal Analogy, Symbolic Analogy, Fantasy Analogy) are psychological tools which at the conscious level almost everybody has experienced to a greater or lesser degree. Therefore it is possible to introduce them without making the individual feel that he is being manipulated. Because he correctly feels that his natural potential is being enhanced, his resistance is considerably reduced. It is absurd when dealing with rigidly conventional people to say, "let us balance a variety of irrelevancies now." On the other hand, they do not feel threatened, for instance, by an analogy from another science to compare with the technology implied by the problem at hand.

REFERENCES

Freud, S. *An outline of psychoanalysis.* New York: Norton, 1949.

Hadamard, J. *The psychology of invention in the mathematical field.* Princeton, N.J.: Princeton University Press, 1945.

Keats, J. *The letters of John Keats.* M. B. Forman (Ed.), London: Oxford University Press, 1935.

Koenigsberger, L. *Hermann von Helmholtz.* Oxford: Clarendon Press, 1906.

Libby, W. The scientific imagination. *Scientific Monthly,* 1922, 15, 263–270.

MacKenzie, C. *Alexander Graham Bell.* New York: Houghton Mifflin, 1928.

Reiser, A. *Albert Einstein.* London: Thornton Butterworth, 1931.

Tyndall, J. *Faraday as a discoverer.* London: Longmans, 1868.

Whitehead, A. N. *The aims of education.* New York: Macmillan, 1929.

3 | The operational mechanism of Synectics

GEORGE M. PRINCE
Synectics, Inc.

Reprinted from the Journal of Creative Behavior, *1968, 2, 1–13, by permission of George M. Prince.*

As president of Synectics, Inc., George M. Prince has been intimately involved in the two major industry-related functions of that organization: solving problems for business and industrial clients and training creative problem-solving groups. Supplementing the two previous chapters, Prince reviews many of the central principles of synectics theory, describing the inhibiting, rule-and-logic conscious mind (which censors many flights of imagination before they lift off) and the use of the irrational unconscious for finding highly unusual viewpoints for a given problem. The unique contribution of this article is Prince's step-by-step outline of the various phases of a "formal" synectics problem-solving session, phases which are carefully guided by a trained and experienced leader. We should repeat, however, that the synectics procedures profitably may be used in elementary or secondary school, as well as in business, without following the precise steps outlined by Prince and without a highly trained synectics group leader. Clearly, the synectics methods constitute a learnable approach to creative problem solving which can stimulate, challenge, and develop the capabilities of both professionals and children.

A theory of creative behavior

One's conscious mind contains all that one knows which is readily available. This information is well organized and interconnected on a logical basis. The conscious mind is a square shooter, characterized by its desire to organize, to make rules of thumb and live by them. These characteristics of the conscious mind are invaluable for learning, putting items in order, and testing hypotheses in a logical way. On the other hand, one can see that the conscious mind tends to be inhibited by the very qualities that make it useful. It lives by the rules and by logic; it resists "irresponsible" speculation. People who rely heavily on their analytic ability find it very difficult to entertain ideas that are foreign to the "rules" they have learned.

The unconscious or subconscious is another remarkable part of the whole. It is a storehouse of immense capacity. According to Freud, it contains everything one has experienced since conception. Jung believed that it contains memories that go back to one's forefathers. Perhaps the most persuasive evidence of the contents of the unconscious comes to us from hypnotists and neurosurgeons. For example, a hypnotist can regress a 45-year-old to his sixth-grade days. The subject can name the children in his sixth-grade class; a check of his yearbook will prove him nearly always completely accurate.

As for neurosurgeons, Dr. Wilder Penfield, operating on a woman's brain, using local anesthetic, prodded some brain cells. The woman exclaimed that he had just caused her to reexperience a long-forgotten episode in her life "in living color." Another prod produced another episode, also complete with sensations. The doctor theorized that the brain has a continuous recording device which stores all that one experiences.

In sum, there is strong evidence that the unconscious mind is a reservoir of information so vast and rich that it challenges the imagination.

The censor

During the problem-solving process, the preconscious, like a problem-oriented file clerk guided by interest and emotional commitment, goes searching for relevant suggestive data. Its criteria for relevance do not seem logical, because so often the data that are "presented" do not appear to one's conscious mind to be connected even distantly with the problem at hand. For this and other reasons, people gradually build in a censor to protect the conscious mind from the overt "interrupting" thoughts from the unconscious by way of the preconscious.

The censor is below conscious control. An individual cannot open his mind simply by resolving not to block the signals from his unconscious. Yet, the censor is not infallible. Given desire on the part of a person to solve a problem and given time and pressure, chances are good that the message or, rather, a message that will be helpful will get through.

Each of us has come to depend upon one technique or another for getting ideas. Usually we have arrived at a procedure by almost unconscious trial and error. A key element in all these procedures is the "mulling-it-over" step, sometimes called incubation. This is a point, which may come early or after much work, when one seems to have gone as far as he can and is still without a new viewpoint. He puts the problem out of his mind (this is a matter of degree; some seem to completely forget the problem, others temporarily turn their attention to something else). A clue usually comes to him—while he is shaving, bathing, cutting the grass, driving a familiar route to work, waking from sleep, or going to sleep.

A second observation about the censor is that it appears to have a direct connection with the use of creative potential. If a person has developed sensitivity to the proddings of the unconscious, if his censor is easily bypassed or weak, he is able to behave more creatively and use more of his potential. A characteristic of the great discoverers is that they are very responsive to their own impulses or intuitions.

A third observation about the censor has to do with its formation.

> Years ago some psychologists at a university were discussing creativity and age. They agreed that by age 45 one is over the hill, and creativity is pretty much gone. They decided it would be useful to establish this fact experimentally. They selected test instruments and tested a universe of 45 year olds. To no one's surprise only 2% tested were highly creative. Discussing the results, one psychologist suggested that it would be interesting to find the age when creativity seemed to "wear out." The others agreed, and they tested universes 44 years old, 43 years old and so on. This proved to be a monotonous task, because the 2% highly creative remained the same until the weary psychologists reached the universe of seven-year-olds. Highly creative jumped to 10%. At five years old the figure was 90% creative.[1]

This suggests that nearly all of us begin life highly creative and that by eight or nine years of age we are seriously undermining our creative potential because of bad habits in thought and behavior. We have been brainwashed with our own active cooperation. The result is that we think too well of our good intentions toward others and ourselves and far too little of our capabilities for creativity and constructive change.

Tipping the balance

As adults, we come equipped with a full set of constructive and destructive behaviors; and if one permits himself to do what comes naturally, these modes of operating to solve problems have a very high content of destructive and defensive behavior which seriously inhibits creative accomplishment. To capitalize on his creative capabilities, an individual must make a deliberate effort to change and make his behavior more cordial toward and curious about the new and strange. The Synectics Procedures have been designed to encourage constructive behaviors and to control or modify destructive behaviors in such a way as to increase the probability of success when innovation is necessary.

Furthermore, how well an individual's approaches to problem solving will work for him at any given time can fluctuate widely from day to day.

[1] Papanek, V. J. Solving Problems Creatively. *Management Views, IX* (Pt. 3). Selected speeches, academic year 1963–1964. U.S. Army Management School, Fort Belvoir, Va., 169–196 (1964).

Some days the system works for us, other days it fails. When faced with a difficult problem, we often think it best not to force things, but to let the problem sit for a time until inspiration strikes—that is, until one of those days occurs when we are at our best.

By utilizing conceptual devices called operational mechanisms, the Synectics discipline strives to teach an individual how to imitate, *whenever he desires,* the way he works on his "on" days. Use of these mechanisms forces new ideas and associations up for conscious consideration, and the individual need not wait for them to arise fortuitously.

Synectics, then, is a structured approach to creative problem solving. The purpose of the methodology is to provide the individual with a repeatable procedure which will increase the probability of his success and hasten his arrival at an innovative solution.

Synectics: the process

The Synectics process involves two basic activities: making the strange familiar, and making the familiar strange.

Making the strange familiar

The human organism is basically conservative. Any strange thing or concept can be threatening to it. When faced with strangeness, the individual tends to force it into an acceptable pattern or change his mind's private geometry of bias to make room for the strangeness. The mind compares the given strangeness with data previously known and in terms of these data converts the strangeness into familiarity. Three basic procedures are involved: Analysis, Generalization, and Model-seeking, or Analogy.

Analysis is the process of breaking down a complexity into its component parts. Generalization is the intellectual act of identifying significant patterns among the component parts. Model-seeking, or Analogy, is the equivalent of asking oneself, What in my knowledge or experience is like this? Lord Rutherford, for example, after analyzing the data relevant to the structure of the atom, sought a model of the system he had proposed and found it in the solar system. Later experimenters accepted Rutherford's analogy and generalized about the structure of the atom on the basis of it being a micro-solar system.

Analysis is, of course, an obvious and necessary part of problem solving. The great pitfall, the traditional danger, in making the strange familiar is in becoming so buried in analysis and detail that these become ends in themselves, leading nowhere. The process of making the strange familiar, if used alone, can usually lead only to a variety of superficial solutions. But basic novelty demands a fresh viewpoint, a new way of looking at the problem. Most problems are not new. The challenge is to view the problem in a new way. This new viewpoint in turn embodies the potential for a new basic solution.

Making the familiar strange

To make the familiar strange is to distort, invert, or transpose the everyday ways of looking and responding which render the world a secure and familiar place. This pursuit of strangeness is not merely a search for the bizarre and out-of-the-way. It is a conscious attempt to achieve a new look at the same old world, people, ideas, feelings, and things. In the "familiar world" objects are always right-side-up; the child who bends and peers at the world from between his legs is experimenting with the familiar made strange. (The layman sees the familiar tree as a collection of solids in an otherwise empty space. The sculptor consciously may invert his world and see the tree as a series of voids or holes carved within the solid block of the air.)

The attempt to make the familiar strange involves several different methods of achieving an intentionally naive or apparently "out-of-focus" look at some aspects of the known world. And this look can transpose both our usual ways of perceiving and our usual expectations about how we or the world will behave. The experience of sustaining this condition can prove an invaluable one in creative problem solving.

Operational mechanisms

Having identified psychological mechanisms that are useful in making the familiar strange, we fitted them into a Flow Chart, a schematic which contains all the mechanisms of Synectics. Following the chart diagram is an explanation of each step, after which is a typical, though condensed, Synectics problem-solving session.

The leader

But first, a word about the group leader. Synectics group sessions are always conducted by a leader. The leader's functions, however, are quite distinct from those usually implied by the word. He is neither a judge (passing on the merits of a contribution) nor a moderator (comparing disparate contributions) nor a chairman (who prepares an agenda and keeps out extraneous contributions). The Synectics leader is primarily responsible for keeping the problem investigation within the confines of the flow chart, and for insuring the most efficient generation, development, and use of analogical material.

Which analogical route to take, however, is an important decision. It is made by the leader on the basis of this criterion: constructive psychological strain. In a people-oriented problem that means he would seek analogies from the exact sciences. In a mechanical problem he might look to biological models.

The leader seeks analogical responses by means of so-called Evocative Questions. The EQ is the bridge between the analysis and analogy. The leader always specifies which type of analogy he wants—Example, Personal, or Book Title. Perhaps a more accurate title for the leader of a Synectics session would be "interlocutor." For in his role of developing this evolving, ever-changing agenda, he is most often merely filling in the gaps "between speeches."

Explanation of steps

Problem as Given (PAG)—A general statement of the problem to be solved as it may have been given to the group members by an outside source or as generated by themselves.

SYNECTICS FLOW CHART

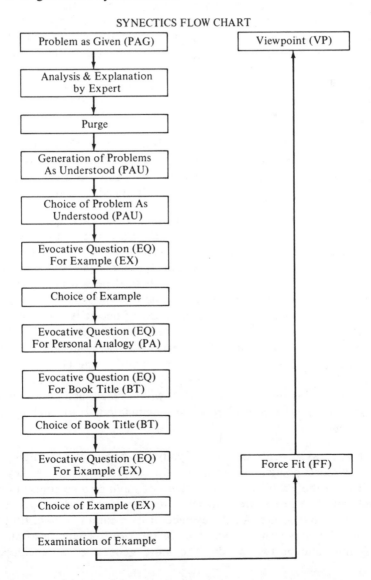

Analysis—An explanation of the problem by the expert, making the strange problem familiar. This should be in enough detail so that there is an understanding of the problem, but since the expert will be a participant, he need not try to make everyone as knowledgeable as he is.

Purge—The universal response to the statement of a problem is "How about solving it this way?" We have found it constructive to encourage people to air these immediate solutions. In some cases they are good viewpoints and, if not, as the expert explains why the suggestion won't work, everyone understands the problem better.

Problem as Understood (PAU)—After the PAG has been explained, each participant writes a restatement of the problem as he sees it or a goal he believes would be desirable. It is useful to write several PAU's which imply different approaches to the problem. We tell participants to feel free to wish for *anything* they can imagine, even if it violates laws they know hold true.

Evocative Question (EQ)—This is a question that requires an analogical or metaphorical answer. We have EQ's that produce three different kinds of analogy:

EXAMPLE (DIRECT ANALOGY) This mechanism describes the actual comparison of parallel facts, knowlege, or technology. The procedure requires searching one's experiences and knowledge for some phenomenon that is like or has some similar relationship with the subject at hand.

PERSONAL ANALOGY The simplest form of Personal Analogy is the casual introductory phrase "If I were he. . . ." Role playing is the kind of Personal Analogy often used as a rudimentary aid in solving problems which are "people-oriented" rather than technical—marketing problems, for example. One identifies oneself with a hypothetical person in a given situation and speculates on how that person would feel and act.

A more demanding form of conscious self-deceit is called for in the Synectics use of Personal Analogy, however; for Synectics uses one's own highly personal emotions and characteristics to gain insight into purely technological or abstract problems. One identifies oneself with a purely nonhuman entity which figures in the problem, investing it with one's own vitality, speculating on how that THING would "feel" and act in the problem situation. The device has proven an invaluable tool for making the familiar strange.

BOOK TITLE (SYMBOLIC ANALOGY) Symbolic Analogy is a highly compressed, almost poetic, statement of the *implications* of a key word selected from the Problem as Understood or having some connection with the problem. The procedure is to select the key word and ask yourself (or a member of your group) for the essence of its meaning to *you*. Empathize or feel for the important connotations of the word. Then try to put those feelings into one or two words. The more general or all-encompassing these words are, the more potentially useful in suggesting areas for speculation. Some typical Book Titles, or Symbolic Analogies, are:

Ratchet	Dependable intermittency
Viscosity	Hesitant displacement
Solidity	Enforced togetherness
Forest fire	Progressive ingestion
Machine-gun burst	Connected pauses
Target	Focused desire
Mixture	Balanced confusion
Multitude	Discrete infinity
Acid	Impure aggressor
Receptivity	Involuntary willingness.

The reader will note that it takes a moment's hard study to follow the connections between the analogy and its subject in some of the above couplets. The reason for the difficulty lies in the fact that the Symbolic Analogy is based on someone else's *personal* view of the key word and its implications. The utility of a Book Title is related to its "strangeness." How much psychological strain does it require for understanding? How surprising is it? Often a symbolic analogy embraces an apparent paradox (e.g. involuntary willingness). It is in the effort to resolve this paradox that insight usually arises.

Examination (Exam)—It is customary in this step to examine factually a selected Example, to play with one of the Examples. Two sorts of facts are produced: (a) descriptive facts about the Example and (b) super facts; statements that are more speculative and strange.

Force Fit (FF)—Although the analogical mechanisms lie at the heart of the Synectics method, they must be "force-fitted" to the problem if they are to be effective. Through the strain of this new fit the problem is stretched and pulled and refocused in order that it may be seen in a new way. If no deliberate attempt is made to find relevance in apparent irrelevance, then one analogy can merely lead to another and another, and potentially fruitful viewpoints will be bypassed. A Force Fit suggests new contexts and thus provides the raw material for new lines of speculation.

Viewpoint (VP)—"Give me a place to stand," boasted Archimedes, "and I can move the world." In Synectics, this "place to stand" is the material of the Examination, strange angles from which to view the familiar facts of the problem. A usefully strange Example can suggest not one but many different potential solutions or viewpoints. One of the basic differences between the Synectics method of operation and traditional problem-solving procedures is that the latter seek solutions. Synectics seeks new lines of speculation, and these in turn lead to potential solutions by means of the Force Fit.

Excursion—A term describing the Synectics procedure from selection of

PAU through Force Fit. If no new Viewpoint is developed, another "Excursion" is begun through all or part of the procedure. That is, sometimes new Examples can be made to the same EQ; or a new EQ may be used; or, when FF reveals a new aspect to the problem, a new PAU may be stated.

A typical session

PAG: How we determine oil saturation in reservoir rock.

Analysis: Expert: "In wells we are drilling now it is a serious problem to get a sample of the reservoir rock that is representative. The best method so far is to put down a hollow bit (on the drill pipe) and cut a core. We bring up this sample of the reservoir rock and then try to guess how representative it is. Trouble is that we may have 3000 psi pressure at the reservoir. As we bring the core up through six or seven thousand feet of muddy water this pressure is released—that and sloshing around in the muddy water makes a big difference between the core we have in hand to examine and the reservoir. If we had accurate data on oil saturation, we could calculate the reserves, get better information on our recovery percentages. It would really do us a lot of good."

Purges: None.

PAU's:

1. How make reservoir rock tell us the truth.
2. How to have oil tell me how crowded it is in the reservoir rock.

LEADER: Number 2 has a look of appeal.

LEADER: Now please put the problem out of your mind.

Evocative question: Example.

LEADER: My Evocative Question is for Example from biology of a crowded situation.

TOM: I don't mean it to be facetious but flies on a cow flop.

LEADER: Yes?

TOM: Well, it's a crowded situation . . . I mean those flies are two or three deep on there.

BOB: Ant hill.

HARRY: Virus culture.

LEADER: Say more about virus culture.

HARRY: It is a funny kind of crowd. It might start out very thin, but it multiplies and makes itself into a crowd.

LEADER: Do you mean it is sort of dedicated to making a crowd of itself?

HARRY: Partly that, but I was thinking that it has a deadly intention and needs a crowd to win.

TOM: Womb with triplets.

DICK: Drop of sperm.

HARRY: Seedling.

LEADER: Let's take this virus culture. Now take a couple of minutes . . . don't say anything while you get into your new skin . . . You are one virus in this culture . . . How do you feel?

Leader writes: EQ:PA (Personal Analogy), Virus Culture. (He waits.)

BOB: I am very small but so is everyone else. I am curled like a corkscrew.

LEADER: Anyone feel differently?

DICK: It's nice and warm in this culture, but I feel itchy . . . I am dissatisfied . . . because I want to go out on my own. . . . These guys are too self-satisfied and smug for me . . . I'm going for a sensitive spot where I can set up my own culture.

TOM: I feel a sense of real urgency . . . panic because I keep turning into two of me and then four . . . and everyone else is doing it . . . I can feel the food getting hard to get . . . got to die . . . want to do something fast but nothing to do—except multiply. My only mission.

LEADER: Your only mission? Who sent you on your mission? (Pause).

TOM: Fate . . . no, not fate really, it was evolution. I wasn't always this way . . . this prolific and deadly. I have evolved . . . you know . . . natural selection—man, I have ancestors who came over on the Mayflower.

LEADER: Great! Does anyone feel differently about being a virus?

BOB: I hate the world. I want to get into some other place—out of this culture where I can kill other things alive. It's a black world . . . I want to murder.

HARRY: I feel I am a very successful virus. With the way these other guys feel I can sit back and relax, enjoy life and play a guitar. One is going to take care of reproducing and killing. Why should I worry?

TOM: I resent his playing his guitar while I'm panicky.

LEADER: This is a rich haul . . . Now my Evocative Question is for a Book Title. Can you give me a two word title—poetic and compelling that captures the essence of virus culture and contains a paradox?

Leader writes: EQ:BT for Virus Culture.

(Long Silence)

LEADER: How about Dick's idea of "warm" and Bob's murderous feelings. Can we make something of that?

DICK: How about warm hate?

LEADER: The paradox is there, but I miss the essence. Say what you were thinking.

DICK: I just picked my "warm" and substituted hate for murder, but I guess a virus doesn't bother with hate.

TOM: Indifferent destruction.

LEADER: You got some of the essence. Can we improve on "indifferent" so the words fight more?

HARRY: How about affectionate destruction.

LEADER: Neat!

BOB: Indifferent purposefulness.

LEADER: What are you thinking?

BOB: From Tom's idea, the virus couldn't care less about his host, but he has a strong sense of purpose. Like Dick said in his Personal Analogy . . . he's ambitious and wants to grow and multiply.

DICK: Compulsive indifference.

LEADER: Let's go with that. My Evocative Question is for an Example from nature of compulsive indifference. (EQ:EX)

DICK: Queen bee.

LEADER: Say more about this Queen bee.

DICK: Well, I was thinking of their mating . . . She has the compulsion, but she flies away from males . . . higher and higher. . . . When one of the males finally mates with her, she is indifferent enough to kill him.

LEADER: Do you mean that the way she plays hard to get . . . the flying high and then when she does let a male make it . . . killing him—is a mixture of compulsion and indifference?

DICK: Yeah.

TOM: Cat.

LEADER: Yes?

TOM: A cat has compulsive curiosity, for instance, and yet the cats I know are quite indifferent to their owner.

LEADER: If I get you, this is a strange combination in cats; being curious implies interest, even concern . . . yet a cat doesn't give a damn about her best friend—her owner.

TOM: Yes, cats are a queer combination.

LEADER: Let's examine cat. I've spent a lot of time wondering about them. Tom, tell us more about cats.

TOM: It seems to me that each tomcat has a territory. He chases out the other toms and keeps the females for himself.

HARRY: We had a big tom once, and he had a huge territory—several square blocks. He'd come stumbling home each morning with pieces chewed out of him. My 5-year-old son who owned him said to him one morning, "Sniffer, is it worth it?"

DICK: You know the way cats lie perfectly still and relaxed. Every once in a while the tip of their tails flip as though to warn anyone, "I'm alert, baby!"

TOM: Cats can be responsive though; you pat or stroke them and gradually they'll relax and purr.

DICK: I think of cats as loners. They don't travel around in packs like dogs.

LEADER: Let's move into Force·Fit. How can we take this idea of cat and use it to help us have the oil tell us how crowded in the reservoir rock it is?

DICK: Something comes to me. If a cat gets crowded he loses all his indifference . . . He gets into a rage.

LEADER: You mean, we might crowd the oil a little in some way and then it would yell and tell us how crowded. . . .

TOM: I think I have a viewpoint.

LEADER: Are you going to build on Dick's?

TOM: Well, no, it's different.

LEADER: Please make a note; we'll come back to you. Is there some way we can put this oil in a rage so it. . . .

BOB (THE EXPERT): If you take the pressure off it becomes in a rage. It boils and fumes and carries on. But you would like it . . . calm. You want to talk to it while it is not in a rage, because then it is oil-like. It's got the essence of cat . . . You don't want to talk to the cat when he is in a rage . . . he's not communicating.

LEADER: How can we calm the oil down?

HARRY: Stroke it!

LEADER: OK, let's stroke it. What does it mean to stroke that oil?

HARRY: You stroke it just like a cat, and it calms down . . . maybe it purrs. You stroke that oil.

BOB (EXPERT, MUSINGLY): Yeah, you got to stroke that oil.

TOM: It even arches its back as you stroke it. It will react to your stroking.

BOB (SOFTLY): Chill it. . . . cool it down.

LEADER: If you want, we'll *freeze* it. Pump liquid. . . . what is that stuff?

BOB: Nitrogen! By God, maybe that's it. . . . We pump down liquid nitrogen and freeze the hell out of that formation.

LEADER: We're with you. . . .

BOB: We'll freeze the water and the oil and everything and core right into it. Everything will stay right put.

HARRY: Petrified candy!

BOB: We'll drill some and keep it cold some way. We'll freeze it and keep it cold as we bring it up. . . . We just might have something.

In the Expert's view this was a new and worthwhile way to view the problem, and it was written up as a Viewpoint.

4 | Bionics

THE ADVANCED TECHNOLOGY STAFF

Martin Company, Orlando, Florida

Reprinted from Engineering Digest, *1963, April,
21–22, 25; and 1963, May, 16–18.*

Bionics is a system design strategy based upon the study of the structure,
function, and mechanisms of plants and animals. As with synectics,
new ideas for man-made systems spring from analogous systems found in
nature. While the two parts of this article will be of interest primarily
to design engineers, they may serve as an inspiring lesson to
nonengineers: first, in the value of idea-finding through deliberate
metaphorical activities and, second, in the wealth of enlightening new
ideas to be drawn from nature's adaptive devices found in botany and
zoology.

BIONICS—PART I

Further exploration of outer space may depend on devices which can
adapt successfully to unpredicted and unpredictable environments. Bionics,
which uses living things as engineering prototypes, may provide these devices. Only living systems can adapt to a changing environment by changing their organization or structure. By contrast, today's machines perform
only those tasks which the designer has anticipated. Unpredicted situations
cause them to work erratically or not at all. Future satellites, space vehicles, and weapon systems will require sensors and computers that can
adapt to changing environments.

What is bionics?

Bionics is a new approach to system design. It is the study of the
structure, function, and mechanisms of plants and animals to gain design
information for analogous man-made systems. Bioncists seek to incorporate in man-made systems such characteristics of living things as self-adap-
tivity, learning, self-organization, self-optimization, and recognition. They

hope that their approach will make possible the design of machines, vehicles, and systems with greater reliability, sensitivity, selectivity, strength, maneuverability, speed, and acceleration, with reduced size, weight, and power requirements.

The broad subject matter of bionics requires individuals trained in both the life and physical sciences, and in engineering—or teams of specialists from those disciplines. Though electronics is the most obvious field for the application of bionic techniques, it is not the only one. Bionics is also applicable to mechanical, thermal, hydraulic, and chemical systems.

Why the bionics approach?

One reason for trying the bionics approach is that, in computer technology for instance, we may be at the point where conventional techniques can no longer answer new requirements. With a great deal of effort, we may be able to build a general purpose digital computer that can perform arithmetic operations 20 times faster than today's machines, but only at a great increase in cost, complexity, and unreliability. Such increases in rates and capacities will not provide pattern recognition, speech recognition, photo interpretation, and other adaptive capabilities that are the possible fruits of bionics research.

Another inducement to bionics research is the discovery in nature of systems similar to man-made ones. After the development of radar and sonar, it was discovered that bats have similar systems. Bionic studies might have uncovered these techniques earlier. Some sensors have been developed through bionics research. The Air Force's Aeronautical Systems Division (ASD) is now testing an aircraft ground speed-altitude indicator based on the beetle's eye, probably the first hardware to come from bionics research.

Various living organisms possess characteristics superior to those of man and his creations. The sensors which we share with animals are often less sensitive or selective than theirs. Some creatures have sensors which we do not possess at all and some have sensors whose function we do not yet understand. Some of these sensors have capabilities which would be desirable in many weapon systems and space vehicles.

Problems

There are problems in the bionics approach. While biology has an extensive literature, much of it is descriptive and classificatory. To be useful to engineers, data must be mathematical or quantitative. Much bionics research, some say as much as 90 percent, will be fruitless from the hardware standpoint. There are no principles of selection that will ensure that any particular biological subject can be adequately enough described so that mathematical and hardware models can be constructed. Because of the interdisciplinary nature of bionics, there are few individuals with training broad enough to handle bionics research projects alone; most projects which range from biological studies to engineering models must be handled by teams. To make a greater contribution to this work, biologists will have to learn to present their materials in a manner usable by engineers or mathematicians, or the latter must learn the language of the former.

Bionics approach

The bionics approach involves three steps: (a) Study and description of the biological model; (b) Translation of the biological description into mathematical or logical models as far as possible; (c) Development of hardware models (usually electronic) from these mathematical models.

The Air Force's Aeronautical Systems Division divides its bionics efforts into three areas which parallel this approach: Medical Bionics—Theoretical Bionics—Engineering Bionics.

In many cases, merely understanding the living system—knowing how it functions—may be sufficient to suggest a solution to an engineering problem. Quantitative investigation, construction of an analog, or duplication of the organism in any form may be entirely unnecessary.

Thus, in the approach outlined above, only the first step may be required in some instances. But this first step can be a time-consuming process, probably the most time-consuming in the bionics approach, and it can be mostly fruitless in terms of hardware development.

Major areas of bionics research

The major areas of current bionics studies are: Self-organizing systems—Sensors—Neurons.

Self-organizing machines are machines that can recognize, or learn to recognize, such stimuli as patterns, characters, and sounds, and which can then adapt to changing environments. Some are based on conventional computer construction techniques, but unconventional programming; they are called programmed machines. Others are based on nets of rudimentary artificial neurons; they are called network machines.

Today's machines operate with almost complete rigidity. Typically, if something happens the designer has failed to anticipate, the machine grinds to a halt. Biological systems are not so limited. For example, human body temperature is maintained at 98.6 °F in spite of changing external temperatures, and the composition of the blood is held nearly constant.

Sensory organs are a class of transducers. Sensory transducers in living systems detect mechanical, thermal, electrical, and chemical forms of energy and transform it into nerve impulses—electrochemical energy. In man-made systems the detected energy is typically converted to electrical energy. Studying living sensors to find the means to extend the range and sensitivity of man-made sensors is an important bionics objective; understanding the data processing which living sensors perform as they detect inputs is perhaps even more important.

The neuron is the basic building block of the human nervous system. It is a specialized body cell that can conduct and code an electrical impulse. An artificial neuron is the essential part of the neuron net self-organizing system. Artificial neurons, sometimes called neural analogs or neuromimes, are designed to incorporate the key logical functions of the biological neuron.

Most studies of the artificial neuron are directed at self-organizing systems, but some of the currently rudimentary artificial neurons are studied for what they can teach about the biological neuron.

While studies of the nervous and sensory systems of men and animals constitute about 90 percent of present bionics research, and electronic hardware is the goal of most of this effort, bionics is not restricted to those areas. For example, studies of the skins and shapes of the porpoise and whale may improve submarine design and studies of human muscle and bone structure may aid in the design of artificial limbs.

Self-organizing machines

There are two types of self-organizing machines, the network machine or biocomputer and the programmed machine.

The network machine performs functions usually associated with animal nervous systems and is modeled after them. That is, it is composed of neural analogs. It is truly bionic. The programmed machine is marginally bionic; it uses ordinary computer techniques to perform a limited number of adaptive tasks.

Network machines improve their recognition ability solely as a result of repeated joint occurrence of stimulus and desired output.

In learning, a circuit in these machines detects the success or failure of the machine to correctly identify the input signal or pattern of signals. Depending on what it sees, it sends either "positive or negative" signals to another part of the machine. These signals cause the machine either to increase or decrease its tendency to make this same identification in the future.

Generally, programmed machines recognize patterns by comparing them on a bit by bit basis with patterns stored in their memories, or by sequential scrutinizing to determine whether the object has certain properties which are stored in the machine's memory. The major efforts in programmed machine research are directed toward finding key unchanging properties of images and in developing filters which recognize these properties while rejecting all others. Methods based on statistical comparisons are also under consideration.

Most of these machines are being built as experiments to learn the characteristics and capabilities of self-organizing machines, but some people, like Rosenblatt at the Cornell Aeronautical Laboratory, are using their machines to help understand the structure and function of the brain and nervous system.

All of the devices developed thus far have been experimental. They imitate living systems in varying degrees: some are made up of nets of rudimentary artificial neurons, others are like conventional computers but are programmed for neural net logic, and still others attempt to duplicate the human learning process. No single approach has yet demonstrated overwhelming superiority.

The self-organizing machine, with suitable sensors and transducers for input and output functions and constructed of small, inexpensive neural analogs, is probably the major hardware goal of bionics. As much as 80 percent of current bionics research and development funding supports this effort.

BIONICS—PART II

Sensors

Sensory mechanisms in both animals and machines detect energy and convert it to a form suitable for processing. In living systems, thermal, electrical, and chemical forms of energy are converted to nerve impulses or electrochemical energy. In man-made systems, energy inputs of all types are typically converted to electromagnetic energy.

Various living creatures have capabilities in the following areas: airborne anti-collision, underwater detection, electromagnetic guidance in heavy jamming, and height finding. Man-made devices exist for all of these functions, but most biological organisms exceed the capabilities of any man-made system.

Bionics can extend the frequency response and sensitivity, and reduce the power requirements and weight of man-made sensors. They can unfold new techniques of detection previously not used in man-made systems.

Visual sensors

A study that has become a classic is the work of Lettvin, et al., at MIT on the eye of the frog. Their research demonstrated that the frog's eye performs five separate functions. In operation, the frog's eye doesn't respond to backgrounds, moving or still, but gives its full attention to objects moving against a background—potential bugs. Bell Telephone Laboratories has created an electronic analog of the frog's eye. The ultimate objective is a property filter. A property filter suppresses certain phenomena while passing others.

The Applied Physics Lab of Johns Hopkins University is working on machine interpretation of radar displays using processes patterned after the frog's eye. An experimental machine has demonstrated the ability to distinguish targets from background noise on a radar screen.

One of the first devices developed through bionics research is a ground speed-altitude indicator for aircraft based on the way the beetle's eye functions. Background work was done at the Max Planck Institute of Tübingen, Germany, by biologist Bernhard Hasselstein and engineer Werner Reichardt. After a series of experiments they concluded that the beetle lives in a world of shadows; it perceives motions by gathering changing light signals on each facet of its retina, correlating their times of arrival at the brain center, and integrating the information to judge speed and direction. The ground speed-altitude indicator uses two photocells, one in the nose of the aircraft, the other in the tail. It measures speed by measuring the time it takes for the photocell in the tail to receive the same changing light pattern the one in the nose has observed. In application, the device will be used to advance film at the proper rate in airborne cameras.

IBM is doing research on the eye in the tail of a variety of crayfish. They say they are maintaining this research so that the company will have some experience in bionics in case a significant breakthrough in the field is made elsewhere.

Auditory sensors

Hearing is another sense that has come under the scrutiny of bionics researchers. The Air Force Cambridge Research Center is studying the hearing system of moths for application to computation and communications equipment development. The moth's ear, which consists of only two cells is able to separate almost imperceptible hostile bat sounds from background noise. This requires greater selectivity than our most selective microphones possess.

The bat's ear and larynx provide a sonar for detecting food and finding its way in the dark. In night flight the bat is able to avoid wires as fine as 0.5 millimeter in diameter and to catch mosquitoes at the rate of 10 a minute. The bat apparently is not disturbed by the sounds of rain or a cave full of other bats. It can pick up the echoes from a mosquito in a background 2,000 times stronger than the signal. Its auditory system weighs only a fraction of a gram. It is hoped that a radar anti-jamming device may be based on the bat's ear. One species of bat of special interest to the Navy can function in two mediums—it locates fish by skimming over the surface of the water.

Exotic sensors

Some creatures, like rattlesnakes, have sensors which humans don't possess. The rattlesnake has IR receptors which will respond to an increase or decrease of 10^{-11} small calorie in 0.1 second, equivalent to a change in tissue temperature of 0.001 °C. Dr. Theodore Bullock, working at UCLA, experimented with the rattler by displaying two balls of equal shape but differing by as little as a tenth of a degree. The snake invariably struck the warmer.

Several varieties of fish have electroreceptors. At Cambridge, England, Dr. H. W. Lissman has been testing fish which are sensitive to electric potential gradients in the range of one microvolt per foot. This sensitivity is adequate to detect the lines of force in the earth's magnetic field when the fish is swimming at a rate of 0.25 feet per second. Some fish will respond to a comb run through the hair and placed in front of their tank. They can distinguish between conductors and nonconductors, or respond to a permanent magnet outside their tank. Fish emit pulses of low voltage with frequencies characteristic of each species. The frequencies range from 50 to 1600 cycles per second. The fish can detect the alteration in the pattern of the electric field resulting from objects, apertures, or other fish in the surrounding waters.

Other studies of animal sensors are underway. At the California Academy of Sciences in San Francisco, biologists are studying bird navigation. They theorize that the European warbler, for example, navigates by the sun during the day and by the stars at night. They are trying to find principles applicable to navigation aids.

The first hardware based on the bionics approach to research will be in the area of sensors. Some of the first results will be improved TV and radar displays and groundspeed indicators for aircraft.

Neuron

The neuron is the basic functional and structural unit of living sensing and intelligence systems. It is a specialized cell that can conduct and code an electrical impulse, and, in some cases, act as an ac/dc converter. Design of an artificial neuron which can be produced cheaply, approach the living neuron's small size and low power consumption, and perform its key logical functions is a major goal of bionics research. Dr. M. C. Yovits, head of ONR's Information Systems Branch, thinks that it will take 10 years to build a successful artificial neuron.

The artificial neuron is the essential part of the network self-organizing system. It is also being studied apart from this application by some groups such as GE and ASD who are developing an artificial neuron as a functional component, like a tube or integrated circuit, for use in advanced data and signal processing systems. Others are studying the artificial neuron to learn more about the biological neuron.

Other areas of bionics research

While 90 to 95 percent of current bionics research concerns the nervous and sensory systems of animals and men, other significant studies are being conducted. Such studies deal with the human motor, circulatory, and nervous systems as clues for the design of artificial limbs, communications system, and efficient methods for designing redundant electronic equipment.

Porpoise and whale

Studies are being made of the porpoise and whale to learn about the very low resistance and very high propulsion efficiency they exhibit. Their unusual capabilities are attributed to the laminar or streamline flow condition which exists at the skin-water interface and is believed to be the result of oily skin, the elastic and damping characteristics of the skin, and the undulating motion of the creature's body. Such studies may permit the design of improved marine propulsion systems, especially for submarines.

Mathematics

The development of new mathematical techniques is important to bionics. Complex electronic systems have created a need for a new mathematics of unreliability. Understanding unreliability is important because the checkout equipment for a complex system sometimes costs more than the basic system itself. Life scientists, too, are interested in a mathematical analysis of unreliability because, while biological neurons are unreliable, animal nervous and sensory systems are not.

An understanding of how humans make decisions—subjective probability, as opposed to the more familiar mathematical probability—is also an area of interest. The Rand Corporation is doing work in computer programming based on research on the way humans solve problems. These studies were used to formulate computer programs based on trial and error methods, simulating human behavior. The system enables the computer to predict final correct results without being specifically programmed to do so.

Dr. David Ellis and a group at Litton Industries are studying the electrical impulses that are known to precede all muscular activity. He says that understanding these may make it possible for a person to perform work merely by thinking about it. Litton has human electrical impulses running tiny servo motors. This research has potential application in the area of artificial limbs.

Evaluation and prospects

The urgent, complex needs of the electronics and aerospace industries require that bionics be among the research techniques employed in the immediate future. The result of early experiments (beetle's eye ground speed-altitude indicator, the various perceptrons), while modest, cannot be ignored when linked to the promise of molecular electronics and advanced efforts to describe the biological neuron. They especially command our attention when the limitations, increasing costs, and complexity of conventional techniques are considered. Certainly a further stimulus to the use of the bionics technique is the discovery in nature of devices previously developed by man. The opposite road ought to be explored.

It is impossible to anticipate and describe all problems and environments that man will encounter as he ventures further into space. Because of this, the most sought after characteristic for spacecraft sensing and control mechanisms is self-adaptation, the ability to adapt to changing environments with incomplete prebriefing. Even the most simple living systems exhibit this characteristic. In a primitive way, early perceptrons have shown an ability to do this, such as the device which can learn to distinguish submarines from porpoises in a few hours, rather than in the several months required for human operators.

The key to real progress in this effort is a more successful artificial neuron. It will not be sufficient in most applications for an artificial neuron to be built from conventional electronic components because of the great numbers which will be required. Developments underway in miniaturization and molecular electronics will probably be able to provide the necessary circuits when they are needed. Redundancy will be an important characteristic because of the impossibility of individual circuit repair and the excessive cost of obtaining extremely high reliability. Mathematical descriptions of the redundancy by which living systems achieve high reliability with the relatively unreliable neuron will be an important contribution. The key biological contribution to bionics research will be a complete description of how the biological neuron works. This is close. Techniques for analyzing systems composed of billions of circuits are being developed.

Bionics is a high risk venture. It is a field for a research minded company not interested in a quick return on its investment.

5 | The techniques of creative thinking

ROBERT P. CRAWFORD
University of Nebraska

From the book Techniques of Creative Thinking *by Robert P. Crawford. Copyright © 1954 by Hawthorn Books, Inc. Published by Hawthorn Books, Inc., 70 Fifth Avenue, New York, New York.*

Virtually every course, program, or book devoted to training imagination includes instruction in Crawford's *attribute-listing* procedure. One of the most simple yet effective means of innovation, attribute listing constitutes not only a method but an explanatory theory of the creative process. In Crawford's own words, "Each time we take a step, we do it by changing an attribute or a quality of something, or else by applying that same quality or attribute to some other thing." In this selection, abridged from his 1954 book of the same title, Crawford elaborates on his attribute-listing procedure and presents examples of its application to such diverse fields as architecture, music, clothes designing, painting, and professional cooking. Note, however, that even the youngest school children can be taught to identify and improve such attributes as the color, shape, material, and, perhaps, function of any simple object.

Some years ago I thought of this business of creating ideas as something very mysterious. Like many others, I believed that it could not be developed, that it either happened or did not happen. But I soon found that creation was a process. I found that certain university students could develop this power and that, as they did so, they became resourceful.

It is as foolish to say that the process of creative thought cannot be taught as to say that medicine or engineering cannot be taught. There is a reason for anything that happens in the world. We can find the reason. When we actually learn how, it is an easy matter to go ahead and make things happen.

Creation, around which we have always placed an aura of mystery, consists in turning the mind forward. Few of us have ever learned the art of thinking forward, because education and experience have always emphasized thinking backward. Strange to say, in most of our educational processes, we deal rather consistently with the past, but without much definite understanding as to how it fits the future. We remember, remember, and then remember some more. But the real object of this remembering is to give ourselves a better future, unless we are to do like so many thousands about us and crawl back into the past for safety's sake.

The great names in the world, however, are those of men and women who have moved forward. Without the comparatively few hundred men like Watt, Pasteur, and Einstein, civilization as we know it would not exist. Ideas have made the world.

The strange thing is that I, we, you—most of us—have done so little. In nearly every office there are individuals—men and women—on very modest salaries, always reported to have "bright minds." In those same offices are other men on relatively high salaries who seem to be taking life easy. In most cases the high-priced men and women are those who have the knack of furnishing their companies with bright, new ideas. These are not always so-called "brilliant" men and women. I venture to say that many of the poorly paid would top more successful men and women in intelligence tests. I see all about me people who were known as very brilliant individuals in school, who were graduated from universities with honors, and yet to whom nothing seems to have happened. Look about for yourself.

Again I say that the difficulty in getting into this practice of creation is that our existence up to now has often been opposed to it. It is almost as if there were a constant battle between past and future. We see and feel our past but not our future. Education usually studies the past, but emphasis upon the past, unless we make use of it, is almost directly opposed to creative thought. We have made too much of a mystery of the future. Yet ideas put into execution *are* the future.

Progress—what is it but a succession of ideas put into effect and piled one on top of the other? A progressive age is an age in which there is a multiplicity of these changes. A progressive company is one that creates and executes many ideas. Ages, companies, and individuals that originate few things are backward. Without these new ideas and consequent changes all of us would be living in a world no different from the times before Christ—even like the days of the caveman.

Everyone, it seems, talks about ideas, but few people are specific about how to get them. A person starting to teach creative thinking encounters blank looks on the faces of his students during the first few weeks. To them it seems strange that anyone should tamper with "those mysterious laws of creation" and assume that they, just students, could have ideas. After a few weeks, the blank looks fade and, by the end of the semester, the students usually have a surprisingly large number of workable ideas.

Everything that man does starts with an idea, or a succession of ideas. The steam engine was an idea. The automobile was an idea—many ideas. The flying machine was an idea. Great books and paintings are ideas. Everything is an idea down to the tube of tooth paste or the wrapper on a candy bar.

This matter of creation or invention—for it is really one and the same process—is fundamental to life. Men and women are measured in the world not by their drudgery but by their ideas, particularly when these ideas are translated into action.

To start off, we are going to take a trip and see what we shall see. Many highly successful businessmen take trips with the sole purpose of gathering ideas in their respective fields. But we are not committing ourselves to one field. We are going to take a look here, there, and everywhere.

"What gorgeous buildings!" I exclaimed one day as I was walking over the campus of the University of Colorado at Boulder. The buildings seemed to violate the rules of traditional college architecture. They were unsymmetrical in line. They sloped at various heights and angles. They were built of local sandstone which varied in color from yellow to reddish-purple.

But now we come to the significant point. Where did the style of those red-tiled buildings originate? They came from the barns and houses of rural Italy. Charles Zeller Klauder, the Philadelphia architect, had planned, like so many architects of university buildings, to follow the traditional Gothic style, but he became so impressed with the site and the materials lying right at hand on university property that he evolved this "new idea" in architecture. And yet we know where it came from.

A famous designer of women's clothes raids the Brooklyn Museum for "new creations." In one recent year her creation of a new woman's suit jacket came from a man's hunting jacket shown in the museum. A "domino coat," which possessed the doubtful asset of making a woman appear as if she were leaving a tent, was the old pyramid coat of 1866. One year the designer managed to get ideas for fifteen dresses out of the museum—not a bad record! Do not think that she simply copies these things. She adapts them to modern use.

The Costume Institute of the Metropolitan Museum of Art featured a "Casablanca to Calcutta" exhibition. There you saw an exhibit of fabrics that had been based on source material in the museum. Side by side you could see the original from which the adaptation had been made and also the new design itself. A peacock and floral design embroidered on an Indian skirt became part of a design for several different fabrics by Hafner. Wesley Simpson had noticed a head of Krishna designed for a mural in the palace of the Maharajah of Jaipur. Just one item there, the tear drop pearls, furnished the foundation for a green rayon dress with black scallops and white tear drops.

There are today great machines for mathematical computation. They grew out of the idea of the machines used for automatic telephone operation. Officials of the Bell telephone system were not satisfied with the scope of the calculating machines used for their mathematical computations and decided to build their own—using the same principles they were using for automatic switching.

In California the Mediterranean style of architecture is developing so fast that standing on the deck of a steamer, one might well imagine himself on the Italian Riviera. That architecture is particularly suited to sunny climates.

In the prosaic field of cooking a professional caterer makes his beets, carrots, sweet potatoes, and radishes so attractive that they might be taken for exotic flowers. An artist not in paints and crayon, but in ordinary food.

As a musician, you adopted the theme of the Indian song for your waltz or light opera number. As a painter, you used the attribute of the cartoon. A sculptor might have done the same in his field.

As a restaurant keeper, you took your rib steak and, instead of broiling it, you reached over to the rib roast idea and created the idea of roasting it. Or you might have started with the rib roast idea and reached over and created the idea of roasting it in *individual* pieces to order—the attribute heretofore applied to steak. Of course, it is not so important where you start in this business as where you end up. Our minds, fortunately, are more concerned with the end of a process than the beginning.

Now! What have we learned so far?

Each new development or bit of creation starts from something else. It does not come out of a blue sky. You make use of that which has already entered the mind, or that which you cause to enter the mind. That is the real reason, the great reason for accumulating knowledge.

In order to test this principle, carefully analyze ideas that came to you suddenly—those that you can recall—and determine what was really their foundation. Talk with your acquaintances who have created something new—whether it be invention, new ways of selling goods, writing, music, anything—and ask them how it came about. Don't their experiences agree with what we have said?

Occasionally you may run across individuals who do not know how they did it or who like to make great mysteries of their accomplishments, but most people who really make a business of creating things know the process they went through.

You have a question here. You say to me: "You have made things very simple. But everything cannot be so simple. Many things are very complex."

"Yes," I answer. "That is true." Most pieces of creation as they stand today do not represent just one jump but many successive jumps. For example, hundreds and thousands of scientists and inventors each did at least one bit in the field of electricity. And sometimes that one bit was sufficient to get their names in the encyclopedia. Civilization represents millions of pieces of creation, each put there by someone or other. Ideas are piled one on top of the other and thereby make history.

Creation generally consists in the *shifting of attributes from one thing to another*. In other words, we give the *thing* with which we are working some new *quality* or *characteristic* or *attribute* heretofore applied to something else.

What this is not—a brief review

We should understand quite clearly what this technique is not as well as what it is:

1. First, our basic process is not just inspiration except in so far as inspiration means that the body and mind are active—in good trim, so to speak—and able to work as quickly and readily at creating as they would work quickly and readily at anything else.

2. The method of creation is not just a matter of combination, as some have implied. You do not pick up an armful of different things and throw them together in that rather vague way that some have called creation. *Each time we take a step we do it by changing an attribute or a quality of something, or else by applying that same quality or attribute to some other thing.* The pattern of great pieces of creation may involve hundreds of successive changes. The creative step is the same, but it is repeated many times with many variations. If you doubt this, examine any notable building and count the adaptations. In any piece of music you will find scores and scores of these adaptations. The mind takes just one step at a time, and it may do this very rapidly. It may consider several changes at one time, but only when they can be considered as a unit, as for example, the general style or architecture of a house. Usually there is just the one dominant change with which you start.

3. An important point, which we again emphasize, is that we do not generally see these attributes or things as simple abstracts. When we reach out and pick up some quality or attribute, it is always in relation to some particular thing. Even when we think of such a highly abstract quality as softness, we usually think of it as the dominant quality of a pillow, a piece of velvet, or something else with which we may be familiar.

4. In making an adaptation, another consideration arises, one that we have already mentioned, but which we again emphasize. When we change our attribute, we usually change it to something that stands in close association to it. In the development of the commercial possibilities of fruit juice as a breakfast drink, we proceeded from orange juice to grapefruit juice to other juices. When we change the thing and apply our same attrib-

ute to it, we generally pick a thing that is closely related to the other. We sell men's shirts by mail so why not sell men's socks by mail? That means that creation is generally a progressive and orderly procedure.

5. Creation is not stealing another's work. Of course, the line between new creation and plagiarism is often a very fine one, because the change may be slight. Any patent attorney can tell you how slight the change and how narrow the interpretation may be in determining that something is really new. Then, as we have pointed out, a "new" thing usually involves not one but dozens of adaptations before it is finally complete. Often the original idea with which we began is no longer seen at all in the complete product. Any man who just sits down and copies something is plain dumb. The process of creation is so simple and so easy, when one understands it, that even the best of things is usually susceptible of improvement.

6 | Conference: How to develop engineering creativity

In 1962 *Hydrocarbon Processing,* a petroleum refining journal, held a conference on creativity intended to answer such basic, yet critical, questions as "Just what is creativity?", "What is the creative technical man like?", and "Can creativity be learned by the engineer who is not 'naturally' creative?" Directing their answers toward both engineering and management, all five contributors clearly represent the "business" world. However, much of the content of these articles has been carefully sifted from the available psychological literature and will relate easily to classroom creativity—its understanding and training.

Addressing himself mainly to identifying traits of creative individuals, Charles H. Vervalin summarizes (in the first and third reports) many of the most recurrent personality characteristics of individuals identified as "creative," plus some traits which interfere with a creative imagination. After presenting a "stage" analysis of the problem-solving process, plus itemizing some hints for changing attitudes and habits in a more creative direction, Vervalin reproduces an interview with the late Alex F. Osborn, originator of brainstorming and author of *Applied Imagination,* in which Osborn summarizes his most important principles of deliberate creativity.

Supplementing Vervalin's trait analysis, and drawing heavily from the work of Guilford, L. C. Repucci further discusses some intellectual and nonintellectual factors contributing to creative productivity. He also summarizes the creativity research at Dow Chemical, which focuses upon both the identification and training of creative talent.

Nothing can be more stiffling or, on the other hand, more encouraging than the "atmosphere" of an organization or classroom. Recognizing this critical determiner of creativity, Arthur B. Wintringham presents some concrete *do's* and *dont's* for executives and managerial-level supervisors.

In the final article of this conference, F. D. McMurry and H. T. Hamblin spell out Hector-the-engineer's possible constructive or destructive reactions to a suppressive environment. They also discuss the dynamics of selling an idea, a problem of no small importance, explaining the nature of both the predictable resistance and possible countermeasures.

While these articles clearly were written with problems of industry in mind, the interested educator will find that such topics as the traits and abilities of creative individuals, barriers to creative behavior, and the nature of the creative process are quite meaningfully related to classroom creativity.

Just what is creativity?

CHARLES H. VERVALIN
Hydrocarbon Processing *staff*

Reprinted from the article of the same title which appeared in Hydrocarbon Processing, *1962, 41 (10), 109–111. By permission of the author and Gulf Publishing Company, Houston, Texas.*

Creative thinking is the process of bringing a problem before one's mind clearly (as by imagining, visualizing, supposing, musing, contemplating, etc.) and then originating or inventing an idea, concept, realization or picture along new or unconventional lines. It involves study and reflection rather than action.

In other words, to achieve something new or different, a person must discover a different combination or application previously unknown to him. This combination might include an existing device, mechanism, fundamental law, effect or change in attribute such as size, shape, color, capacity, etc. Creativity, then, is the obtaining of a combination of processes or attributes that are new to the creator.

The creative person

Just who is this person with unusual capacity to innovate—to change? Many people see him as an offbeat, nonconforming, individualist who has little interest in anything aside from his own imaginative pursuits. The perfect stereotype of such an individual is the coffee-house, beatnik-type artisan who lives in a curious world of daydreams, paintbrushes, poetry, or music. The more sophisticated stereotypist may visualize Da Vinci, Beethoven, Poe, or, in science, some other such "creative genius" as Einstein or Newton.

The fact is, that while such people may be the epitome of creativity, there is another side of creativity people seldom consider—*the cumulative, innovative efforts of people in all fields, using each others' ideas as building blocks.* Our own HPI is a good example of this. For every Dubbs,

Houdry, or Kalichevsky, there are thousands of HPI engineers and scientists who hold patents—and additional thousands of non–patent-holders who have contributed to genuine innovation and change in a product, process, technique, or what-have-you.

Creativity—esthetic and nonesthetic

Just as there are different *levels* of intelligence and different *types* of intellect, there are different kinds of creativity. There is creativity in music, literature, and art—the common forms with which we are all familiar. But there is also *technological* creativity, of which we can think of many examples within our own industry.

Thus, we can start with the fact that creativity takes many forms. The great Leonardo Da Vinci was both artisan and technologist—both an esthetic and a scientist. Perhaps no single individual in history has been as creatively productive and diversified as Leonardo. However, he was an exception. By and large, creative persons have *one* specialized talent in which they excel. This does not mean, of course, that the creative engineer cannot paint or compose music. It does mean that he need not necessarily do so to be classified as creative.

Just what, then, is a creative person? How does he differ from his noncreative contemporaries?

Many things were learned about the creative individual in a recent research project at the University of California's Institute of Personality Assessment and Research. Some 600 persons were studied, representing the fields of writing, architecture, physical-science research, engineering, and mathematics. Persons studied were recommended by experts in their respective fields on the basis of proven capacity for creative innovation.

Creative people understand themselves

Qualities of the creative person

Basically, here is what this intensive research showed about the creative person.

1. There is no clear stereotype of the creative individual, although some similarities exist in all such persons. Some of these similarities follow.

2. All exhibit great intellectual curiosity. As for intelligence, it was usually high—but it is important to understand that intelligence is a many faceted thing—so naturally some of the study's subjects scored higher in some areas than others, and vice versa. For example, writers showed unusual verbal intelligence (ability to perceive and construct verbal relationships and ideas) while the scientists scored much higher than others on spatial relationships (geometrics) and mathematical concepts.

3. They are discerning and observant in a differentiated way. They are alert and can concentrate and shift attention appropriately.

4. They have a wide range of information in their minds which they are able to combine, sort, and extrapolate to solve problems involving creative construction.

5. They are sensitive to their own psychological intricacies and, being so aware, have few repression or suppression mechanisms (mental "blocks") in their makeup.

6. While intellectually well endowed, they are also emotionally responsive, i.e., exhibit empathy for people and divergent ideas (tolerance of ambiguity). They make little attempt to repress unpleasant or troublesome problems in seeking solutions.

7. They almost unanimously report relatively unhappy childhoods.

8. They "understand" themselves, in the sense that they can easily see and react to the components of their personalities, and are more perceptive of their own psychological characteristics.

9. In tests for introversion-extroversion, most of the subjects showed a tendency toward introversion—but those rated as extroverts scored as high on creativity potential as the introverts.

10. They are not particularly conscious of what others think about them, and are thus freer from conventional restraints and inhibitions.

11. They are not conformists in their ideas, but are not nonconformists either. Rather, they are genuinely independent.

12. They are flexible with respect to means and goals. They do well when independence in thought and action are called for, and don't respond to situations that call for too much conforming behavior.

13. They are less interested in facts as such, and are more concerned with *meanings* and *implications* of facts.

14. They are intellectually verbal and communicative and are not

interested in policing either their own images or impulses or those of others.

A substantiating study

In a similar study at Pennsylvania State University by Professor Viktor Lowenfeld, eight key characteristics of the creative person were determined. These were later confirmed by Professor Guilford at the University of Southern California. These eight characteristics are as follows:

1. Sensitivity. The creative individual is sensitive to problems, needs, attitudes, and feelings of others. He has an acute awareness of anything odd, unusual, or promising in the person, material, or situation with which he is dealing. (The studies showed no differences between perceptual and social sensitivity.)

2. Fluency. This refers to the ability to take continuous advantage of a developing situation—to use each completed step as a new vantage point from which to assess the problem and move on.

3. Flexibility. People with high creative ability adjust quickly to new developments and changed situations. Unforeseen obstacles in a problem-solving situation are often used to advantage by the creative person.

4. Originality. This is self-explanatory. It was measured, in this study, by uncommonness of the individual's responses to problematical situations and the number and diversity of solutions given.

5. Redefinition Skill. Creative people have unusual ability to rearrange ideas, concepts, people, and things—to shift the function of objects and use them in new ways. Inventiveness is not always a factor here—rather, the imaginative use of old things or ideas for new purposes.

6. Ability to Abstract. This might be referred to as skill analysis. It involves proficiency in analyzing a project's components and comprehending the relationships between components, i.e., getting details from the "whole."

7. Ability to Synthesize. This is the opposite of the ability to abstract. It means ability to combine several components to arrive at a creative "whole."

8. Coherence of Organization. The ability to organize a project, express an idea, or create a design in such a way that nothing is superfluous. In other words, "getting the most out of what you have to work with."

Because of obvious space limitations, we have had to place emphasis upon the generalities of these research findings. There are many paths leading to the full development and expression of creative potential. And, there is no single slot into which all creative people fit. But if one insists on a "canned" listing of the creative person's characteristics as revealed in research, the following is as close as we can get:

Creative people are not necessarily beatniks

High level of intelligence (intelligence here being broadly defined)
Openness to experience
Freedom from inhibitions and stereotyped thinking
Esthetic sensitivity
Flexiblity in thought and nature
Independence in thought and action
Love of creation for creation's sake
Endless quest for new challenges and solutions

Barriers to creativity

Now that we have conceptualized the creative person, what are some of the psychological barriers to creative thinking? And, can creativity be taught to a person who does not have a "natural" capacity for it? This topic is covered in the article on page 76. But first, let's take a closer look at what research shows about creativity, *specifically among scientists and engineers*. This information is in Dr. Repucci's article on the following page.

What research reveals about creativity

L. C. REPUCCI

The Dow Chemical Co., Midland, Mich.

Reprinted from the article of the same title which appeared in Hydrocarbon Processing, *1962, 41 (10), 112–117. By permission of the author and Gulf Publishing Company, Houston, Texas.*

Any attempt, ten short years ago, to report on what research reveals about creativity would have been difficult, because in 1952 research data on creativity was very limited. In ten short years, the task has become even more difficult because the subject matter has received a lot of attention, resulting in a tangle of research reports. The tangle, like all tangles, seems hopelessly confused and meaningless. But this confusion is really a tribute to the apparent vigor and progress in creativity research. Here is what some of this research has revealed about creativity among scientists.

Creativity can be measured

Great progress has been made in creativity measurement. Despite many objections about the type and nature of measurements employed, creativity can be and has been measured.

The issue of what is measurement versus what is legitimate measurement is a serious problem in the philosophy of science. However, it is not appropriate to enter into this discussion here. It *is* appropriate to point out that physical scientists tend to feel that social science measurement is not very sophisticated. Such people overlook the fact that sophisticated measurement in any field of science does not arrive spontaneously, but only as a result of many little refinements. *The refinements in creativity measurement will come.* Some crudities exist now, but each day brings more and more sophistication—so much so that certain factors seem quite clear.

Cognitive factors

Since creativity is generally seen as some form of mental operation, it is no surprise to find that much research has been done to discover the factors of intelligence crucial to creativity.

Creativity can be measured

A consistent finding is that intelligence does not, in and of itself, account for creativity. A certain minimum level of intelligence is generally required—but beyond this level, creativity is accounted for by other factors.

The minimum intelligence needed is about 120 IQ. Hence, if you have an IQ of 160, this fact does not account for whatever creativity you may exhibit. The best that can be said is that you have intellectual capacity to be creative. Conversely, if you have an IQ of 90, the odds are against your being creative because you do not have minimum intellectual capacity.

This finding powered a whole new area of research. It was thought that if intelligence did not account for creativity, then perhaps creativity could be accounted for in terms of some type of specific mental ability or intellectual manipuation not tapped by measures of overall intelligence.

Guilford's findings

The driving force behind this effort has been Guilford at Southern California. Using the tool of factor analysis, he isolated specific aspects of intellect which might account for creativity. In his investigations, Guilford has isolated 53 such factors (Guilford, 1959).

Rather than working with intelligence as a simple concept, he distinguishes between intellect and intelligence. He defined intellect as the collection of memory and thinking functions and processes. These functions he calls factors.

Intelligence, on the other hand, is seen as a very limited aspect of intellect. It is defined by Guilford as a shifting collection of intellectual factors. Starting with these definitions, he isolated 53 factors which he found fit nicely into a unified, three-dimensional matrix. For practical purposes, we will not "three-dimensionalize" intellect as Guilford has done. Rather, we will list the factors in sequence.

He starts with three basic variables. These variables are operations, content, and products. Each variable is subdivided.

Operations

This refers to what the organism does with information. Information is defined as that which the organism discriminates.

    1. Cognition (discovery, recognition, or comprehension)
    2. Memory (retention or storage)
    3. Divergent Production (generating varied information from given or known information)
    4. Convergent Production (generating information from information)
    5. Evaluation (deciding as to the goodness of information)

Content

This refers to the general variety of information.

    1. Figural (concrete or perceived)
    2. Symbolic (composed of signs)
    3. Semantic (meaning—usually verbal)
    4. Behavioral (presently a theoretical category dealing with the behavior of others or self)

Products

Form that the information takes as a result of processing by the organism.

    1. Units (items of information with "thing" character)
    2. Classes (collections of units with common properties)
    3. Relations (connections between units)
    4. Systems (organized structures)
    5. Transformations (changes or redefinitions)
    6. Implications (extrapolations, such as antecedents or consequents)

Basic findings lead to other factors

As Guilford sees it, these basic factors theoretically converge so as to yield other factors. For instance, verbal comprehension is the result of convergence of

    Cognition (which is an operation)
    Semantics (which refers to content)
    Units (which are products)

Consequently, he defines verbal comprehension as "cognition of semantic units."

Creative people have great motivation

Once he isolated these factors, Guilford turned to the "input" problem. That is, he concentrated on the question "What type or types of stimuli will best elicit these factors?" The stimuli he has settled on are a series of tests, which have been used in a variety of research situations. The results indicate that some are very useful and some require further work.

Certainly, the Guilford tests are not the only ones available. I chose to discuss his approach to provide a feel for the amount of work and the depth of thinking that has gone into research on creativity testing.

Personality factors

Unfortunately, the intellectual factors do not, in and of themselves, account for differences in creative ability. These intellectual factors seem to be a necessary—but not sufficient—ingredient of creativity. A large portion of the variance in different creative abilities seems to depend upon personality factors.

Studies in this area generally show there are personality differences between Hi and Lo creative subjects. When these studies are examined collectively, the results often seem contradictory. That is, one study will report a difference in terms of such variables as independence and dominance. Another will report either no difference or a difference in the opposite direction.

These contrasting views which keep appearing in the literature can be integrated if we keep in mind that different studies involve scientists from different occupational environments. One well known study deals exclusively with industrial scientists. Another deals with scientists in a public institution. Yet, both reports contain some contradictory findings.

The creative scientist's work environment

If we look at the data, there seems to be a natural selection of work environments based on personality factors. For instance, one study of industrial scientists reports that the more successful and creative ones were optimistic, extraverted, nonanxious, independent, and confident. The least successful ones were the opposite on all these variables.

The studies done on institutional scientists describe them as passive, introverted, and anxious. This area needs to be studied more carefully.

Another variable is motivation. If there is any agreement regarding the personality of creative people, it lies in the area of motivation. The literature consistently reports that creative people have great motivational drive. This finding has been consistent and there was a need to measure this drive. So, at Dow we decided to try to devise a measure of motivational drive.

Starting with the idea that scientists can be differentiated into Hi or Lo creative groups by the way they convert problem-solving tension into problem-solving drive, I devised a Word Discrimination Test for which there were no right answers. I administered this test along with a Chemistry Test and a Progressive Additions Test to 94 industrial scientists.

The Chemistry Test was a simple multiple-choice test and the Progressive Additions Test was a simple arithmetic additions device. The specific predictions were that the more creative scientists would be more attracted to the nonanswerable items (not confirmed); they would produce more items (confirmed significantly); and produce more complex items (confirmed significantly). The latter two prediction confirmations bear out results reported in the literature that more creative people are more productive. They also prefer more complex tasks.

Personality and work

A fascinating research study in the personality area, which has implications for environmental studies, is work done by Gough and Woodworth (1960). They sought to determine whether there were distinctive or stylistic variations in the personalities and work habits of research scientists.

To answer this, they prepared a set of 56 diagnostic statements they believed pertained to scientific activity, scientific values, and modes of research activity. A sample of 45 professional industrial research scientists were asked to Q-sort these statements. From this study, the authors identified eight different research styles.

Personality styles among scientists

These are the eight personality styles arrived at by Gough and Woodworth.

1. The Zealot. He is dedicated to research activity but does not get along well with others.

2. The Initiator. He is the rapid generator of ideas and a good "team" man.

3. The Diagnostician. He has a knack for improvising quick solutions in research trouble spots. He has a live-and-let-live attitude.

4. The Scholar. He is well informed but indecisive and unconfident.

5. The Artificer. He has a knack for taking the poorly formed ideas of others and making them workable. He is open and responsive to others.

6. The Esthetician. He favors analytical modes of thinking to other types. He tends to be undependable.

7. The Methodologist. He is interested in methodological issues. He is not inclined to competition.

8. The Independent. He favors thinking in terms of physical and structural models rather than analytical. He tends to be a "loner."

What we need here is research to determine the best "product mix" to maximize research effort. It would be a great stride forward if we could start new laboratory groups and use some of these findings in the selection of the personnel. Then if we were to take into account the research findings regarding environmental variables, it should be possible to maximize creative output.

The environmental findings suggest that if we keep mixing scientists of different specializations together in a work situation, the creativity factor is greater than if we mix scientists of similar specializations together in a work situation.

A later study done by Scofield (1960) tested this finding and obtained positive results. Scofield took some seventh-grade pupils and divided them according to whether they were close friends or nonfriends. He gave both groups a task, and found that the nonfriends outproduced the friends. Then he took a group of college sophomores, repeated the procedure, and obtained the same results.

Biographical data

An inocuous way to measure potential creativity is by biographical measures. This approach has not been fully utilized yet, partially because it seems so naive and partially because great contradictions *seem* to exist.

Apparent contradictions

For instance, Roe (1951) reports that 75 percent of her Hi creative scientists had parents in a business or profession. But Stein (1956) reports that parents of his Hi creative subjects had not gone as far educationally as parents of his Lo creative subjects. Furthermore, he reports that the socioeconomic status of the parents of his Hi creative subjects was *not* so high as that of his Lo creative subjects.

Then Taylor (1957) reported that scientists who came from middle-class families were rated much higher on creativity by their supervisors than scientists from either the Hi or Lo income groups.

These different findings, and what they could possibly mean, puzzled me until I decided to investigate the reasons for differences. Faced with the fact that the criteria used in each of the three mentioned studies were different, I decided to manipulate the criterion variables.

The first thing I did was to administer a biographical data sheet to approximately 80 industrial scientists. Then I examined the response differences between a group of nine chemists who had a patent rate of one or more per year (the average actually was 2.91 patents per year per man). I compared them with a group of seven chemists who had a patent rate of .00 per year. The sample size is necessarily small because these two groups represent extremes in the patent rate distribution.

The mean number of years of professional experience for the Hi group was 9.6 years and for the Lo group, 10.7 years. With respect to age, the mean age for the Hi group is 39.7 years and for the Lo group, an even 40.0 years. All subjects had a Ph.D. in chemistry.

This study revealed many interesting differences between the two groups.

I then studied 29 subjects who were rated on the dimension of creativity by *both* the supervisor and their peers. There were only 16 subjects whom both the supervisors and peers rated as Hi creative and 13 whom both the supervisors and peers rated as Lo creative.

Not only did the biographical information of the rated group differ from that of the patent group, but it also differed in direction. That is, the results were reversed for the two groups.

If we examine only the differences between the biographical information found in Hi patent versus Hi rated subjects, we can see clearly the need to keep our criteria in mind when we speak of biographical differences between Hi and Lo creative subjects.

Difference between patent holders and ratees

The major differences seem to be that the Hi patent people are more aggressive, more self-sufficient, more unsocial. They are less given to joining either organizations or social units than are subjects rated Hi creative.

The Hi patent subjects are not inclined to run PTA's or serve on church boards or fraternities. The Hi rated subjects seem to be involved in many such functions.

Another difference between the groups lies in the area of academic achievement. The Hi patent producers seem to emphasize academic excellence more than the Hi rated subjects. For instance, 77 percent of the Hi

Inventors are aggressive, not necessarily social

patent producers belonged to one or more honor societies but 66 percent of the Hi rated subjects belonged to no honor societies.

Space does not permit a full discussion of all the results nor of a comparison of Lo patent producers versus Lo rated subjects. It is interesting that the Lo patent producers more nearly resembled the Hi rated subjects, while the Lo rated subjects more nearly resembled Hi patent producers though they did not tend to be Hi patent producers themselves.

To illustrate, both the Hi patent producers and the Lo rated subjects tend to read a large number of scientific journals. Both the Hi rated subjects and the Lo patent producers tend to read few scientific journals.

What are the differences?

These differences perhaps reflect either variances in motivational level, personality makeup, or environmental factors. Further work in this area is needed.

It would be interesting to give the same biographical data sheet to a group of academic scientists who are Hi patent producers, a group who are Lo patent producers, a group who are rated Hi creative, and a group who are rated Lo creative—then compare the results with those obtained for industrial scientists. Such a study might clarify the issue of biographical differences as a selection device or as a predictor of creative performance.

If the data were in the expected direction, then companies would have to decide which type of subject they wanted in their environment. This is a crucial point. To employ a lot of Hi patent producers may be disappointing if your environment cannot tolerate many Hi patent producers. Our data suggests they are somewhat difficult to get along with and direct.

If the environment cannot tolerate the ambiguity and change which this class of people thrives on, then the environment will stifle them. This consideration represents just one of many which both management and the individual might consider when deciding either what company to work for or what kind of people they want to employ.

Creativity research at Dow

Because of the conviction that creativity can be measured and that such measures are useful to industry and education, Dr. J. H. McPherson and I are engaged in a series of projects to increase understanding in this area. Mention has already been made of several completed studies. Some of our other efforts revolve around the following investigations.

Dow publishes results of study

The first project is the continued publication of the "Creativity Review." This little multilithed abstract service is an attempt to keep Dow personnel and others abreast of current developments in the field.

A second project is an attempt to develop a Technical Exceptional Success scale from the Minnesota Multiphasic Personality Inventory. This scale is based on an item analysis of the MMPI profiles of Hi-Lo patent producers. A similar analysis will be made for the Hi-Lo rated subjects. The object is to obtain as much verification of differences as possible. If we can obtain differences from the biographical data and validating differences from the Technical Exceptional Success scale, we will have increased assurance that whatever predictions will be made will have greater validity.

Evaluating group leaders

In the training area, Dr. McPherson is conducting an experimental group leaders program. The first step in this program is to evaluate the group leader himself. This is done in three steps.

1. The group leader evaluates himself and his behavior with the aid of a special set of questions.
2. He is then given a battery of psychological tests.
3. Each subordinate evaluates the group leader by means of a special set of questions.

All this information is then fed to the group leader by Dr. McPherson in private.

Following this, each subordinate undergoes the same three operations. An added dimension is that the group leader evaluates each of his subordinates with the help of the "Supervisor's Evaluation of Research Personnel" put out by Science Research Associates.

The object of this study is to find out what perceived differences exist between supervisors and subordinates. If there are perceived differences, then the question becomes "How do these perceived differences aid or hinder the creative productivity in the specific laboratory group?"

The underlying assumption is that if perceived differences exist, and if they are hindering creative productivity, then any positive change in the perceived differences should result in increased creative productivity.

Seeking the right stimuli

A related study is one I am doing. In this study, problem-solving discussions of one of our creative laboratory groups were recorded. Later, these recordings were printed so a careful analysis could be made of various types of associations that each problem (stimulus) evoked.

The underlying assumption behind this study is that if we can determine the types or classes of verbal or ideational stimuli which set off productive chains of creative associations, perhaps we can train our people to concentrate on productive stimuli and avoid unproductive stimuli.

This study has another dimension—to see if creativity is related to the independence-dominance dimensions. The procedure here is to:

Administer a group of tests to members of the laboratory group.

Have them listen to the taped sessions.

Train them to recognize for themselves where they stand on the independence-dominance dimensions.

Attempt to train the dependent-submission ones to become more independent and dominant.

Retest them to determine whether the changes are permanent or transitory. The tests will include creativity tests and personality tests.

Creativity for salesmen

Dr. McPherson is experimenting with a creativity training course for salesmen. Each sales trainee is given ten of Guilford's creativity tests. Dr. McPherson is relating the performance on these measures to the sales testing battery and to sales performance in the field.

In the course of his sales experiments, Dr. McPherson has found that when individuals brainstorm alone, using standard brainstorming instructions, they produce a greater number of ideas for product uses than they do when in a group.

He also found that in brainstorming sessions, the shape of the object influenced the type of responses given. He is using this information to help sales trainees understand what is meant by blocks to creativity.

He also is attempting to devise procedures whereby trainees can learn to be more flexible in their approaches to problem-solving situations.

These procedures include a series of lectures, interspersed with practice sessions. These sessions include efforts to help men recognize within themselves when they are faced wih a perceptual block, and the development of an internal feedback system to help overcome such blocks.

Effectiveness of brainstorming

In a similar vein, the author experimented with a group of sales trainees to determine the effectiveness of brainstorming sessions. The trainees were randomly divided into two groups. Group A was instructed to think of as many positive uses for a product as they could within a ten-minute period. Group B was instructed to think of as many limitations of the product as possible within the same period.

The groups were in separate rooms. After the ten-minute period, instructions for the two groups were reversed. That is, Group A was asked to think of as many limitations as they could. Group B was asked to think of as many positive uses as they could, again within a ten-minute span.

The initial finding is that Group B, which was asked to be negative first, produced more positive ideas when called upon to do so than did Group A, which started with positive instructions. This study will be repeated because there was some question of response-recording accuracy. It certainly will be a startling finding if it holds up in subsequent studies. It will reinforce a long-standing psychological adage that people can begin to think more positively if they first relieve themselves of all the negatives.

There seems to be a guilt reaction process operating here. If I tend to destroy a thing first, then I develop an internal need either to rebuild it or to replace it. If this process truly works, it has some great implications for the creative process.

Brainstorming alone is effective

Helping men become more creative

Most of these studies are proceeding concurrently. The final results are not yet known. We are convinced that each tentative step taken in the creativity domain will help our people to become more creative.

We are also convinced that the quality and quantity of research done in this field has carried us a long way from the oversimplified notion that creativity is simply a result of preparation, incubation, inspiration, and verification.

We know that the powering forces behind creative effort are more tangible and measurable than heretofore suspected. We also know that within the next ten years, the measurement and specification of variables involved in creative effort will be spelled out more clearly than at present.

We also know, in an intuitive sense, that perhaps within 10–20 years, each individual will have within himself enough knowledge and enough understanding to recognize the direction of his creative talent. He will then be able to maximize this talent. If *we* are really creative, we might hasten this ten-year period and reduce it to five.

REFERENCES

Gough, J. G., & Woodworth, D. G. Stylistic variations among professional research scientists. *Journal of Psychology,* 1960, 49, 87–98.

Guilford, J. P. Intellectual resources and their value as seen by creative scientists. In C. W. Taylor (Ed.), *The third (1959) University of Utah research conference on the identification of creative scientific talent.* Salt Lake City: University of Utah Press, 1959. Pp. 128–149.

Roe, A. A psychological study of eminent biologists. *Psychological Monographs,* 1951, 65 (Whole No. 331).

Scofield, R. W. Task productivity of groups of friends and non-friends. *Psychological Reports,* 1960, 6, 459–460.

Stein, M. J. A transactional approach to creativity. In C. W. Taylor (Ed.), *The (1955) University of Utah research conference on the identification of creative scientific talent.* Salt Lake City: University of Utah Press, 1956. Pp. 171–181.

Taylor, D. W. Variables related to creativity and productivity among men in two research laboratories. In C. W. Taylor (Ed.), *The second (1957) University of Utah research conference on the identification of creative scientific talent.* Salt Lake City: University of Utah Press, 1957. Pp. 20–54.

How you can develop a creative imagination

CHARLES H. VERVALIN

Hydrocarbon Processing *staff*

Reprinted from the article of the same title which appeared in Hydrocarbon Processing, *1962, 41 (10), 118–121. By permission of the author and Gulf Publishing Company, Houston, Texas.*

"Creativity" is a whale in a vast sea of deep partially unexplored psychological factors. And the whale, like all mammals, must occasionally come up for air. In other words, we must not forget that, while it is a mistake to oversimplify the creative process and ways it can be developed, creativity can be learned by the person for whom it does not come "naturally." After all, when you have always lived with a feeling of creative "drought," there is only one direction you can go—UP!

Furthermore, research as to creativity's "learnability" is opening new inroads and substantiating many of the existing approaches to developing applied creativity technique. This research and a cautious, systematic study and disciplined application of the principles outlined here is our whale's "breath of air."

You *can* increase your creative ability. In fact, a long-range study by General Electric showed that company engineers who had received creativity *training* produced three times more patentable inventions than those who did not have this training. (The company has taught creativity for many years.)

Following is an approach that has been very successful for a great many companies and individuals.

Assessment of creative capacity.

The first thing you must do is make an objective appraisal of your present capacity for creative perception. There are a number of tests in current use that will reveal this (you'll recall from Dr. Repucci's article that Dow Chemical gave a group of salesmen no fewer than *ten* such tests).

There is obviously not space to discuss these tests here, but you can probably get information from your Training Department, from a competent consulting psychologist in your community, or from the Psychology Department of your state university.

Other good sources of creativity-test information are (1) Creative Education Foundation, Buffalo, N. Y., (2) Ohio State University Psychology Department, (3) The University of Chicago Psychology Department, (4) Institute of Personality Assessment and Research, the University of California at Berkeley, and (5) Pennsylvania State University Psychology Department.

Self-testing

If it is not possible for you to take a battery of creativity tests, the next best thing is to try your hand at a few creative problem-solving puzzles. A number of such problems and a comprehensive bibliography of recommended reading on the subject of creativity is available from HP/PR Reprint Department, P.O. Box 2608, Houston, Texas, at a cost of 25 cents (to cover handling).

Such puzzles will help you to determine if you are stereotyped or conformative in your thinking. Intolerance of ambiguity is one of the major "blocks" to creative thinking.

Finally, you should make a careful self-appraisal, studying your past efforts and accomplishments that seem creative. What is your capacity for innovation on and off the job—in your work, hobbies, social activities, etc? How do your characteristics compare with those of creative persons previously described?

Hindrances to creativity

The next step in your self-development program is to have a firm grasp of the psychological "blocks" to the creative process. Having considered these "blocks" and determined a course of action to remove or alter any you may have, you can then consider creativity technique. Technique will be discussed later, but first let's consider the inhibiting factors in creative thinking.

There are four basic psychological "blocks" to the creative process.

1. Feelings of insecurity. Manifested in lack of confidence, fear of chastisement, fear of failure and of making errors, worry over personal esteem, fear of authority, and feelings of dependency upon others.

2. Need for conformity. Manifested in a security based on order and norms; a need for repetitive, familiar environmental surroundings and conditions; fear of being different or of not fitting into psychological and cultural patterns. This is a more-or-less "don't rock the boat" quality.

Blocks to creativity: insecurity and conformity

3. Incapacity to use unconscious perception and evaluation freely. This shows up as an unwillingness to try anything new, a general lack of zeal and "drive," and a weakness of sensitivity to problems.

4. Occupationalism. These are barriers related to the job speciality or occupation and involve stereotyped patterns of habit, perception, judgment, motivation, and other factors related to choice of occupation and the ways the occupation is practiced.

Naturally, some of these "labeled" qualities overlap. And, it is important to remember that they are interrelated and psychologically integrated as a part of the "whole" person and his reaction to environmental stimuli.

Without a great deal of hard work and close, introspective self-examination, any attempt to cope with the above "blocks" is bound to be superficial and certainly not permanent. The reason is that most of the barriers have a deep psychological base, and only by fully *understanding* this base (call it a form of self-psychoanalysis, if you will) can we expect dramatic and lasting results.

Developing creativity

Assuming that you have developed a consciousness of creative "blocks" and ways to cope with them, you are ready to apply the techniques of thought process that will lead to new ideas and innovation.

The Osborn Method

Dr. Alex Osborn, the "Father of Brainstorming" and a leading pioneer of creativity education, divides the creative process into these phases:

Orientation (picking out the problem)
Preparation (gathering relevant material—the organizational effort)
Analysis and Ideation (seeking possible solutions)
Incubation (a time lag for the mind to synthesize the problem and solutions)
Evaluation (putting the pieces together and verifying the solutions through further testing or evaluation)

We should not be deceived by the seeming simplicity of this procedure. It is simple enough to be effective, but it certainly isn't automatic. There is no substitute for *work* involved in using the formula. In fact, the creation of new ideas will require tremendous mental effort. Perhaps that is why it is often said that creativity is "painful." Thomas A. Edison once commented that "Creativity is 90 percent perspiration and 10 percent inspiration."

In addition, while the formula approach is the product of considerable thought and experience, it is not infallible. There are probably better techniques to be found on an *individual* basis—that is, ones that will work better for you. But only through study and application will you find them.

Finally, you must be prepared for any challenge that might unexpectedly come up during the creative process—so look for the unusual and offbeat.

Now let's take a closer look at the creative steps previously outlined.

Orientation

Try to define and limit the problem area. At first, forget about specific ideas. Rather, clearly define your problem—your objective. It is important here not to be discouraged by problems that seem to have no possible solutions. As the Seabees said during World War II, "The difficult we do immediately—the impossible takes a little longer."

Preparation

Gather, define, and organize your raw material and knowledge that bears upon the problem. This is very likely the most difficult part of the creative process because a great deal of painstaking mental effort is necessary. You cannot be superficial at this stage and hope for a creative solution.

Direct your search over a broad field, using data that seem even the least bit pertinent to your problem. You must exhaust every source, and this requires considerable self-discipline.

Exploration and preparation must continue until no known raw material or data have been overlooked. Then, your data should be classified on a logical basis for later reference and evaluation.

Creativity can be learned

Analysis and ideation

Digest all the information you have gathered, analyzing and organizing your knowledge into a usable form. One technique for this is to place information in a card file. In other words, set up a retrieval system, perhaps along lines similar to the AIChE technique (see HP/PR, July 1962, page 148. Also, HP/PR, May 1961, page 263).

Whatever system you choose—put everything in writing, systematically, for fast reference.

The next step is to refine your data. Within the mass of information you have gathered are the keys—the interrelationships—that will open the right avenue to a creative solution to your problem.

Ideation involves either group or individual brainstorming or both. The technique includes four "ground rules,"

1. Criticism of another's ideas (in group situation) is forbidden until the "idea session" is over.

2. All ideas will be considered no matter how irrelevant or ridiculous they seem at the time. To see how effective this can be, read the article "Thinking Unlimited," on page one of the *Wall Street Journal,* September 13, 1962, issue.

3. Quantity of ideas—the greater the better—is a must.

4. Combination and improvement of all ideas presented is desirable. In other words, group members draw upon each others' ideas.

More about brainstorming in the interview with Dr. Osborn, later in this article.

Incubation

After all of the previous steps have been completed, your mind must be allowed time to "incubate."

The whirlwind of ideas and research has now passed and a time lag is necessary during which you should actually avoid consciously thinking about your problem. The human mind is intricate and complicated, and psychologists do not yet claim to understand why this time lag is helpful —but consistent research has shown that it is absolutely essential.

Evaluation

After all steps have been completed, including incubation and deference of judgment, you are ready for evaluation and solution—the final, ultimate creative product of the mind.

Some additional tips

Here are a number of ways you can orient your mind toward more creative pursuits. You will have to review this list every day until you get into the habit of practicing the recommendations unconsciously.

1. Make a careful evaluation of your psychological makeup. Does it include any of the blocks previously mentioned, and, if so, to what degree?

2. Develop interest along creative lines. You might try music, painting, tinkering with electronics—any pursuit that involves ingenuity and for which you feel you may have a talent. There is a good chance that such creative pursuits will "carry over" into your job.

3. Dig for ideas—from friends, good literature, other sources, on a variety of subjects. In other words, expand your horizons, using every available source.

4. Get plenty of mental exercise that requires depth thinking, such as brain-teaser puzzles, unusual mathematical or mechanical applications, etc.

5. Seek the answer to a specific problem each day, considering all of the alternative solutions regardless of how foolish they may seem at the time. Start off with ideas that can help you on the job or at home.

6. Start an "idea file" on the job and at home.

7. Set aside time each day to let your thoughts flow freely. Choose a specific time, and preferably an isolated place for your "quiet time."

8. Brainstorm individually and in groups every time you get an opportunity. This encourages a steady idea flow.

9. Try to think of alternative solutions to all problems—in your engineering work and otherwise. Turning out ideas is habit forming.

Now let's see what a leading creativity educator has to say on the subject.

An expert's view of creativity

Here's what HP/PR learned in an exclusive interview with Dr. Alex Osborn, president of the Creative Education Foundation, Buffalo, N. Y.[1] Dr. Osborn is an internationally renowned authority on creative education and the author of four books on the subject, one of which is in its 15th printing.

Q   In nonacademic terms, what are the principles of deliberate idea-finding, as you see it Dr. Osborn?

A ' First of all, you can think up almost twice as many good ideas, in the same length of time, if you defer judgment until after you have created an adequate check-list of possible leads to solution. Secondly, the more ideas you think up, the more likely you are to arrive at the best leads to solution. The basic principle calls for deferment-of-judgment during ideative effort to keep the critical faculty from jamming the creative faculty. This principle is just as productive in individual effort as in group collaboration.

Q   Has this "deferment-of-judgment" principle been borne out in research on the subject?

A Yes. Several research projects have confirmed its potency. For example, in one study, a group attacked an assigned problem while an equal number of ideators individually attacked the same problem, but in the ordinary way—*without* deferring judgment during the ideative effort. The brainstorming group produced 70 percent more good ideas than the non-brainstorming individuals, in the same length of time.

Q   What if those individual ideators had adhered to the deferment-of-judgment principle, instead of allowing judgment concurrently to intrude? Would they then have produced more good ideas?

A The finding on this question showed that when individuals practice deferred judgment they generate almost twice as many good ideas as when they allow judgment concurrently to interfere.

In ideative effort, quantity breeds quality. Until recently, this principle could be substantiated only on the basis of the laws of probability, plus empirical evidence. Those who think up twice as many ideas are likely to think up more than twice as many *good* ideas in the same length of time.

Q   Has research confirmed this principle?

A Yes, indeed, a great deal of it. In one such study, ideas produced during the first half of a sustained effort were compared to those produced in

[1] Editors' note: The late A. F. Osborn, of Batten, Barten, Dursten, and Osborn, New York Advertising Agency, founded the Creative Education Foundation in 1954. The current president of the CEF is Sidney J. Parnes.

the second half. The second half of the session provided 78 percent *more* good ideas than did the first half.

Q   What are the steps in setting up such group brainstorming sessions? Are there any pitfalls here?

A   Well, of course no one should attempt to conduct group brainstorming without at least learning the do's and don'ts. For this purpose, the best Manual to date is the one recently published by the University of Chicago. Copies are available free from the Creative Education Foundation, 1300 Elmwood Ave., Buffalo, New York, 14222. Also available free is a list of idea-spurring questions, compiled at M. I. T. Leaders of brainstorm sessions find that these queries can do much to insure success.

Q   How do you evaluate individual efforts at idea-getting, compared with group brainstorming?

A   As a matter of fact, despite the virtues of group brainstorming, individual ideation is usually more usable and can be just as productive. In fact, the ideal methodology for idea-finding is a double attack: Individual ideation and group brainstorming. And, of course, these procedures can be far more productive if the deferment-of-judgment principle is constantly observed.

Q   As a close observer of creativity education trends, where are some of the places in education and industry you see it being applied?

A   More and more professors are weaving creative principles into their regular teachings. Some 50 types of existing courses have thus been made more creative. These include standard courses such as economics at the University of Chattanooga, English at Findlay College, marketing at Harvard and decision making at Columbia.

The University of Texas is also incorporating more and more creative teaching into courses.

As to separate courses in creative problem solving, some 1,000 such courses have been inaugurated in industry and in education. Over 50,000 members of the Air Force have taken this subject in the ROTC, on some 200 campuses.

In addition, many, many, large companies have had great success with creativity courses—A.C. Sparkplug Division of General Motors, and General Electric, Alcoa, and Westinghouse, for example.

Q   Can you give some examples of where creativity training has measurably increased ability to think up good ideas?

A   Yes. In one scientific investigation I know of, covering 330 students, a course on creative problem solving almost doubled the ability of the average member of the group to think up good ideas. More specifically, it shows that those who take these courses are able to average 94 percent better in production of good ideas than those without benefit of such training.

Q   Practically all of our readers are engineers. Can you give them an example of engineers and scientists that are benefiting from developing creativity?

A   Indeed I can. More and more research scientists are recognizing that even they can benefit from creative education. For example, after a creative problem-solving seminar conducted by Battelle Memorial Research Institute, a survey showed that 85 percent of the participating Ph.D's concurred in these reactions: First, they had learned something new. Second, it was worthwhile to them personally. Third, it would help them in their work. A five-year program of creative training has since been inaugurated at Battelle.

I want to thank you, Dr. Osborn, on behalf of HP / PR and our readers, for this interview.

Management's role in the creative climate

ARTHUR B. WINTRINGHAM
Rexall Chemical Co., Los Angeles, Calif.

Reprinted from the article of the same title which appeared in Hydrocarbon Processing, *1962, 41 (10), 122–127. By permission of Gulf Publishing Company, Houston, Texas.*

What exactly is meant by "Management's Role in the Creative Climate"? The title contains four key words:

1. Management
2. Role
3. Creative
4. Climate

"MANAGEMENT" is like Caesar's wife; that is, "All things to all men." Definitions of management are almost without number. However, the addition of one adjective outmodes all other definitions of precisely what *good* management is. This adjective is *enlightened*. Therefore, we should begin the definitive approach to this subject by assuming we have enlightened management, because without it there can be *absolutely no creativity*.

"ROLE" needs no specialized definition. For our purposes here, "role" indicates and implies a willingness of our enlightened management to do or provide a creative "climate."

"CLIMATE" within our frame of reference is the atmosphere peculiar to the company. This atmosphere must contain the several elements dealt with in the paragraphs below in order to nurture and sustain the other concept in our title—creativity.

"CREATE" is defined by Webster's New Collegiate Dicionary as follows:

1. To bring into being; to cause to exist. Hence: (a) To invest with a new form, office, or character; to constitute, (b) To produce, form, or bring to pass, by influence over others; as, to create a favorable opinion.
2. To produce as a work of thought or imagination, especially as a work of art.

Thus, creative, for our purposes, may be defined as ability to create or bring into being, cause to exist, or produce thought or form.

What, then, can management do to create this all-essential climate?

Management credo

The atmosphere which surrounds an entire organization is conditioned almost without exception by what top management ordains as its modus operandi. There are, of course, many types of managements—from the tight-fisted, inner-directed, tightly controlled operation to the kind in

Chief executive is a pacesetter and a coach

which too little control or two few guide lines exist. This latter type of management develops an organization which does not usually last long.

Somewhere between these two extremes lies the ideal. This is the company whose management credo is that only by permitting and encouraging creativity can their company succeed, grow, and develop in an age where a new product line or technical innovation can mean the difference between a very successful or a mediocre firm.

The chief executive

The top executive of an ideal company is both a creative pacesetter and a coach. He makes the creativeness around him flourish and grow. He respects ideas and their potential. The corporation founded by Walter Chrysler was so instilled with this credo that, many years after his retirement, the corporate credo still is expressed in its motto, "Creative Imagination."

More experienced executives and line supervisors must guard against the cynical attitude of the experienced man. Clarence Francis, head of General Foods, warns, "Younger executives come to me with what they think are new ideas. Out of my experience I could tell them why their ideas will not succeed. But instead of talking them out of their ideas, I have suggested that they be tried out in test areas in order to minimize losses. The joke of it is that half of the time these youthful ideas, which I might have nipped in the bud, turn out either to be successful or they lead to other ideas that are successful. The point I overlooked was that, while the idea was not new, conditions under which the idea was to be carried out were materially different."

Chance to fail intelligently

In this atmosphere the creative employee is encouraged to develop the willingness to fail intelligently. In research, (presumably our most creative field) there are over 999 failures to one success.

Failure takes many forms. Failure in school is an inability to measure up against a standard or aim. Failure in research, on the other hand, can be a learning mechanism or an opportunity to change the approach or research route to achieve a goal.

In school our future employees are taught that failure is shameful. Serious failure means expulsion. How can this attitude be reserved? By patience! We can encourage a creative man to learn from his failures and to press on toward the objective in spite of repeated setbacks. This encouragement requires the use of prudent management techniques.

Motivation in "creative climate"

Generally, the techniques of good or enlightened management are the same for motivation of the individual as they are for developing a creative

Engineer needs a chance to fail intelligently

climate. Several of the more important tools management can use to achieve these aims are listed below:

1. Delegation
2. Communications
3. Morale (sensitivity and development)
4. Pressure

Let's consider each of these items individually.

DELEGATION. Our ideal management has now decreed that it has the kind of company in which creativity is important. Certain management techniques are set in motion to bring about the atmosphere in which creativity can flourish.

One of those techniques is the complete delegation of responsibility and authority. Creativity will flourish only in an atmosphere in which the creative individual is free of management obstacles such as overguidance or overdirection. The creative employee requires a climate of free thought. Furthermore, he needs authority to carry out experimentation without undue supervisory shackles. This means an adequate budget and freedom to use it, plus other tools described later in this article. To achieve full delegation and assure the creative employee that management is not giving only lip service to it, a free flow of communications is needed.

COMMUNICATIONS. The company that recognizes the importance of communications is one step ahead. The company that actually *does* something about it is a dozen steps ahead. Much has been written—books, articles, treatises, etc.—on the subject of communications and communication techniques. Perhaps so much has been written and said that the subject is becoming a bit hackneyed. It is, however, one of the intangible elements of

Environment can thwart or enhance creativity

every company's climate. No other single factor even approaches the importance of communication.

While communications may consist of many media—written, spoken, implied, etc.—from management downward and outward, it also includes the reversed pattern of upward and inward from each employee. Good communications has the added benefit of being a major factor contributing to good morale. And, an idea man needs both good communications and good morale to keep his ideas flowing.

MORALE. The importance of good morale is well known. Major contributing factors will be repeated here just as a review:

1. Keep employees advised of changes that affect them.
2. Let employees know where they stand.
3. Keep the chain of command clear.
4. Be courteous to all employees all of the time.
5. Listen when an employee speaks.
6. Control your temper.
7. Treat each employee as an individual.

This list could go on forever. But even the most unsophisticated supervisory training courses contain more complete listing of the supervisor's responsibilities, most of which depend upon good communications.

PRESSURE. In order to achieve useful creative results, management should keep pressure on the idea men. Management should have specific aims and deadlines for achieving these aims clearly spelled out.

During periods of strife or war, many more creative developments are forthcoming than during similar periods of no pressure. There is a definite correlation between the need to create and its achievement. Therefore, a

Even creative people need a timetable

dynamic management which emphasizes to its men the need for progressive aims will achieve a higher degree of creativity than will a complacent, laissez-faire management.

The importance of the four major items above cannot be overstressed in developing a creative atmosphere.

Mechanisms for creativity

We have discussed management *attitude* toward creativity. Now let's look at some management *do's* which will further contribute to development of the creative climate.

There is no panacea for management. There is no easy route—no rules handbook—for developing a creative climate. But some techniques may help set guidelines of behavior and approaches which could improve a creative atmosphere.

Encourage people—avoid overmanagement

How can management develop, nurture, and achieve a truly creative climate? Our ideal management, in establishing this atmosphere, must take two basic approaches. First, it must encourage its creative people. Second, it must discourage itself from overmanagement and discouragement by implication, act, word, or deed.

First let's consider the positive approach. The management of our ideal company is faced with many problems—staffing, providing tools of the trade, educational encouragement, patience, etc. It must consider each of these factors individually.

The creativity of individuals varies, generally, with the degree of inquisitiveness. The mind that is always asking why or how generally belongs to a creative person. Thus, in staffing the ideal company, we should search out the most creative people available, most often the research-oriented scientist or engineer.

Clues to creativity

Some characteristics we look at in seeking the creative potential of an individual are: (1) school work (What was his thesis subject and how was it approached?); (2) home life (Does he make gadgets and devices to solve home front problems?); (3) social activities (Is he contributing in the social or fraternal situation?); (4) every activity (Does he demonstrate the imaginative approach?).

One of the United States' most creative individuals, Charles F. Kettering, upon graduation from college, accepted a job at National Cash Register Co. Several improvements he made in their product are still used, such as the spring-operated cash register. In this machine the force for totalizing and opening the cash drawer is provided by the tension of a spring set by closing the drawer. We all know of the later achievements of this man. He was selected by his first employer because of his "inventiveness."

Providing "tools of the trade"

In the area of providing tools of the trade are many factors. We would not ask a research chemist to work in a barn—but do we truly provide proper tools? Many people think creativity is spurred by the ivory tower approach. And, in fact, some very important ideas have been generated by lone thinking. But most of our major developments have come from collective efforts of many creators. A good example is the steamboat. Robert Fulton is the recognized inventor, but his "Clermont" was but the culmination of many ideas. The ideas did not occur all at once—they were the result of many experiences and evaluations.

Fulton benefited from the experience of Newcomen and Watt who had evolved the steam engine. Another group made up of Symington, Rumsey, Fitch, Stevens, and Fulton all contributed to the idea of harnessing this prime mover to the boat. Fulton was really a coordinator, and with the confidence of Robert Livingston, his financial backer, he turned the ridicule of his critics into cheers on that warm August day in 1807. Thus, free flow of ideas up, down, and laterally, is the tool of the trade— communications.

Equipment and surroundings

Obviously, another tool can be the physical equipment and surroundings of the creative person. Sufficient space and tools are a must. Management is responsible for providing these tools.

An adequate reference library should be made readily available to our creative people. In many cases, an adequate public university or other facility is close enough to the place of employment to satisfy library demands. In any case, a small reference library should be a part of any engineering or research function.

Our ideal management not only provides for an on-location library but allows its employees freedom to visit the nearby library as the case warrants.

Management should also provide subscriptions to the pertinent trade journals. Many creative thoughts have occurred because a man saw how others were solving problems similar to his own.

Encouragement to further education can include anything from tuition refund plans to sponsoring attendance at seminars and meetings. All of these educational programs increase creativity by encouraging the employee's effort and providing an atmosphere in which free flow and exchange of information will be forthcoming, both within and outside the company.

Creativity training

An added educational tool is training in creative thinking. There are many good books on this subject which can be used as a text for on-site education. There are also many workshops of various levels sponsored by such groups as the American Management Association and others. But selection of a specific workshop should only be made after careful evaluation by management of its needs and quality of the proposed course of instruction.

In the area of education, Boss Kettering is said to have destroyed his college diploma when he received it because he did not want this to be the end of his learning period. He went on to be one of the nation's most creative individuals.

Another important item in creativity is management patience. Many managements curtail expenditures on projects when success is not rapidly achieved. This can be a serious mistake.

Top management should take a middle-of-the-road course—not quick to cancel nor to pour too much effort and money into a project that appears to be making little progress. Management's best attitude is to keep enough pressure on employees to achieve rapid improvement, but not so much that it thwarts the thought and exchange of ideas in the problem-solving phase.

Our ideal management will attempt to instill in its employees the attitude so well expressed by Charles Kettering when he said, "I have always told my gang that I don't want any fellow that has a job working for me, but I do want some fellow whom the job has. In other words, I want the job to get the fellow, not the fellow to get the job."

Management can make its jobs attractive by increasing the challenge —following good management principles. This may sound trite, but many

Creative success should be openly rewarded

of the items in management credo and attitude which develop a creative atmosphere also are basic motivation principles of management.

What about awards?

There are many successful company suggestion systems which incorporate awards to employees for valuable ideas. In these companies, management will often argue far into the night about the creativity that awards generate. But creativity cannot be turned on or off like a spigot at the creator's discretion when he is tempted by awards. Not that the creative individual should not be rewarded, but, rather, that the rewards for the truly creative man should come through the normal merit and advancement reviews. This is a more lasting and acceptable award.

The last positive item is encouragement. Every company manager, from the president down, should encourage his employees to self-improvement, greater achievement, etc. Here again, a sound management principle is a spur to creativity. When a man's idea proves unworkable, he has reached a low mental point. Here, a pat on the back will improve his attitude and show him that management is backing him—win or lose. An encouraging word has often turned failure into success.

There are many more areas of employer-employee relationship that could be discussed here if space permitted, but any responsible management is quite capable of exploring these for itself.

Pitfalls in the "climate"

There are many pitfalls into which management can fall in establishing a creative climate. Some they do wittingly—others occur by default or ineptitude. They may seem obvious but let's try to enumerate and define some of the management attitudes that affect the creative climate.

BE A LISTENER. How many of us have tried to explain an idea to our supervisor and failed because we felt he wasn't listening? Perhaps the boss had some thing more important (?) on his mind. This is a sure way to stifle ideas. The employee will not face the "closed ears" boss twice.

LOOSEN THE REINS. The tight-fisted manager (and we have all seen him) says, "We are going to do it my way or else." Can you imagine the reaction of an idea man to this statement? He will freeze and will very likely seek an atmosphere where his ideas are received and nurtured.

ACCEPT CHANGE. Then there is the resistance-to-change managerial group. They becloud the issue with, "Well, we have done it for the last 20 years this way. And, since we are successful, you cannot argue with success." These are the managers who apparently would rather cross our western deserts at ten miles per day in a prairie schooner than in an air-conditioned airplane at 600 mph.

LET THE BOAT ROCK. There is another management type that is effective in stifling creativity. This is the status quo or let's-not-rock-the-boat group. They express themselves in devious ways and sometimes state, "We have never done it that way before," or "No one has ever tried that, and if the idea were any good someone would have used it." More generally, however, this group talks the subject to death without any clear statement, leaving the idea man with the impression, "What's the use?"

AVOID SIDESTEPPING THE ISSUE. There is an even more insidious procedure used by some managements—that is to listen carefully and assure the idea man, "We must try that sometime." The key here is the word "sometime." In many cases, "sometime" never comes. These are the sit-it-out, don't-move managers. They generally have a little of the status quo in them but are more devious in their handling of their people. There is no more insidious technique that this do-nothing group uses to kill initiative and creativity.

ALLOW ENOUGH MONEY. A more direct approach used both directly and under cover is the withholding of experimental funds. This is known as the "poor boy" technique. The direct application of this technique is evidenced by, "That's a fine idea but we cannot fit it into our budget now." Left unsaid is, "or ever." The more insidious (and here I label the man a nonmanager) approach is to fail to come up with the required funds. Then —when asked about it, says, "The board cut it out of our budget."

WATCH THOSE "KILLER PHRASES." Many are the devious ways some managements use to kill creativity. Their actions have given birth to a group of phrases in the language of creative thinking known as "killer phrases." In addition to those in the above paragraphs, here are a few more:

"A swell idea, but . . ."
"It won't work."
"It's not part of our job."
"We haven't the time."
"Too expensive."
"Not ready for that yet."
"Good idea but our plant is different."
"Too academic."
"Hard to administer."
"Too early."
"Too late."
"Let's be practical."
"There are better ways than that."

You can think of many more. There are as many "killer phrases" as there are creative murderers.

All of us have seen companies which, after careful screening, hire very capable and sometimes highly paid men only to prostitute and kill their desire to win. The destructive force used is poor day-to-day handling of the men's problems. An organization that has poor employee relations can rarely be expected to be creative. So, if management is not sensitive to the morale of its employees, creativity will be suppressed.

Summary

In summary—management's role is to generate an atmosphere for creativity. If it is not generated, it will not develop spontaneously. Management should work at establishing the proper corporate environment to allow creativity to grow, flourish, and bloom.

Management must first have a credo which should be stated.

Second, management should establish and encourage effective delegation. Without delegation, creativity will wither on the vine.

Third, management should encourage good communications to provide an atmosphere in which creativity can flourish.

Fourth, management should work at the establishment of good morale. Without this, creativity is nonexistent.

Fifth, but not by any means less important, pressures for results *on a specific timetable* should be developed. This should be tempered by a degree of patience and encouragement of men to fail intelligently when failure is imminent.

How to cope with a noncreative climate

F. D. McMURRY and H. T. HAMBLEN
Humble Oil & Refining Co., Houston

Reprinted from the article of the same title which appeared in Hydrocarbon Processing, *1962, 41 (10), 128–132. By permission of Gulf Publishing Company, Houston, Texas.*

Hector Goodfellow is a bright, imaginative, young engineer. He has eight years of service with a manufacturing company that employs several hundred people. Over a period of years he has nurtured his creative ability to a high level of development. He is a creative person by almost any standards. This, he believes, is his greatest asset and potentially his greatest contribution to the organization.

But Hector does not think his talent is being used. He has come to believe that his organization is rigid, autocratic, nonpermissive, and to some extent old-fashioned. He reacts negatively to certain answers which he receives to his suggestions: "Don't rock the boat"; "We didn't do it that way

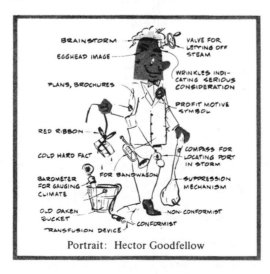

Portrait: Hector Goodfellow

in the old days"; "We tried that and it won't work"; "It costs too much money"; "Sounds good but I don't have time to try it"; "It may be fine, but nobody has actually *done* it before"; "The present way was good enough for grandpa . . . ," etc.

Alternatives to management's idea-suppression

Hector believes his talents are not recognized, far less utilized. He, like many others, is a creative individual in a noncreative climate. He has needs for being productive, for releasing his creative energy, and for gaining recognition. These needs are thwarted. Hector is thus in a conflict situation which produces frustration. The more he thinks about it the more frustrated he gets.

What can he do? Many alternatives are open to him. The choice is not always made at the conscious level. That is, an individual often selects one alternative without realizing it. He is thus surprised at the consequences and implications as they develop. Let's consider a few of the alternatives which are most commonly chosen. Hector may behave in any one or a combination of several ways.

DO NOTHING. As one alternative, he can remain in the situation and make no attempts to alter or adjust to it. He can continue operating in the same manner. He may accept the problem stoically and perhaps even begin to enjoy his difficulties and become a martyr. This alternative is not likely to lead to an adequate solution of the problem.

FLIGHT, WITHDRAWAL. If the conflict is severe enough and he sees no way of solving it, he may choose to withdraw from the situation entirely. He may choose to leave the organization. He may retire or, if he does not have sufficient income, he may seek other employment.

Withdrawal–flight from uncreative climate

Blaming the boss is one "escape"

In a democratic society, he is fortunate to have this alternative open to him, and it may indeed solve his problem. Very often, however, one finds that the new organization provides him a climate very similar to the old one. It may be even less encouraging than the old.

Many individuals, after years of job-hopping, conclude that a non-creative climate is a fact of life and that it must be reckoned with as a reality. Actual withdrawal may solve Hector's problem, but more likely it will not.

AGGRESSION, HOSTILITY. He can attempt revenge on the system which has thwarted his needs. He can "fight city hall" in various open and disguised ways. He can become quite sarcastic and cynical. He may project the blame onto his boss. He can invent clever means for undermining the goals of the organization.

He may grow to hate the system although his hate may or may not be apparent. Expressions of hostility may serve to vent some of his pent-up frustration—i.e., they may allow him "to let off some steam." But while this may reduce his frustration temporarily, it is very unlikely that this alternative will prove adequate in the long run. No matter how adequately he expresses his hostility, the problem is still unsolved and may even be compounded.

FEAR, ANXIETY. He may develop specific fears, or he may become a victim of a free-floating anxiety. If this happens, there are many psychological defense mechanisms available to him which will help him maintain the integrity and worth of his ego, e.g., he can and will to some extent rationalize: "Well at least I tried. This outfit is just not ready for new ideas. They turned it down but at least now they are thinking about it. They just don't know how to use good staff men."

He may insulate himself from exposure to future conflict by refusing to submit ideas and refusing to identify himself with creative projects. If he does make progress up the organizational ladder, he is more likely to insulate himself to avoid frustration. He may become so bogged down in paper work and administrative trivia, that "he has no time" for the creative work he professes to enjoy.

OTHER EGO-DEFENSE MECHANISMS. Other "escapes" commonly used include internalization, inhibition, repression, suppression, regression, displacement, compensation, etc. These may be consciously or unconsciously used, separately or together, to reduce Hector's anxiety. He may study sculpture. He may start painting. He may write poetry or otherwise engage in some creative activity which provides an outlet for his talent and energy.

He may come to accept substitute goals. He may compromise with reality by lowering his aspiration level and accepting that which seems possible, thus "doing the best he can."

All individuals use these mechanisms in some degree. However, if carried too far, they are likely to produce more problems than they solve. Hector Goodfellow, for example, may come to feel better about his "self-picture," but his problem is likely to remain unsolved. These mechanisms may thus help his morale, but his creative productivity in the organization may remain at a low level.

CONSTRUCTIVE PROBLEM SOLVING. Another alternative is to attack the problem constructively. The ego defense mechanisms mentioned above operate largely at the unconscious level. If he is able to analyze himself objectively, Hector may determine the extent to which he is employing these mechanisms. Then, once they are exposed, they become of less value to him and he may seek a more constructive alternative.

He will probably find the most effective alternative is to take constructive action to solve the problem. His actions may thus be channeled in one or both of two directions: (1) he may work toward improving the climate, or (2) he may strive to improve himself.

Let us explore what might be involved if this general approach is selected.

Improving the climate

Can a young engineer make the situation more receptive to his creative ideas? Evidence suggests that he can. It is unrealistic, of course, to presume that Hector will effect major changes in his department or company overnight. However, perseverance, planning, and resourcefulness will enable him to make the climate more receptive. This is chiefly a long-term proposition.

A certain amount of training "from the bottom up" is possible. That is, a subordinate is often able to influence his boss to some degree so that the boss, over a period of time, comes to understand, accept, and even encourage creative effort.

Hector can work with and stimulate other innovators. He can set an example by proving that some new ideas are actually sound. He can interest other people in the organization in the creative process by talking with them, sending them literature, and exposing them to other stimuli.

He may find it effective to "bootleg" some of his ideas, putting them into practice on a small scale as needs arise. His talent is thus utilized without official approval, but if the ideas are sound they come to be recognized after the benefits are reaped by the organization. This, in fact, is often done successfully. It has also been known to cause trouble for innovators who show too much initiative.

If the barrier is primarily administrative, Hector may be able to influence the establishment of new procedures, channels, and routine recovery methods for innovations. This provides a means for facilitating the recognition and application of ideas.

Of course changing the climate takes time and effort. However, if Hector is willing to spend the necessary time in mapping his strategy, his perseverance and planning will yield some reward as long as he is realistic about it.

Success generates further success. The more the climate is changed, the more it can be changed. Thus, he should expect that his initial achievements will be gradual and infrequent. However, before Hector launches forth on a campaign of organizational change, he needs to look at both sides of the problem—the company and also *himself*. It is possible that the organizational climate is more permissive than he believes. Frequently, it is not *what* is suggested, but *how* it is suggested—and this requires Hector to make some changes.

Improving himself

One thing Hector might do is to improve himself and to accept the situation for what it is. This does not mean that he gives up. It does mean, however, that he comes to face the realities of corporate existence. He will probably "philosophize" (rationalize) about the unfortunate limitations of the system. He will likely come to accept certain norms of conformity which, whether good or bad, are necessary for his personal achievement.

He may place new value on hard work and perseverance. It is also possible that Hector will finally realize he is perhaps not the most creative individual in the world after all. He finds, perhaps to his surprise, that there are many other people in his same organization with great intellectual capacity and great creative talent. This insight, however, should not deter his ambition. It should only circumscribe it within realistic limits.

In changing himself, Hector may also find it quite possible to sharpen his own creative ability. Even in the most imaginative mind there is great room for improvement. Experiments have shown that efficiency in the creative process can be significantly increased with proper understanding and practice.

Another way Hector might change himself is in developing his own ability to *sell* his ideas. No matter how great his intelligence and talent, and no matter how many good ideas he produces, his ability is not likely to be used unless he is able to put the ideas into practice. This requires selling.

It is unfortunate that many creative people never achieve their potential because they lack ability to persuade others of the value of their ideas. Often, these people can't present ideas in a fashion that is attractive enough to command attention, or communicate well enough so that the idea is understood. Hector must remember that new ideas mean change, and that people naturally resist change. So, in addition to having new ideas, his problem is not solved until he does a selling job that motivates management to accept the change.

Selling ideas

Most innovators will readily accept the above premise. But so what? How do you sell ideas? The obvious answer to this question is that ideas should be accepted or rejected on merit alone. As the saying goes, "If the idea is a good one it will sell itself."

It is unfortunate but, people being what they are, this answer is not realistic. Merit, of course, is *one dimension* in the acceptability of an idea. In addition, there are many *psychological* factors which play an important part in selling ideas. Let's examine some of the main psychological techniques which have proved useful.

BANDWAGON. Some people tend to accept ideas which will allow them to "get on the bandwagon." If it can be shown that "everybody else is doing it," particularly competitors, the new idea stands a better chance of being accepted.

PROGENY SUPPORT. People tend to support that which they help create. People in authority are more likely to accept a new idea if they have participated in developing the idea. Hector Goodfellow would thus do well to invite people to participate in the early developmental stages of the innovation. They will then be familiar with the idea and committed to its value.

PROFIT MOTIVE. Proposals perceived to contribute to additional dollars and cents profits or savings tend to be approved. Some of Hector's ideas, of course, will contribute to the advancement of science or humanity.

Aside from the scientific value of an idea, it is also very desirable to stress the profit motive as a reason for seeking approval.

OLD OAKEN BUCKET. A new procedure is more likely to be accepted if it seems to involve only minor change from the present or past method of doing business. Similarities between the new way and the old way should be pointed out, if it can be shown that the new way is really not a drastic departure from the old.

PORT-IN-A-STORM. If a sense of urgency seems to show a new idea as the only alternative, the idea is likely to be approved. A dilemma is created which may or may not be real. Example: Patrick Henry's "Give me liberty or give me death."

PLAIN VANILLA. Acceptance often depends to some extent on the amount of "common sense" involved in the proposal. Sometimes called the "plain folks" device, this technique is valuable to politicians, salesmen, and engineers alike. For example, a political candidate may take great pride in displaying a hole in the sole of his shoe.

PROOF BY PILOT. A new procedure stands a much better chance of being accepted if the proposal involves trying it out on a pilot basis before making it general practice. Hector's proposal might well stipulate that the innovation should be tried on an experimental basis for a certain time. Then, if it is successful, it may become general practice.

This technique is good for two reasons: first, it may prove or disprove the value of the idea; and second, people in the organization become familiar with the practice and are committed to it before it is instituted. Their commitment sometimes stems from what is called "halo effect," which is the additional enthusiasm manifested by most groups who gain recognition by participating in experiments.

INCOMPLETED STAFF WORK. Committees are often more likely to approve an idea if they can exercise their authority in deciding a few additional details about the project. If their decision involves only a yes or no (approve or disapprove) their approval is less likely to be gained than if they have a detail or two to discuss in addition to the yes or no. For example, Hector asks the executive committee to decide not only whether or not to accept his proposal, but also the date on which it is to go into effect.

RED RIBBON. Many ideas die on the vine because their *presentation* lacks polish, lacks completeness, and leaves too much unexplained. If an idea is to be submitted to a decision-making group, it is often desirable to make a polished performance out of the presentation. This might involve organizing and rehearsing the subject to the point where it seems both logical and spontaneous.

Successful preparation and use of visual aids and an attractive report or brochure may prove valuable. There is sometimes more reluctance to turn down or change a proposal that is presented in a finished fashion —tied up with a red ribbon—than one which obviously is poorly presented and lacking in preparation.

PROOF BY PRINT. People tend to place extra value on the printed word. The proposal and background material seem to carry more authority if the material is mechanically reproduced. For example, Hector might have the proposal reproduced for distribution before or during the meeting at which he is to discuss it.

UNDERSELL. The undersell and soft sell are very often effective for sophisticated groups. This technique works well with the red-ribbon technique mentioned above, particularly where some resistance to the idea is anticipated.

Example: Hector, in presenting his idea to the group, enumerates the advantages of the proposal. Since the group is likely to know the disadvantages, he then discusses these disadvantages in detail. Then he points out how the advantages outweigh the disadvantages. He realizes that it is usually a mistake not to give the other side of the picture to a sophisticated group.

SCIENTIFIC AUTHORITY. Added value is sometimes given to a proposal by quoting statistics, books, scientists, and various research data. Hector, being an engineer, should have no trouble in selecting data to report.

CREDIT ASCRIPTION. A wise man once said, "There is no limit to what you can accomplish if you don't care who gets credit for it." The use of the first person plural is often valuable in discussing the development and application of an idea.

Giving credit to others, especially those with authority to approve an idea, often has good results. Example: Hector in his presentation may recall that the chairman's earlier discussion of a problem stimulated the entire idea and that certain people assisted in the development of it.

GROUND FLOOR. This principle is paradoxical to the bandwagon technique. It involves placing certain value on the fact that this particular idea is brand new and perhaps represents a competitive advantage for that reason.

Example: "Of course this has never been tried before but if we want to continue to be leaders, rather than followers, this is something we can't afford to wait on. We can be in on the ground floor if we do it now."

COAT TAIL. Ideas tend to assume additional value if they are identified with reputable persons or groups who have technical or organizational authority. This kind of identification implies that certain people whose opinions are respected are in support of the idea.

PROPITIOUS TIMING. Executives are generally more receptive to new ideas at certain times of the day. As a rule of thumb, it is best to present a proposal to an executive after ten in the morning or after a big lunch. When the executive is hungry, immediately before lunch, is the poorest time. It is said that bills presented to Congress stand a better chance of being passed if they are presented late in the afternoon. This, of course, varies depending on the particular individual or group to which the idea is presented.

INDIRECT BENEFITS. A proposal is likely to be received more favorably if secondary, long-term, or indirect benefits are anticipated. The major emphasis, of course, will be on the primary benefits which most often involve the immediate results. In addition, the secondary and long-term benefits or by-products should be enumerated.

A specific method of measuring the effectiveness or economics of the idea should accompany the proposal. For example, Hector's idea will not only save X number of dollars this year, it will also, in the long run, insure more regular maintenance on the equipment and will improve the morale of the operators.

TRANSFUSION OF UNDERSTANDING. People tend to distrust that which they do not understand. Nor can they comfortably control, guide, or utilize that which they do not understand. Thus, they are unlikely to accept such an idea. Therefore, Hector should insure that his proposals are understood by the people in authority. They should have a good overall grasp of the principles, assumptions, variables, and implications involved.

This transfusion of understanding will sometimes be difficult for Hector, but it will pay big dividends. It may mean a refresher session in mathematics for his boss or a short course in catalytic reactions for the committee.

BARNUM EFFECT. People sometimes seek that which is new and different. In contrast to the Old-Oaken-Bucket effect, this device stresses something rare and exotic. By knowing his audience, Hector will be able to decide which of the paradoxical effects to employ at a given time. The Barnum Effect accounts for the success of such side-show displays as the "Wild Man from Borneo," who may actually be a resident of a nearby village. It also explains why some managers send subordinates to executive development courses at geographically remote universities when an equally good program operates in the same city where the subordinates live.

ELOQUENT EDICT. There will be little question about peoples' acceptance if a top management authority issues a "thou-shalt-support" type of edict. If Hector can secure the publicized support of the organization's top man, others will more readily find merit in the new idea, and there will be no attempt at suppression.

Techniques are valid

Psychological researchers have found these and other techniques to be effective in many situations. Hector Goodfellow will probably accept the validity of these techniques, but he might well ask whether it is honest to do these things. What ethical principles are involved? Isn't this a manner of manipulating people? Isn't this Machiavellian politics? What dangers are inherent in using these techniques?

These practices have no doubt been used in the past by unscrupulous men who wished to be persuasive at all costs. These are fairly powerful devices and should be used with caution. They may be used to great advantage where they can be applied with honesty and sincerity.

The ethical question of whether to use these techniques or not might be analogous to the question of whether or not to use gun powder, since it is a powerful tool. The ethical value depends not on the tool, but on the motives of the user.

A word of caution should be in order. The application of any and all of these techniques can be overdone. For example, Hector should not become known as a "name-dropper" by always using the leverage of big names or important people to impress management with the value of an idea. It is quite possible to lean too heavily on techniques. Hector should not lose sight of the fact that the *merit* of the idea should receive primary emphasis. The psychological techniques may increase the probability of acceptance.

In Conclusion

Assuming that Hector Goodfellow is successful in improving both the climate and himself, he is likely to find that the climate is still somewhat rigid. There are advantages to resistance. Hector should realize that climates are sometimes rigid for good reasons, and ideas generated in a non-permissive climate *may* be better ideas than those too easily sold. Tough-to-sell ideas may be better thought out and better presented. When new ideas do go into effect they are more likely to prove workable.

Hector must realize that his development or improvement requires him to *change*. Change is probably as painful to Hector as it is to the organization. Innovators often become frustrated because they demand that others change, while they themselves refuse to do it. If Hector can apply the same pressure and encouragement to himself as he applies to others, his path of self-development will indeed be less arduous.

All things considered, the best advice to Hector Goodfellow would be to look both at the organization *and himself*. He should set up his objectives and work seriously on the improvements he desires to make, realizing that his initial successes may be minor and infrequent. Even though improvement is a gradual process, he should be optimistic about his efforts as long as they are well planned.

Good luck Hector. Have faith, keep trying, and don't give up the ship.

7 | How to squelch ideas

CHARLES H. CLARK
National Association of Manufacturers

From Brainstorming *by Charles H. Clark, copyright © 1958 by Doubleday & Company, Inc. Reprinted by permission of the publisher.*

For a thorough discussion of principles, procedures, and problems of brainstorming, the appropriately titled book *Brainstorming* by Charles A. Clark is excellent. One of Clark's most striking contributions in *Brainstorming* is his summary of (perhaps familiar) idea-squelching "killer phrases" and apologetic "self-killer phrases" which neatly serve to thwart new ideas, inhibit the flow of future suggestions, and prevent the acceptance of carefully nurtured "brain children."

The most dramatic way I know to show how most conferences are negative and firmly opposed to new ideas is to have each member of the group write on three-by-five cards three killer phrases, such as: "It's against policy," "It won't work," "We've never done it before," "The boss's wife likes blue." Then I have the cards shuffled and passed around in the group. They are read aloud by panel members.

On the following pages there is a list of the most prevalent killer phrases. You know them well; everyone does who has ever attended a meeting, but read the list over carefully. You will hear echoes from wasted conferences, and you will know what to avoid in the future. In a brainstorm session killer phrases are strictly ruled out. In fact, I place a bell in the center of the table, and whenever a killer phrase pops up the bell is rung by the person nearest it.

Here they are:

We've never done it that way before . . .
It won't work . . .
We haven't the time . . .

We haven't the manpower . . .
It's not in the budget . . .
We've tried that before . . .
We're not ready for it yet . . .
All right in theory but can you put it into practice?
Too academic . . .
What will the customers think?
Somebody would have suggested it before if it were any good . . .
Too modern . . .
Too old-fashioned . . .
Let's discuss it at some other time . . .
You don't understand our problem . . .
We're too small for that . . .
We're too big for that . . .
We have too many projects now . . .
Let's make a market research test first . . .
It has been the same for twenty years so it must be good . . .
What bubblehead thought that up?
I just know it won't work . . .
Let's form a committee . . .
Let's think it over for a while and watch developments . . .
That's not our problem . . .
Production won't accept it . . .
They'll think we're long-haired . . .
Engineering can't do it . . .
Won't work in my territory . . .
Customers won't stand for it . . .
You'll never sell that to management . . .
Don't move too fast . . .
Why something new now? Our sales are still going up . . .
Let's wait and see . . .
The union will scream . . .
Here we go again . . .
Let's put it in writing . . .
I don't see the connection . . .
Won't work in our industry . . .
We can't do it under the regulations . . .
Nuts . . .
Political dynamite . . .
Sounds good but don't think it will work . . .
It's not in the plan . . .
No regulations covering it . . .
We've never used that approach before . . .
It's not in the manual . . .

It'll mean more work . . .
It's not our responsibility . . .
Yes, but . . .
It will increase overhead . . .
It's too early . . .
It's too late . . .
It will offend . . .
It won't pan out . . .
Our people won't accept it . . .
You don't understand the problem . . .
No adolescent is going to tell me how to run my business . . .

Besides the killer phrase, you have to ring the bell on the killer glance and the man who jumps at repetition. Repeating an idea may spark a new chain reaction.

A twin brother to the killer phrase someone else uses to swat your idea is the apologetic phrase you often use to give a deadly introduction to your own idea. In a brainstorm session it's outlawed too, but don't ring the bell. Notice how these killers disappear as you cultivate a creative atmosphere receptive to new ideas. Edward J. Walsh of General Foods calls these "Self-Killer Phrases."

Can you hear yourself in this list? If you can, discipline yourself to present ideas not with apology but with confidence.

This may not be applicable, but . . .
While we have only made a few preliminary tests . . .
This may not work, but . . .
This approach is screwy, but . . .
It isn't clear that we need this, but . . .
I don't know if the money can be appropriated, but . . .
It might be a dead end, but . . .
Would it hurt if we did . . .
Do you suppose it would be possible to . . .
It may sound hair-brained, but . . .
It may take a long time, but . . .
I don't know just what you want, but . . .
You probably have ideas about this too, but . . .
You aren't going to like this, but . . .
This is contrary to policy, but . . .
This may not be the right time, but . . .
This idea seems useless, but . . .
You can probably do this better, but . . .
If I was younger and had my health . . .
I suppose our competitors have already tried this, but . . .
I'm not too familiar with this, but . . .

This may be too expensive, but . . .
I don't know what is in the literature on this, but . . .
This is not exactly on this subject, but . . .
I haven't thought this one through, but . . .
You'll probably laugh, but . . .
My opinions are not worth much, but . . .
I'm no genius, but . . .
Perhaps we can't sell this to the old man, but . . .
I don't get enthused over this idea myself, but . . .
It may not be important, but . . .
This will need further study, but . . .
If you'll take the suggestion of a novice . . .
I'm not aware of all the complexities of the issue, but . . .
Joe doesn't agree with me, but . . .
I realize this doesn't solve the problem, but . . .
If I'm out of line, correct me, but . . .
Now here's a sketchy idea of what I have in mind, for you to kick holes in . . .

The brainstorm session is not the time for apologies or modesty; it is not the time for cold water or wet blankets. The chairman must stop the use of all killer phrases. By ringing the bell and having others ring the bell as soon as one is heard, he can do it with humor but with telling effect. Once the danger of the killer phrase is pointed out, most of us try to avoid the habit, but they are so much a part of our conference personality we need a reminder to retrain ourselves into thinking creatively, positively instead of negatively.

8 | Try these six steps to more ideas

EUGENE RAUDSEPP

Princeton Creative Research, Inc.

Reprinted from the article of the same title which appeared in
Hydrocarbon Processing, *1966, October, 45 (10), 207–210. By
permission of the author and Gulf Publishing Company, Houston,
Texas.*

In his *Six Steps to More Ideas,* Raudsepp suggests numerous activities,
attitudes, and strategies for increasing creative productivity, nearly all of
which are consistent with known principles of creative problem solving.
Briefly, he describes specific means of acquiring knowledge in new fields,
developing a deeper understanding of one's own field, sensitizing oneself
to problems needing creative solutions, learning to systematically find
ideas, maintaining enthusiasm, and preparing to show one's ideas.
Although written for managers, many of Raudsepp's suggestions can
contribute to understanding the nature and nurture of classroom creativity
as well.

Every day, you have to use creative ability in your job. Every manager
does. Some bring stronger creative ability to their problems than others.
As a result, they're worth more to their companies.

These are not "favored" men, exercising a special God-given power.
Most have acquired their creative problem-solving ability through disciplined practice. If you were to examine their technique, you would probably find they follow six key steps to increase their creative power. So can
you!

Step number one: Stretch your horizons

One mainspring of creative power is a broad background of accumulated knowledge. The manager with a knowledge of many fields can spot
analogous situations and find creative ideas. The manager with only a de-

tailed knowledge of his special field limits his creativity by the narrowness of his field.

Thorough immersion in one field has to be coupled with a breadth of experience and knowledge in many other fields. To increase the fund of your total experience you can:

SET TIME ASIDE TO READ IN OTHER FIELDS. This will broaden your perspective and provide you with new information.

Start with related fields and gradually spread to areas further removed from your specialty. Keep this question in mind while reading: "How might I be able to use this?" Take notes while reading. Anything that strikes you as significant, stimulating, or interesting should be preserved for later reference.

COLLECT AND FILE CLIPPINGS, NOTES, AND IDEAS THAT SEEM ORIGINAL. Keep them organized and available. Look them over occasionally to stimulate your idea production.

ATTEMPT TO WORK OR WRITE ON A PROBLEM OUTSIDE YOUR OWN FIELD. This will increase your ability to incorporate new information and ideas into your own problems.

MOVE ABOUT IN YOUR ORGANIZATION AND EXCHANGE IDEAS WITH OTHERS. Creativity is contagious and such exchanges may spark new ideas for you.

LISTEN TO COMMENTS AND COMPLAINTS. Be alert for noting the unusual.

CULTIVATE HOBBIES LIKE CHESS, BRIDGE, AND PUZZLE SOLVING. Aside from exercising your problem-solving abilities, they help you relax and frequently open your conscious mind to the flashes of insight and hunches lodged in your subconscious. Keep in mind that constructing and building hobbies are more stimulating creatively than collecting hobbies.

Travel stimulates in the same manner as hobbies. Any kind of relaxation permits unconscious ideas to emerge.

Unremitting, continual exercise of your creative powers is necessary. For this reason try to approach every problem you encounter as imaginatively and creatively as you can. Observe things around you with the questioning attitude: "How could this be done differently or better?" You should also form the habit of asking yourself questions about as many facets of the problem as you can.

Step number two: Cultivate your field

Although the creative manager needs a broad background, he can't afford to neglect his own field. He has to have more than the mere skill to manipulate the things he works with. He has to have an intimate knowledge of the basic principles and fundamental concepts of his field of specialization. Deep understanding of your field will allow you to bring a multitude of approaches to any specific problem.

Experience shows you can increase your understanding of your area of work if you:

SEEK OUT ALL AVAILABLE SOURCES OF INFORMATION. Talk to others about your problem and listen attentively to what they have to say. Personal exposure to things, personal experience through seeing, hearing, and feeling will increase your creative powers. All outstanding managers know the importance of personal investigations.

READ AND EXAMINE THE LITERATURE IN YOUR FIELD. Keep both a critical and imaginative attitude. Be aware that what you read is not the last word on the subject or even the best possible position. Findings and facts are fluid and dynamic and they change frequently.

George Bernard Shaw had a high opinion of his tailor because he took Shaw's measurements each time he had a suit or coat made. Everyone else Shaw dealt with expected old measurements to go right on fitting him year after year. The same applies to facts. Since facts refer to situations and since situations are always in a state of flux, facts never remain static.

QUESTION EVERY ACCEPTED ASSUMPTION ABOUT YOUR PROBLEM. How did they emerge? Who made them? How valid are they really? Strong beliefs and inaccurate assumptions are frequently treated as established facts or self-evident truths. They can stifle the creative process even before it gets started.

DON'T BE TOO QUICK TO THROW OUT UNORTHODOX OR UNUSUAL IDEAS. Don't try to demonstrate how untenable they are. Think of minor changes that would make them practical.

LOOK FOR THE KEY FACTORS OF YOUR PROBLEM and try to isolate them. Remember that lack of thorough analysis of your problem may often cost you invaluable hours spent on a wrong problem or on a side issue not really relevant to your problem. Don't be discouraged in advance because others who had tried to solve the same problem had failed. Remember that conditions change, and what did not work once might work now.

If your problem requires further study and the mastery of new knowledge, don't discard the problem. Rather, proceed to put in as much effort as you can in learning the requisite materials to achieve the solution. The rewards of effective creative solutions far exceed the effort and perseverance put into them.

Step number three: Pinpoint the problem

Almost every manager these days is besieged by problems. So the question—where to find problems—should not preoccupy us much. The manager who is not able to spot problems can best develop or stimulate his sensitivity to potential improvements by asking himself such questions as: "What am I doing, or what is done that could be done more effectively, better, cheaper, differently?" Sometimes the negative approach, "What's wrong with this?" will furnish a list of irritants that can provide a source of problems.

Because of the many problems thrust upon managers in every realm of activity, the real difficulty often is to spot the *real* or *important* problems. So it is best to arrange problems hierarchically in terms of their importance, difficulty, and feasibility of possible solution.

You should first make a list of problems to be solved—then proceed to pick out for special attention the problems that combine your optimum interest and understanding with the importance of the problem.

The next step is to define the problem. The correct problem definition is crucial to effective creative solutions. It is frequently half the battle. Incorrect problem definition will prevent solutions. Fluency of ideas and flexibility of thought are likewise affected by incorrect problem definition.

It follows from this that the first problem definitions should be considered tentative. You might have to modify or expand the meaning of your initial definition several times. Frequently, further information must be first collected in order to define the problem at all. With this in mind:

STATE YOUR PROBLEM IN A SIMPLE, BASIC, BROAD, GENERIC WAY. Don't structure the problem statement too much. Don't hide it with modifying adjectives, adverbial phrases and side problems.

DON'T SUGGEST SOLUTIONS IN YOUR PROBLEM DEFINITION. One executive said, "Costs are too high. Should I ship by parcel post to save money?" This not only limits his cost cutting to shipping, but also eliminates alternative ways of shipping.

KEEP ASKING YOURSELF: WHAT ARE THE PROBLEM'S ACTUAL BOUNDARIES? What are its unusual aspects, its common aspects? Can these aspects be taken for granted? These questions will help you clearly define the boundaries of the problem.

BREAK DOWN THE PROBLEM'S VARIABLES THROUGH ANALYSIS. At the same time keep an overall view of the problem in your mind's eye.

Step number four: Hunt for ideas

Here's a checklist that will help you get started on solving a specific problem:

LIST THE IDEAS AND VARIOUS APPROACHES THAT MIGHT SOLVE THE PROBLEM. Take off in wide directions—amassing as many ideas and leads as you can. Note all the ideas, even the insignificant ones. Following one line of thought too early could prevent others from occurring. Even if you feel that you have hit upon a sound idea, don't stop the idea process. You have written the idea down and it won't get lost.

Many fleeting thoughts that in isolation look inconsequential may contain a new vital germ of an idea. Or later, these thoughts in combination with other thoughts combine into a new meaningful idea. Remember no idea should be rejected at this stage as of no consequence until later proven so.

BEWARE THE DANGERS OF EARLY COMMITMENT TO AN IDEA OR STRATEGY. In the perceptual laboratory, for example, individuals who make an early, incorrect interpretation of a picture in an "ambigu-meter" (a device that gradually brings a blurred picture into focus), will tend to retain the wrong perception. They actually fail to "see" even when the picture has been fully and clearly exposed. Similarly, it is a common occurrence in many organizations that managers will "stick to their guns" to support a position they have taken publicly, beyond its validity and usefulness.

Seemingly "undisciplined thinking" in the initial stages is necessary. It expands the range of consideration and raw material from which creative solutions will emerge.

Look for analogous situations and their solutions in other areas, at the same time remembering that none of these solutions will fit your problem precisely.

Relax your binding faith in reason and logic when thinking up ideas. Let your imagination soar. See if there is a relationship between things that nobody has seen before. Reach out for explanations that go beyond your own experience. Even if the facts don't seem to warrant it, keep on speculating and guessing.

REFUSE TO BE DOWNED BY INITIAL FAILURES. Continue working at your problem in the face of any discouragement you might come to feel. Resist the temptation to give up. Patience and perseverance are some of the most valuable assets in creative problem solving. Most successful managers are willing to try again and again, in spite of discouragement. They thus overcome many failures before achieving success.

DON'T BE DISCOURAGED IF YOU EXPERIENCE A SENSE OF STRESS WHEN LOOKING FOR A SOLUTION. Without the feeling of pressure you won't be able to marshal aid from subconscious sources or from your past experience. Have faith in yourself and believe that the answer will come.

Sustained creative thinking, when the problem is tackled from every angle, will usually yield enough material for you to put into a systematic, orderly outline. Frequently, to your surprise, you may have come up with many more ideas than you thought you could produce.

Even if no satisfactory solution emerges at this stage, the unremitting, sustained concentration will leave your subconscious with a wealth of material to work on. After a few days away from the problem, when you renew attacking it again, you may find that you are much more productive than you were during your previous session with the problem. "Sleeping on the problem" has been proved extremely valuable by almost all creative individuals. But it is always preceded by intense preliminary spadework and analysis.

WHEN YOU AGAIN TACKLE YOUR PROBLEM, GO OVER THE APPROACHES AND IDEAS YOU HAD LISTED PREVIOUSLY. Try various combinations of them. Often one idea will start you off in a completely new direction. Follow it freely, even though it may seem that the new train of thought departs from the area of the problem with which you are immediately concerned.

IF YOU STILL DO NOT MAKE PROGRESS TOWARD A SOLUTION, REEXAMINE YOUR PROBLEM DEFINITION(s). Is it too broad, preventing anchorage points? Is it too limited, narrowing your field of thought? Should you divide your problem into several subproblems and work on them one at a time?

In any case, the previous efforts at analysis and definition have given you a better understanding of your problem. Now, after you have redefined it, you may be on the last lap of a determined surge toward solution.

Step number five: Boost your lagging enthusiasm

Creative ability tends to lag after sustained efforts at problem solving. Here are some ways to increase your lagging creative drive:

SUSPEND JUDICIAL THINKING. Learn to turn your judgment off and on at will. During the heat of creative problem solving, criticism and judgment must be suspended.

The acceptance of proposals as they emerge from the subconscious, while one is actually working on a problem, is a delicate affair. One has to resist the increasing pressure of criticism and judgment that the progressively articulated portions of ideas inevitably elicit.

Nothing can inhibit and stifle the creative process more (and on this there is unanimous agreement among creative individuals) than critical judgment applied to the emerging ideas at the early stage of the creative process. Critical judgment at this point will inhibit, if it does not completely shut off, the forward propulsions of further ideas.

SET IDEA-QUOTAS FOR YOURSELF. But set realistic deadlines. When you set idea-quotas, be sure your time is not too limited. A sense of freedom from time restrictions is an important factor in the solution of problems, even though a subjective sense of pressure and need are there.

ALWAYS CARRY A NOTEBOOK WITH YOU. Ideas strike at any hour and under the strangest of circumstances. If you don't make a notation of them they may disappear back into the subconscious.

Don't trust your memory. We often let a good idea slip away from us because we think we will remember it. More often than not, however, an idea that occurs during a brief moment is irretrievably lost if not recorded on the spot.

PROPER MOOD IS IMPORTANT FOR CREATIVE PROBLEM SOLVING. Don't wait for it. Pick up the pencil and start writing down the different aspects of your problem, the different approaches you might use, and the directions you might want to explore. As appetite comes by eating, so creative mood will come when you are actively engaged in writing things down.

Sometimes the effort or ritual of preparing for work may produce the proper mood or emotional tone. You should deliberately perform such acts which create the atmosphere for your best concentration and creative thinking.

DURING THE CREATIVE PROCESS, PRACTICE EMPATHIC INVOLVEMENT. That is, attempt to *feel* the ramifications of your problem. You should, in a sense, imaginatively become the thing you are creating or the problem you are solving. After a period of involvement, detach yourself from the problem and view it objectively from a distance. Effective creative process requires continuous shifting between involvement and detachment.

IF YOU ARE NOT MAKING ANY HEADWAY, EVEN AFTER YOUR "SECOND WIND," DROP YOUR PROBLEM AND DO SOMETHING DIFFERENT. Break off and relax. Unremitting pressure or inability to "let go" of problems sometimes actually prevents "illumination" or insight from occurring. Effective solutions frequently have a habit of occurring when conscious attempt to solve the problem has been suspended.

ORGANIZE YOUR TIME WITH LONG PERIODS WHEN YOU CAN ENGAGE IN HOBBIES OR BE COMPLETELY ALONE AND SILENT. Make a game of the images that come to you during periods of relaxation. Felicitous insights often occur in relaxed or dispersed attention.

To gain a respite from judicial orientation and conservative thinking, inventors often seek complete relaxation. They claim that the ideas they value most occurred to them during passive and relaxed states, or even under fatigued or half-waking conditions. It is, for example, well known that Newton solved many of his problems when his attention was waylaid by complete relaxation. Similarly, Edison knew the value of half-waking conditions. Whenever confronted with a seemingly insurmountable hitch that defied all his efforts, he would stretch out on his couch in his workshop—brought there for just this reason—and try to fall asleep.

SOMETIMES IT IS INADVISABLE TO DISCUSS YOUR PROBLEM-SOLVING IDEAS WITH OTHERS, particularly before you have had a chance to develop and crystallize them to some degree. A discussion too early in the process might make your ideas disappear into thin air, or it might give you false leads or change your original mode of approach. It might also abate the driving power behind your motivation.

On the other hand, meeting with congenial associates who work in the same problem area, may give you additional enthusiasm to continue with your work. There are no hard and fast rules here. You have to discover for yourself whether initial discussion helps or hinders you.

SOMETIMES DISCUSSING YOUR PROBLEM WITH PEOPLE UNFAMILIAR WITH YOUR LINE OF WORK CAN GIVE YOU A NEW SLANT. Such people have a fresh, naive point of view. In the process of explaining your problem to them you are often made aware of certain obscurities or incongruities in your approach that you may have overlooked before. Also, naive questions have a surprising way of triggering fresh, new viewpoints.

A few times in your life you may be lucky enough to have the so-called "avalanche experience," when ideas come in a flood after a major solution to a difficult problem. One idea seems to spark the development of others and these, in turn, others. Many of these ideas are related, but even dissimilar germinal ideas occur during this period. Failing to record them promptly may cost you months or years of fruitful ideas.

DETERMINE THE PHYSICAL CONDITIONS DURING WHICH YOU REGULARLY DO YOUR BEST THINKING. If you find, for example, that certain physical postures, e.g., pacing the floor, sitting quietly at your desk, tilting the chair back, lying down, or relaxing in an easy chair, are conducive to your best work, you should not hesitate to use them. In fact, you should deliberately make an effort to ascertain what sort of physical activity accompanies your most productive efforts, and then deliberately assume it when attempting to solve problems.

DURING PROBLEM SOLVING, AVOID DISTRACTIONS AND INTRUSIONS AS MUCH AS POSSIBLE. Choose a time when you can stay with your problem even hours on end and without interruptions.

You have to free yourself from the usual environmental distractions and routine duties. Otherwise your absorption in the problem must be so intense that you become completely oblivious to existing distractions. You have to develop the knack of closing out the external environment at will. You must detach yourself instantaneously and whenever necessary from whatever you depended upon as a stimulus to set your ideas in motion. Real creative problem solving cannot be done in a distracting environment, or during the rush of regular duties.

Apply the time and energy that many people spend in worry and confusion over irrelevant things, to facing your problem. You can then advance much further with it.

The ability to maintain a basic peace of mind when tackling problems is important. A very successful executive has said, "I'll sweat, but I won't fret, no matter what I'm doing." He understands that concentrated attention and application are essential, but that tenseness and pressure-jitters contribute nothing. He works smoothly, like a long-distance runner, not in bursts like a sprinter. And creative problem solving is almost always more comparable to a cross-country run than to the 100-yard dash.

DEVELOP A "RETROSPECTIVE AWARENESS" OF THE PERIODS WHEN YOU SOLVED YOUR PROBLEMS CREATIVELY. Note the methods that were successful and those that failed. Try to learn why by retracing the routes you followed and those you avoided, as far as possible. Self-knowledge in the area of creativity will aid idea-production.

SCHEDULE YOUR CREATIVE-PROBLEM-SOLVING PERIODS FOR THOSE TIMES WHEN YOU HAVE YOUR MOST FAVORABLE MENTAL SET FOR PRODUCING IDEAS. We all have our personal peaks and valleys of output. Keep a record of periods during the day in which you are most productive. You can then establish a pattern and plan ahead, reserving these peak periods for concentration, problem solving, and uninhibited thinking. Less productive time can be used for investigation, study, and evaluation.

BE PREPARED AND ALERT FOR THE "MOMENT OF SURPRISE." Be alert for ideas when riding in a car or train, when at the movies or at the concert, and especially the brief periods preceding and following sleep. It is incredible how many ideas and insights most of us fail to record and utilize because they took us by surprise.

Step number six: Prepare for premiere

An enormous amount of hard work goes into the polishing of an idea before it becomes a workable thing. Suppress any pride of paternity you may have and continue to examine it critically before showing it to others. No matter what your position, you will have to convince someone else of your idea's practicality.

9 | Obstacles to creative thinking

ALVIN L. SIMBERG

A. C. Spark Plug Division
of General Motors Corporation

From A. L. Simberg, Creativity at Work. *Boston: Industrial Education Institute, 1964, pp. 41–69 (Section V). Reprinted by permission of the author and publisher.*

Rightly assuming that an understanding of barriers to creativity will increase creative potential, Alvin L. Simberg explains carefully the *perceptual, cultural,* and *emotional* "blocks" to creativity, demonstrating these with challenging, but deceptively simple, puzzles. The interfering role of our past experiences, strong habits, and social pressures comes through very clearly: the nature of the "real" problem is obscured, imagination is limited, and the willingness to propose unusual ideas is frustrated. Simberg's main recommendation for overcoming these blocks is to identify them and know how they function.

Kinds of obstacles

Creativity as a process, means being able to develop end results which will satisfy the needs of the organization in a way which they have never been satisfied previously. The heart of this process is ideas. From the previous discussions, it has been pointed out that everyone has within him the basic capacity to be creative. What prevents many from doing so?

There are three different types of blocks possessed by most individuals that inhibit creative thinking. One of these types is the perceptual block—not seeing what the problem is or what may be wrong. A second set of blocks we term "cultural." These are caused by the way we have been brought up, what we have been taught to believe as right and wrong, good and bad. Finally, we have the emotional blocks which are within us because of the insecurities we feel as individuals.

Let us examine these kinds of blocks in detail and see how they stand as obstacles in the path of creative thinking and problem solving.

Perceptual blocks

The family of perceptual blocks is probably the single most frustrating and damaging one. These blocks, as we said, are caused primarily by not seeing what the problems are or what actually may be wrong in the situation. These are the types of blocks that make us "want to kick ourselves" for not having seen the solution previously. Further, they are the type that cause us to begin our work in problem solving without the proper goal in mind. These have to do with our statement of the problem, our biases toward and preconceived notions about the problem. While we are not talking about attitudes as such, it should be recognized that there is very little in our outward behavior that is not colored in some manner or other by our attitudes. This is even more true when we discuss thinking behavior.

To a great degree, our perceptual blocks may be classified as merely having a mental set or predisposition toward seeing the situation in a certain way, no matter how closely or how thoroughly we look at it. Let us look at some examples of this type of block.

1. Difficulty in isolating the problem

This is the case where the individual is unable to separate the real problem from related problems, or as we say, he cannot see the forest for the trees. While this sounds basic and elementary, it is, nevertheless, extremely important to pinpoint the problem specifically. Too often we are not tackling the real problem at all. This might be similar to the physician who treats symptoms rather than curing the disease or to the mechanic who, when unable to figure out whether the car has ignition, fuel system, or other trouble, will eventually decide on a complete overhaul. Trying to keep this first block in mind, attempt the little problem below.

TIME FLIES YOU CANNOT THEY FLY TOO FAST

The problem is to punctuate the above words so that they make sense. (The answer to this and other problems associated with these blocks will be found at the end of this chapter.)

2. Difficulty caused by narrowing the problem too much

This block is caused by paying little or no attention to the environment surrounding the problem. It is not unusual to find in scientific endeavor that experiments are sometimes conducted to determine a particular point, while the effect of other variables of the total situation is ignored. The above block comes about primarily because of our inability to see the problem stated in any other terms than it is. For example, try the little problem below.

HOW CAN YOU MAKE FOUR NINES EQUAL ONE HUNDRED?

(Do anything you want to with the nines)

3. The inability to define terms

Language is the way we have of communicating and understanding. It follows that if you do not understand a problem, you cannot work on it. This becomes more important when there is a group working together on a problem, or when the specific direction a solution will take may depend upon the kinds of words used.

4. Failure to use all of the senses in observing

Ordinarily we think of observation as seeing only. However, it often helps in solving problems to be able to use dimensions other than those provided by vision. For example, the machine repair shop of one company uses a tape recorder to capture the sounds of punch presses because they have found that it sometimes helps them to be able to diagnose the difficulties better from the sound than from watching the machine. In fact, the reason they make a tape recording rather than merely watching and listening is the fact that they find the visual part of the machine operation distracting.

Physiologists today are beginning to talk in terms of not the standard five, but rather fifteen or twenty different senses. It is their contention that many of these senses, primarily internal, may account for the types of things which we today call "hunches, premonitions, etc."

5. Difficulty in seeing remote relationships

This is the ability to form and to transfer concepts. Actually, it is the heart of the whole learning process. It means the ability to be able to see a solution in one area and further to be able to see applications of this solution in other areas.

See how well you can find the relationship below.

This is a drawing of a pran.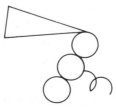

Can you describe in words what a pran is? Probably not. Some might call it a "doodle," others a "figure." At this point, it could be anything. But here is another one.

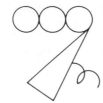

Now what is it?

Analyzing it further, we have a little more to go on now. It might be that a pran is a figure composed of a triangle, three circles, and a curly tail. But let us look at still another pran.

The current year's model.

It looks as though our idea is not right. But the curly tail is still there. Here is still one more pran (not yet even off the drawing board),

And no curly tail.

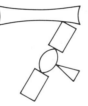

What have each of these figures in common that we term all of them as prans? After a considerable amount of thinking about this problem, we finally get an insight. It is not the kind of parts that compose the pran, whether they are circles, or triangles, or have curly tails. It is the relationship of the parts to each other. They are like a figure "7" with a "tail."

Seeing remote relationships means the ability to look at different objects or situations, or even problems, and to try to see what it is that they have in common. It is not always a physical likeness. It may be merely one of relationship, having functional similarities in one situation which apply in another.

6. Difficulty in not investigating the obvious

Once we have become accustomed to looking at certain situations and problems in a particular way, it becomes increasingly difficult not to do this. Every day we look at the same things, but really cease to "see" them.

We pass the same bulletin board, and even though the notices change from time to time, unless there is something really different about the new notice (a different size or color of paper, etc.), the chances are that we will not see it. So it is with our problems of design.

The first reaction to the assignment of designing a new component is to look for components which are similar and provide the same function. Is it not just as easy to sit down and ask yourself what better or simpler or cheaper method could be used to achieve the same end result?

The individual who first thought of using a flexible ice cube tray got the idea from noticing that some water in his boots, which had been left outside, had frozen during the night and had flipped out quite readily when the boot was turned inside out. How obvious!

Try this problem: Two Indians, a big one and a little one, were walking through the woods. They resemble each other and in truth are related. The little Indian is the son of the big Indian, but the big Indian is not the father of the little Indian. What is their relationship?

It is the "obvious," however, which can sometimes be the most elusive. So often we try to search for the complicated when the simple will suffice. We develop complex processes because we think it is modern; sometimes these are only more costly. See if you can figure out the problem below and try to be aware of your thinking processes as you do so.

The problem: To determine the system being used to place either above or below a line all the letters of the alphabet.

I will start you by telling you that "A" goes on top. Where does "B" go?

A _____

You don't know. You require more information. At this point, it could be either above or below; but I shall help you. "B" belongs on the bottom.

A _____   Where does "C" go?
  B

Probably some will say above, that I am alternating my letters. The more cautious will not be sure of what the system being used is. They want more information. "C" belongs on the bottom.

A _____ .   Where does "D" go?
  BC

You study it, trying to find the system. Is it a numerical one? Perhaps there is a sequence of one up, two down, which would make "D" go above. Or perhaps it is a sequence of one up, three down, which would make "D" go below. Someone, after more deliberation, decides that it isn't a numerical system at all. He believes it is based on vowels and consonants. The vowels go above, the consonants below.

Let us try this system.

A			This is correct.
BCD			

A   E   This is correct.
———————
BCD

A   EF   What has happened?
———————
BCD

"F" is on top and it is a consonant. That must not be the key to the system. What, then, can it be? What have we been missing? We've tried all sorts of systems. Let us try to see if there isn't a simple key. First, we'll look at the letters above the line. Have they anything in common? And the letters below—what is similar about them?

Think about this and if you are still unable to find the key, refer to the end of the chapter.

7. Failure to distinguish between cause and effect

Most people feel quite confident that they know the difference between cause and effect. However, these are not always clear-cut distinctions. Nor do statistics always provide the correct answer.

For example, in a large university it was recently found that engineering senior students who made poor grades were much heavier smokers than those earning good grades. Did the smoking cause poor grades, or did the poor grades cause more tension which led to heavier smoking? Or is it possible that both the poor grades and the heavy smoking were the result of a common cause? Or is it further possible that none of these facts was related to one another except by coincidence?

The person who would be creative must learn not to jump to conclusions regarding causality.

Cultural blocks

Society lays down rules of behavior, thought, and action. If the individual does not obey these, he is considered a nonconformist. But conformity and creativity seldom go hand in hand.

Conformity requires that an individual act in a certain way merely because it is customary. Creativity, on the other hand, requires that the present way be challenged, investigated, and if necessary, changed.

The cultural blocks to creativity are some of the most difficult to eliminate. These are caused by all the forces of society which have shaped our lives. These blocks are first implanted in the home situation in the pre-school years. More are added as we go through the school years, with the emphasis upon good grades, good behavior, etc. Add to this the difficulty of an individual who finds himself a new employee in a company question-ing the policies of the parties in power, perhaps getting off to a wrong start, and it is obvious why changes are not easily brought about.

It requires a certain amount of courage to create. It takes an attitude that not enough people possess—one that enables an individual to strike off in new directions. Let us investigate a little more closely some of these blocks which we have termed "cultural."

1. The desire to conform to an adopted pattern

Most of us do not like to be different. It is not a very comfortable feeling. However, many of our routine actions are really not necessary for conformity. They are the patterns of behavior which, for one reason or an-other, we have developed by ourselves. The human mind is fascinating in that it is able to develop patterns where none exist. We continually try to find meaning even when none exists. We seem to be able to "correct" our perceptions, to organize them into the meaningful objects that we know, instead of looking objectively at what we see.

For example, try the problem of the nine dots below. The task is to join these nine dots by four straight, continuous lines. (Do not raise your pencil from the paper.)

. . .

. . .

. . .

2. We must be practical and economical above all, so often judgment comes into play too quickly

Our lives are composed of a series of paradoxes. On the one hand, we are taught to be practical, thrifty, etc., while on the other, our teachers are the first to admit that "it takes money to make money."

Perhaps your supervisor gives you the assignment of developing a new product. He tells you that he wants something that is really "practi-cal," yet it must be startlingly different. Unfortunately, what often happens is that at the sound of the word "practical," our imaginations cease to function.

Would it not be just as simple to start with the "startlingly different" idea; develop this—no matter where it led us—and then engineer this back to practicality? Learn to try to shoot for the single great idea at the outset. Dream the biggest dream, wish the biggest wish. Take your chance on the "one in a million shot." You can always come back to reality by stages, either because of cost, processing problems, etc.

What happens is that our minds seem to function *either* imaginatively (creatively) *or* judiciously (using judgment). When we are using judgment —deciding, placing values upon something, using rights and wrongs, etc. —we cannot also be creative. Lest it be thought that judgment is of no value, let us hasten to add that it is of the utmost importance. But judgment has its place, and this is after, not during, the time when we are trying to find ideas.

3. It is not polite to be too inquisitive nor wise to doubt everything

People who are curious and ask questions are often considered "nosy." In business language, they are often told that the matter is "out of the realm of your immediate responsibility."

The individual who accepts this code literally, who fails to question methods, processes, materials, and personnel, will not find out things, will remain noncreative. Usually, if a person is properly approached, he is happy to answer questions. Not many modern managements expect complete blind obedience to established procedures merely because they are "policy."

By stifling questioning, we are cutting out the very heart of creativity —curiosity. This is the one factor which should be greatly encouraged. It results in the type of attitude which makes possible finding the highest cost reductions, new processes, and savings. It is only by questioning, through curiosity, that these can be obtained.

Harlow Curtice, former president of General Motors, wrote: "Men of science and engineering. . . . possess what I have called the inquiring mind. This type of mind is never satisfied with things as they are. It is always seeking ways to make things better and do things better. It assumes that everything and anything can be improved."

To worry about cultural taboos on asking questions is to deprive ourselves of needed information. It could mean the difference between solving a problem and not solving it for lack of information.

4. Overemphasis on competition or on cooperation

There is another seeming paradox in our society—that of competition or cooperation. We usually think of these as opposites, while in reality they may be considered in another way. An overemphasis on cooperation could mean that the individual must temper his creative ideas to fit in with the current thinking of the organization for which he works. This situation may be true in some companies. However, in many others there is no such barrier, except that which lies within the individual himself. Furthermore, cooperation means having to work *with* other people.

Competition in itself implies that one is working against someone else. Overemphasis on competing can lead a person to lose sight of his primary goal, that of trying to solve the problem at hand rather than trying to "beat someone else to it."

What seems to have happened is that because of this emphasis either upon cooperation or upon competition, people tend to rely less on their own initiative, resources, and creativity. They seem to feel either that they are in a race against someone else or must cooperate to keep their jobs. Either attitude, on an all-or-nothing basis, leads to stagnation of ideas.

5. Too much faith in statistics

As a nation, we have probably been treated to more supposedly "factual" evidence on the basis of statistics than any other nation in the history of the world. With the rise of TV commercials, this has been compounded to the standpoint of utter confusion and even ridicule.

The problem is that people do not look beyond statistics, tend to take them literally. This becomes important because it is possible that the standard conditions upon which the statistics were based have been changed. Or perhaps some important variables were neglected, either by oversight or intentionally.

For example, it was recently reported that the average daily temperature of a midwestern city for the past fifty years had been about 65°. This figure was put forth to show that the city would be an ideal place for new businesses to locate. Yet an actual check from the weather bureau indicated that over these same years, the range has been from 22° below zero in the winter, to 114° above zero in the summer. As can be seen, it is not such a "hot" place to locate.

The above example will show how important it is to not only ask such things as averages or means, but also to inquire into ranges. What are the extremes which might be encountered? Another important thing to question is who is making the statement. If someone were to tell us that the formula for energy was not $E = mc^2$, but rather $E = mc^3$, the chances are that we would laugh at them. However, if Dr. Teller or some other famous physicist were to say the same thing, we might take the notion more seriously. You see, it really does make a difference who asks the questions.

6. Difficulties arising from overgeneralizations

This is an extremely important block, especially where it involves people. From the standpoint of human relations, there are not very many generalizations which one can make about people. They must be recognized and treated strictly as individuals. Therefore, assignments should not be made on the basis that a person is an "engineer" or that he is "this" or "that type" of person. Rather, investigate a little before making assignments to make sure that the individual, as an individual, would be willing to work on such a problem, would be interested in it, commit himself to it. You will find that it will more than pay dividends for you.

7. Too much faith in reason and logic

This often strikes people as being unrealistic. "How," they some-times say, "can a person be too reasonable or logical?" There was the be-lief in past centuries, for example, that only lighter-than-air craft could fly. If people still believed this, we would not have airplanes today. Yet, was it not reasonable and logical to assume thus?

Try the little problem below and see if you can solve it.

> Just before the nurse dies of the effects of an attack, she said, "He did it, the vil-lain!" referring to one of the three doc-tors in the room. She didn't glance or point in his direction. The doctors were named Green, Brown, and White. Why was Dr. Brown immediately suspected?

8. Tendency to follow the all-or-nothing attitude

The inability to compromise ideas can be one of the most baffling ob-stacles to creativity. It is not that people are stubborn deliberately, but rather we all are fond of our own brain children. We will sometimes de-fend our own ideas against all others to the detriment of the project's suc-cessful completion.

Another inability to compromise often occurs when we talk about feasibility and budget. Probably everyone would love to have all of the money required to make the ideal product, design, or solution work. How-ever, there comes a point at which some sound decisions must be made. There is the necessity to compromise the ideal with what is economically feasible. The individual who can see only his own point of view and not any other will no doubt run into great difficulty at this point.

Still a third kind of a situation occurs where one must set a deadline on revisions or deviations. Many designers and planners are so much the perfectionist that they are never happy with what they have. These individ-uals usually want another week or two—at least a few more days—to try and think of something better.

9. Too much or too little knowledge about the field in which you are working

Probably the obvious part of the above block is the latter, having too little knowledge about your field. Many of us seldom reflect about the fact that the first part, having too much knowledge, can be just as devastating an obstacle.

When one becomes an "expert," a certain attitude or "set" seems to occur that makes him feel that he, and only he, has all the answers. This can be found in many organizations when we have an individual with a great amount of education in a specialized, narrow field. When we find such an expert, it is very difficult to talk to him about his own field, since his feeling is that no one knows as much about it as he does. When we try to talk to him about something else, we learn that we cannot, since he is a specialist in only the one field. He does not feel competent to talk about anything else. In effect, therefore, we are unable to talk to him at all.

Beware of letting yourself become so highly specialized that you are unapproachable, either by your colleagues or by others from whom (perhaps to your surprise) you can learn a little.

10. Belief that indulging in fantasy is worthless

Speculation has always been the forerunner of invention. Most new products at one time were merely the wishful thinking, idle musings—daydreaming, perhaps—of an active, imaginative mind. Our culture, however, does not condone daydreaming. It is viewed, per se, as a waste of time. When the supervisor sees the technical man at his desk, apparently staring into space, he usually finds it difficult to avoid the nagging doubt that he may not be "doing his work." For, after all, how do we really know when the engineer is thinking or merely daydreaming?

The unfortunate thing here is that, because of our cultural insistence on looking busy all the time, the person who sits and thinks feels uncomfortable and the supervisor watching the scene feels equally uncomfortable. And in such an atmosphere of guilt on the part of the thinker and doubts on the part of the supervisor, an atmosphere to encourage ideas is extremely difficult to achieve.

Most supervisors, over a period of time, know who the idea-producers are. If the supervisor is going to worry about these employees, it may be that he doesn't have enough to do. We have to learn to be concerned about the kinds of things which pay off.

Emotional blocks

Emotional blocks to creativity lie within ourselves, partly determined by the stress of everyday living. To help understand their effect upon our creative thinking processes, picture a balance scale with emotions on the one side and clear thinking, or intellect, on the other. We find that as one side goes up, the other goes down. In other words, when emotion is at its maximum, the intellect is likely to be near minimum. Overpowering amounts of emotions—such as fear, love, hate, and anger—can be blinding, make us "freeze." They can be, and most usually are, completely debilitating.

Probably at the root of most emotional blocks is insecurity, whether on the job or in other areas. Whatever the cause, however, the effects can be just as harmfully effective as those caused by the perceptual and cultural blocks.

All individuals feel insecure to some extent. The main thing to keep in mind is that a good deal of insecurity is groundless. Most people are at least a little apprehensive about tackling a new assignment, about trying to adjust to a new situation. But most of us seem ultimately to meet the challenge fairly successfully. However, the fears and anxieties accompanying new situations are sometimes sufficient to block creativity.

Let us look at some of these emotional blocks and see how they affect our creative behavior.

1. Fear of making a mistake or making a fool of yourself

Probably more good ideas have been lost for this one reason than for any other. There seems to be a natural reluctance for anyone, particularly someone new in an organization, to say anything that might be considered "foolish" by his fellow workers or especially by his supervisors. The sad part of it is that in many cases the idea would not seem foolish at all to others; the individual only thinks that it might.

The fact that this is apparently a fairly universal block has caused its inclusion in the rules for "brainstorming." This rule states that "free-wheeling" is welcomed—the wilder the idea, the better; it is easier to tame down than to think up.

Alex Osborn, the coiner of the word and inventor of the process called brainstorming, in a book entitled *Applied Imagination,* discusses the importance of this block. He states that self-encouragement is needed almost as much as mutual encouragement. A perfectionism complex will throttle effort and abort ideas. He relates the following incident.

> One of the ablest members kept mum throughout one of our (brainstorming) sessions. I button-holed him afterward and begged him to spout whatever ideas might come to his mind at our next meeting. He said he would try but that after that last meeting, he had jotted down about fifteen ideas with the thought of bringing them up next time. When he looked them over, he decided they were worthless and tore up the list.
>
> It took quite a while to make him realize that one of his "worthless" ideas could be better than most of ours, or could be improved upon or combined into one which might become the best of all our ideas.

2. Grabbing the first idea that comes along

When under pressure, an individual who has been working on a problem for some length of time is likely to take the first idea that occurs to him. Quite often, he will then quit trying to find more. This can have serious repercussions.

In the first place, sometimes the "really good ideas" come later when we have warmed to the task. There is a great deal of value to the notion that we should always aim for a quantity of ideas. It is useful in two ways. It gives us a choice of alternatives for the solution to a problem. The second value, however, should not be overlooked.

If we go to our supervisor with only one possibility for a solution to a problem, he has only one choice—yes or no. If, however, we approach him with a multiplicity of solutions (we recommend at least three), he does not have to say either "yes" or "no." He can, rather, have the opportunity to look over what we have given him and then say that he might prefer one over the others or that one of these might be preferable if a little more work were done on it. In any event, we can help improve the relationship between supervisor and employee by not forcing him to say "yes" or "no."

As a general principle, we state "never stop at the first obstacle or with the first solution." It may very well be that when we are through, the first one was the best. However, we should certainly consider all the alternatives that we can develop before our final decision is made.

3. Rigidity of thinking (difficulty in changing set)

Everyone has opinions, prejudices, and preferences for certain methods, processes, and materials. Sometimes when someone else suggests a change of any of these, it is felt as a direct threat to the individual. It may make us do one of several things. In the first place, it tends to make us hold on to our opinions more strongly. Secondly, it makes us so defensive that we may look for new reasons to back up our opinions.

Whenever possible, we should try to divorce the idea from any specific individual.

4. Overmotivation to succeed quickly

Anyone who takes his job seriously and is intent upon advancement aims to be "the best." It is only natural, therefore, that a person in this situation will find himself very highly motivated. He may not have too much patience. When he does not immediately see a solution to a problem, he may become frustrated and either give it up or continue to butt his head against a stone wall.

Patience and a great amount of concentrated thinking are often required for the solutions to complicated problems. We have to learn to allow time for meditation, for the continued mulling over of a problem in our minds (sometimes at the level below awareness—called incubation). Just as "nothing succeeds like success," so very often lack of progress serves only to block further progress.

5. Pathological desire for security

Everyone has a natural desire for security. But overconcern with security can be neurotic. In this block, the word "pathological" is used. The reason for this is that we often see employees who have security as the main force driving them; it seems to be an integral part of them. Such individuals may refuse to take a chance on anything that is new or untried.

Any young employee with this attitude in an organization, is in a severely handicapped position to try to develop new ideas.

Quite often such an attitude is instilled through association with senior company employees who may have had unfortunate experiences many years before. There should be no realistic reason for the younger individual, starting in an organization—with his entire career ahead of him—to retreat into a foxhole of security. A good supervisor can do much to help overcome this block through reassurances and proper coaching.

6. Fear of supervisors and distrust of colleagues and subordinates

When an individual distrusts those with whom he works and fears those for whom he works, he is probably the victim of another emotional block. In some cases, of course, these fears may be based upon reality. Perhaps, through improper placement, the individual is "over his head," either technically or because of administrative inexperience. Ordinarily, these fears are not related to reality. They may be caused primarily by a lack of confidence within the individual or a fear of supervisors generally —or any authority, for that matter.

Whatever their basis, they are a definite deterrent to creative activity and problem solving.

7. Lack of drive in carrying a problem through to completion and test

Many of us enjoy starting new projects, but once having gotten things underway, we lose interest. There is a certain glamour in beginning something, being "in on" the start, the planning—in short, the "idea" stage. One of the reasons this phase is so interesting is because this is where an individual can contribute his ideas. He attends meetings, makes sketches, discusses with others, and, in general, feels highly involved and motivated.

Many supervisors have found that they can sustain this high level of motivation by using these same techniques with later phases of the project. Keep the individual knowledgeable about the progress, hold further meetings to solve "smaller" problems which might normally be turned over to the "specialists" without his being invited.

If participation is the key to involvement and motivation, then the lock must be made accessible.

8. Lack of drive in putting a solution to work

How often do we find that problems have been solved but that people won't use the solutions? When this occurs, what does it mean?

One possibility is that others may not have confidence in the solution, either because of technical grounds or some personal reasons. A second possibility, and usually the real reason, is that they had nothing to do with the idea—so why should they use it?

Here again, as in the previous block, we see the value of involvement, personally, by the people you want to use the ideas. This does not mean that we would invite *everyone* to *every* meeting or solicit *everyone's* ideas about *everything*. One way to keep people involved is simply by keeping them informed about what is happening. Let them know of the present status, what the future plans are, what things may be tried, whether you feel this may work. People will more naturally feel proud of something in which they had a part, even if only a vicarious part.

Overcoming the blocks to creative thinking

There is no magic formula for removing the shackles that bind creative thinking. Essential at all times is a positive attitude, rooted in self-analysis and a desire to improve. The person who has been foiled in a creative problem must begin his new attempt by questioning: What caused the block? How can I remedy it?

Bearing in mind that there are three major blocks to creativity—perceptual, cultural, and emotional—the frustrated innovator can assure himself that no matter what their cause, these blocks lie within his own mind.

The perceptual blocks obscure the problem as it really is. They frustrate recognition of the "need area." The cultural blocks, instilled by traditional upbringing in the home, teaching in the school, and the pressures of society, restrain imagination, inquisitiveness, boldness. The emotional blocks are irrational fears and anxieties that make us reluctant to take appropriate action on our ideas and beliefs.

The first step toward a remedy, therefore, is to recognize these blocks. Certainly little can be done about personal shortcomings that we do not recognize and that others cannot or will not point out to you.

Sit down and analyze yourself. Think about the blocks to creativity. To which of these do you feel you are prone? If you are honest with yourself, you can isolate the ones that have been hindering your idea output. If you are having genuine difficulty in recognizing them, ask someone close to you whom you respect—but do not ask unless you are willing to be open-minded.

Now that the blocks are out in the open, have been recognized for what they are and what their effect upon you is, take the next step—admit them. Go back to specific problem situations that were not solved because of blocks like these. Review them and decide how you might have acted had it not been for these blocks. Look for problems that were subsequently solved by someone else. What was it they saw that you missed? Question them about it. Try to see how you might have reoriented your thinking or synthesized the facts to yield a different, unblocked view. Next, look for new situations or problems where you can attempt solutions with your new "frame of mind."

Many design people have developed for themselves a little checklist that they keep in front of them when they are working on problems. Anyone can devise such a checklist. Refer to it regularly when you are temporarily halted on a problem. Do not, however, make the mistake of using it as a crutch. First, let yourself go! Use your imagination! Use all of your creative faculties.

When you run into a roadblock—when you can go no further—then refer to your checklist. Remember, its only function is to help ensure that you are not failing to solve the problem because of blocks within yourself, which are making you either:

1. Unable to see the problem.
2. Not able to take a different approach.
3. Afraid to come to grips with the situation.

Awareness is the key to overcoming creative obstacles. You must be constantly aware of all the different ways in which your thinking and idea output may be blocked.

A word to those who supervise the activities of technical people is in order here. Give the innovators a chance! When making an assignment, do not be so overly specific in what you want done that no room is left for imagination on the part of your employees. State the problem in a general manner, ask them how they would go about solving it or what ideas they have about it.

Above all, have confidence. Everyone has within him not only these blocks but also the capacity to rid himself of them. If you think about it this way—that you are not going to become more creative but are going to try to use more of the ability you already have—the task confronting you may not seem so insurmountable after all.

Answers to Problems in this Section

Perceptual Blocks

1. Time flies? You cannot. They fly too fast!
   (If this still is not clear, try changing the word "flies" to "mosquitoes.")
2. 99 9/9
6. His mother.
   Straight lines on top, curved lines below.

Cultural Blocks

1.

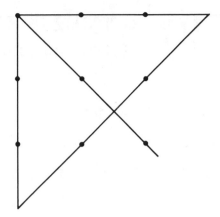

7. The other two doctors were women.

10 | Energizing the creative potential in future engineers

DAVID H. OFFNER
University of Illinois

Reprinted with permission of the author and publisher from the article of the same title, Journal of Creative Behavior, *1967, 1, 15–21.*

David H. Offner describes three agents needed for energizing the creative process in future engineers: realistic challenge, creative involvement, and relevant constraints. Two conditions for "continuing the (creative) reaction" are a reservoir of knowledge and experience plus an integrated conceptual framework. He further describes how his University of Illinois course, entitled "Creativity in Engineering Design," prepares students for developing and using their creative talent by emphasizing these agents and conditions.

Finding:

Engineers are essential instruments of technological innovation; technological innovation, all knowledgeable parties seem to agree, becomes an increasingly vital factor in the achievement of domestic and international goals.

Recommendation:

The development of the inventive and innovative potential of engineer students should, therefore, be an active concern of industry, government, the universities, and in larger perspective, society as a whole.

The two statements are the first of forty significant findings and recommendations that resulted from the National Conference on Creative Engineering Education, held in September, 1965. They put in general perspective the challenge that faces engineering educators. But in what ways should we proceed to energize this creative potential in future engineers? I believe three intermixing catalysts are necessary for training engineering students:

1. Challenge them realistically.
2. Involve them creatively.
3. Constrain them relevantly.

I would like to show how these catalysts have been used in my own courses, and to discuss two other essentials—a reservoir of knowledge and experience, and an understanding of the general theoretical framework of the subject.

Challenge

As to realistic challenge, engineers (and engineering educators) are in an exciting profession. Von Karman reminds us that while "the scientists explore what is . . . the engineer creates what has never been." Students need to grow in their appreciation and understanding of the engineering accomplishments all around them. Examples of creative engineering are found everywhere—a highly-instrumented, orbiting satellite, a deep-sea, roving laboratory, or any of a thousand land-bound technological creations that are taken for granted. Each such engineering system, with its complex or simple combination of subsystems, devices, and components represents a veritable smorgasbord. From such examples a teacher can select for study a number of imaginative working solutions to challenging problems. Current engineering applications of "fall out" from the knowledge explosion provide an almost limitless source of ideas for future use. These applications also help to conceptualize fundamentals for later recall. Stimulating and rewarding students' curiosity by increasing their understanding of known creativity can catalyze their imaginations and release fruitful action. Getting students to read, discuss, and think about the latest engineering feats is also a realistic way of building a stockpile of useful ideas for later exploitation.

Involvement

Secondly, we must involve students creatively. Software and hardware projects, individual and group activities, and oral and written assignments should be carefully planned, experimentally tested, and integrated to provide the kind of involvement that will best develop and strengthen students' creative capabilities. The teacher must avoid or circumvent known barriers, and incorporate idea-generating techniques which will smooth students' paths to personal creative accomplishments. Key words here are enjoyment, satisfaction, and flexibility. Students should enjoy getting creatively involved, and find satisfaction in the ensuing experience. The teacher should be flexible in his approaches and methods, and always sensitive to the kind of modification, deletion, or addition that may improve the energizing process. Enjoyment and personal satisfaction come from successfully tackling a challenging and worthwhile problem. Therefore, projects and assignments should be carefully selected for creative involvement, and should usually be planned so as to allow their completion, evaluation, and presentation. Creative ideas that are developed into working models provide the involvement that makes a student look forward to his next creative opportunity. Versatile creativity kits, which enable students to try out their ideas and develop their concepts into working models, are urgently needed.

Constraint

The third catalyst is constraining students relevantly. While our students are being challenged and involved, they also must be made aware of the constraints required in converting a dream to reality, or a concept to working hardware. Engineering is an iterative, decision-making process for obtaining the means, processes, or systems to satisfy a desired objective. Except for trivial cases, the conception, development, and construction of engineering systems must take place within relevant guidelines if the final creation is to satisfy all original purposes. Such constraining realities as cost, reliability, practicality, efficiency, space, maintainability, and fabricability should be introduced as the types of relevant evaluating criteria for selecting the best ideas and testing subsequent prototypes. The freedom to "dream up" alternate solutions includes the responsibility to judge those solutions in terms of their final purposes. Successful engineering systems are examples of the "survival of the fittest"—they best fulfilled the purposes for which they were created. Systematic evaluation procedures play an important role in reinforcing successful creative activity. They provide the feedback mechanism for refining and evaluating initial engineering concepts.

The actual course

Incorporating these three catalysts—realistic challenges, creative involvement, and relevant constraints—into projects, courses, or a whole curriculum requires careful preparation of material, clearly defined objectives, and appealing presentations. However, a teacher convinced of the importance of these catalysts will discover many ways to stress them. A brief description of several examples I used in a University of Illinois senior elective course, entitled "Creativity in Engineering Design," will show how these emphases can be woven into class activities and assignments. The class in question met for two-hour sessions twice a week.

The general objective of the course was to prepare each student confidently to use and develop his creative abilities whenever he applied his knowledge of natural laws and engineering technology in developing engineering systems. The method for attaining this course objective was described in the University catalog:

A study of engineering systems to show the creative use of scientific principles and design procedures; survey of natural laws and examples of their creative applications; introduction to methods for promoting creativity in engineering.

The first hour, when possible, was spent studying the system to be discussed the following hour. For example, one session concerned an automatic bowling-pin-setter. For the first hour we inspected the pin-setters operating in the Student Union. The class was divided into several teams, each of which was asked to sketch a different subsystem (*e.g.,* pin elevator, pin spotter, sequence controller, ball elevator, *etc.*), and to explain its operation. Later we discussed possible modifications or alternatives to these solutions. Previously each student had been assigned one of these subsystems as a "black-box" exercise, in which he was asked to provide a possible system satisfying the "input" and "output" requirements. In the second hour, we discussed the design and development of the ball-return accelerator. In this way the challenge, involvement, and constraint were used with some degree of continuity.

One of the individual projects was called POM (*Project Operation Moonshine*). The assignment read:

> System designers announce their open season on moon exploitation. Anticipating early development of moon systems of all kinds, they are inviting engineers to submit a system designed for operation on the moon. To assure a certain uniformity in the quality and workmanship of the submitted system, materials from which the system models are to be constructed are limited to the following: 1 piece of aluminum foil, 2 pieces of poster paper, 2 safety pins, razor blade, 12 paper clips, 4 flexible binding pins, 9 rubber bands, 6 thumbtacks, and 4 pencils. Accompanying the models must be a description of the components, and an explanation of the function and method of operation of the system.

Subsequently, the creative system-models, the enthusiastic oral presentations, and the written reports indicated that, having been challenged and constrained in time and material, students had energized their own creative potential. They also enjoyed the exercise and were satisfied with the results.

The systems studied in the course were classified according to one of four principal functions: *m*aterial transfer, *i*nformation transfer, *c*ontrol transfer, and *e*nergy transfer; or MICE. One of the group activities was a card game called "MICE-burgers." Teams of four members were selected and each member was given a card, on each side of which a patent was described. Each student was given time to study his card and record the principal ideas. Team members then exchanged cards, studying them again until each team was acquainted with the eight patents on the four cards assigned them. Each member then was given time (using as many of the individual patents as possible) to sketch ways patent-ideas could be combined to produce a new MICE-system. Finally the team members got together to evaluate their concoctions, possibly evolve still other combinations, and agree on the best one to present to, and defend against, the other teams. Summary sheets were used to record students' findings. These sheets also added to the student's stockpile of possible components for creative answers to future engineering problems. A subsequent individual project involved inventing and describing a device or system that would satisfy one of the needs described in "Inventions Wanted by the Armed Forces." I believe activities of this nature, in which students study and modify carefully chosen existing systems before "going it alone," help them develop confidence in using their creative capabilities.

Case histories

To emphasize the relevant constraints and systematic procedures used in creative engineering design, actual case histories can be studied before involving students in developing case histories of their own creations. One illustration I use is the development of a fatigue-testing machine designed and assembled in our department. The heart of the machine is the mechanical force generator, consisting of two pairs of interconnected, rotating, eccentric weights on parallel shafts, which with associated hardware is capable of generating a sinosoidal varying force of from 0 to 10,000 lb. amplitude. A phase changer permits generating any force amplitude within this range without stopping the machine. Starting with the need, the financial and time constraints, "heart" specifications, and space requirements, I discussed the final concept, verification model, assembly and component drawings, and demonstrated the ultimate physical machine with its 60 cps "heart beat." I believe this demonstration gave the student an awareness of the context in which the engineer must create, and at the same time introduced him to the excitement of seeing a concept develop into a pulsating reality with its own noisy personality.

A seminar-meeting was conducted by an engineer from industry at the end of each month. Each seminar included an overall view of design-steps used in getting the system from the concept to the hardware stage; a discussion of the general design and operating principles of the system; and a close look at one of more specific devices in the system which would acquaint the students with the means, chosen from several alternates, of solving a challenging problem.

The reservoir of knowledge

In addition to the three catalysts mentioned earlier, a basic condition for energizing the creative potential of future engineers is a continually growing reservoir of knowledge and experience. Sir Joshua Reynolds reminds us of this fact:

Invention is little more than new combinations of those images which have been previously gathered and deposited in the memory. Nothing can be made of nothing; he who has laid up no material can produce no combinations.

D. J. Cohen puts the same idea this way:

The most original ideas are nonsense because all sensible ideas have some non-original connection with previously existing facts or relationships.

Among the important "do it yourself" tasks all engineering students should face is the meaningful, enthusiastic, and systematic recording of ideas, principles, and experiences for future creative use. To assure some tangible results in this matter, I recommended that a neat, well-organized notebook be kept, and indicated that its contents would determine part of the course grade.

If students are to get a meaningful start in creative engineering, this formal stockpiling of ideas should not be only enjoyable and challenging, but also relevant and useful. To spur this bookkeeping activity, I used about eighty, boxed sample products collected at design exhibitions and shows. Students were given a summary sheet listing each item, with space for describing its main observed features and suggested uses. After students recorded their findings they read a descriptive brochure that accompanied each item. Such exercises not only increase the student's stockpile of ideas, but also develop his ability to observe details and to use his imagination in relating observations to possible applications.

The conceptual framework

A second condition for creative productivity was noted by Dr. Kurt Lion, speaking at the 20th Annual Conference and Exhibit of the Instrument Society of America. In a lecture entitled "Creative Teaching in a Modern Society" he said:

Teaching to prepare the student for creative accomplishments should . . . be directed to the formation of clear and precise basic concepts. It should also convey to the student a continuity of ideas, *i.e.,* a presentation of a discipline as a coherent entity, an integration of the field rather than a fragmentation of the subject matter.

He suggests that engineers who have an acquaintance only with peripheral matters seldom make basic contributions. Understanding the "big picture" of any discipline, so that the many "bits and pieces" fit together in a meaningful array, is probably one of the most crucial requirements for approaching maximum creative efficiency. Success in solving the unknown technological problems of the future will depend largely on the extent to which this generalized integration within and among fields of knowledge is obtained. Considerable imagination and insight will be required.

One of the best ways I found of impressing students with the importance of seeking understanding at this basic level is to acquaint them with the *Chart of Electromagnetic Radiations* (available from the W. M. Welch Scientific Company). The chart depicts the entire radiation frequency range, with colorful illustrations of the uses, theory, and limitations of radiations within the spectrum. Students can understand and use the creative power inherent in such a unified conceptual tool.

Engineering by its nature is creative; in many definitions of creativity and engineering one can notice a generic relationship. As an engineer, I view creativity as a dynamic process for obtaining a realizable solution to a need. This process occurs in a mental reactor, is fired by imagination, controlled by reason, and results in the critical fusing for the first time of selected elements from a stockpile of knowledge and experience.

Creative engineering is a decision-making process for obtaining the means, processes, or systems to satisfy a desired objective. This process requires both technology and scientific principles, both synthesis and analysis, both ideation and judgment.

Summary

Agents for energizing the creative process in future engineers should include these three: realistic challenge; creative involvement; and relevant constraints. Two necessary conditions for continuing the reaction after the process has begun include a growing reservoir of knowledge and experience, and an increasing understanding of basic concepts at the integrating level. Curricula and courses structured to emphasize and develop these conditions can provide the desired pad for launching our future engineers into life-long creative orbits. It is up to teachers to assure an uninterrupted "count-down."

11 | Value engineering

VALUE ENGINEERING DEPARTMENT
Lockheed-Georgia

Abridgment of pp. 2, 8–15, and 18–19 of "Value Engineering," Value Engineering Department, Lockheed-Georgia Company, Marietta, Georgia, a Division of Lockheed Aircraft Corporation. Reprinted by permission of Lockheed-Georgia Company.

Value Engineering (VE) is a creativity-based tool for industrial cost reduction. Searching both for unnecessary costs and for lower-cost alternatives, the value engineer assumes that the dollar expense of virtually any product or process may be reduced, often drastically. The present selection, abridged from a booklet prepared by members of the Value Engineering Department of Lockheed-Georgia, presents briefly the history, principles, and techniques of value engineering—including the unique "blast-create-refine" strategy—along with some impressive examples of successful, creative cost reduction. The article is topped off with a very concise overview of creativity, clearly intended to acquaint the blossoming value engineer with principles of creative problem solving particularly relevant to his field. The interested reader may wish to obtain further information from the Society of American Value Engineers (SAVE), Windy Hill, Suite E-9, 1741 Roswell Street, Smyrna, Georgia 30080.

History of Value Engineering

During World War II, when some critical materials were difficult to obtain and a great many substitutions had to be made, Mr. Harry Erlicher, Vice President of Purchasing for the General Electric Company, observed that many of the substitutions resulted not only in lower costs but also in improvement in the final product. Although these happened coincidently at first, Mr. Erlicher decided to try to make them occur purposely. To this task he assigned Mr. L. D. Miles. Mr. Miles greatly exceeded the scope of his assignment. He applied the basic principles of creative thinking and developed the systematic functional approach to cost reduction which he named "Value Analysis." This was in 1947. Through his dedication to this science, "Larry" Miles has become known as the "Father of Value Analysis."

In 1954 the Navy Bureau of Ships was looking for a means of reducing the cost of ships and equipment. It had heard of the General Electric program and obtained training for Navy personnel in this new field. The Navy directed its effort primarily at cost avoidance during the design stage and called its program Value Engineering, though it embodied the same techniques and concepts as the General Electric Value Analysis program. For the most part, the two terms are used synonomously.

When Mr. Robert McNamara became Secretary of Defense in 1961, he was determined to bring to military procurement a degree of efficiency and economy comparable to those prevalent in competitive industry. He adopted value engineering as one highly promising approach to cost reduction. The Armed Services Procurement Regulations now stipulate that, with minor exceptions, all major procurement contracts will include a value engineering clause. The contractor is encouraged to develop and submit to the Government cost reduction proposals which require changes to specifications. These contract clauses provide for the contractor to share in the cost reductions approved.

Definition of terms

Value Engineering

A systematic, creative approach to ensure that the essential function of a product, process, or administrative procedure is provided at a minimum overall cost.

For emphasis, the following elements of Value Engineering are listed:

It is an organized creative approach to cost reduction.
It places emphasis on function rather than method.
It identifies areas of excessive or unnecessary costs.
It improves the value of the product.
It provides the same or better performance at a lower cost.
It reduces neither quality nor reliability.

Value Engineering study

An objective appraisal of all the elements of the design, construction, procurement, installation, and maintenance of equipment, including the specifications, in order to achieve the necessary functions, maintainability, and reliability at the lowest cost. Value Engineering entails a detailed review of product designs and specifications, placing a total dollar value on the costs of production and maintenance, and relating these costs to the functional value of each part and assembly. Alternative designs, materials, processes and methods of fabrication, together with standard products available from specialty suppliers, are explored to find the lowest cost way to achieve required functions.

Function

Function is that which makes a product work or sell. The function should be defined in two words, a verb and a noun; for example, "support cable." There are two reasons for restricting ourselves to such a definition of function:

The use of two words avoids the possibility of combining functions and attempting to define more than one simple function at a time.

The use of two simple words will assure us of achieving the lowest level of abstraction possible with words; the identification of the function should be as precise as possible.

Primary or basic function

The *primary* or *basic function* is the most important essential function without the performance of which the product would be virtually worthless.

Secondary function

Secondary functions are essential functions of less importance than the primary function. A more detailed discussion of function will be found on page 147.

Value

Value is the relationship of effectiveness to cost. *Maximum Value* is the lowest cost to reliably achieve the essential function. *Cost* is the sum of labor, material, overhead, and other costs to produce.

Analyzing

In analyzing value, we study what makes up value. The analysis and evaluation of function is the foundation of Value Engineering.

Blast-create-refine

Blast the present concept out of your mind.
Create new or alternative approaches, without any negative criticism.
Refine the possibilities into a lower cost, acceptable proposal.

Evaluate by comparison

The process of comparing the cost of one method of achieving a function with the cost of other methods of achieving the same or similar functions.

Roadblocks

Reasons used to prevent incorporation of a change. Roadblocks result from a natural reluctance to change. They are usually expressed as an honest belief, but they are based on faulty information, lack of information, misconceptions, or simple inertia.

The Value Engineering job plan and techniques

Most of the key value engineering techniques are not new, nor are they revolutionary; they are elements of good engineering practice applied in a systematic sequence to achieve maximum value. The techniques used in Value Engineering are:

1. The Value Engineering job plan

Before starting any job it is not only helpful but necessary to have a plan of action. The job plan provides such a plan and consists of five phases: (a) the information phase, (b) the speculation phase, (c) the analysis phase, (d) the decision phase, and (e) the execution phase. These phases will be discussed in greater detail after you are acquainted with the other techniques.

2. Get all available facts

As a first step in reducing costs, it is necessary to become completely familiar with the product by factual review. This consists of determining what is the primary function—the secondary function. Why was it designed this way? How is it made? How much does it cost? What does it weigh? What are the specifications? How many units will be used? What is the lead time for fabrication or procurement of each part? Only after you are armed with all the facts can you approach the problem intelligently.

3. Get information from the best sources

To save yourself and others time and trouble, it is imperative that you contact people who can give you the information you need accurately and quickly. Examples would be: Materials and Processes for information on metallic and nonmetallic materials, processes, and finishes; Manufacturing Planning for fabrication methods; Material Procurement for vendor information and cost estimates of purchased parts; Contract Administration for contractual requirements, etc.

4. Know costs

To make a complete analysis of any component, it is necessary to know not only the total cost of the component but the breakdown of the total cost. This breakdown will include materials, labor, and overhead. Each operation eliminated will then remove that portion of the cost.

5. Define each function

This technique consists of describing the function of each part with a verb and a noun. For example, a diaphragm (a) holds pressure, (b) seals holes, (c) provides reliability, etc. This is discussed later in some detail.

6. Evaluate each function

After defining each function, set up the relative importance of each function in dollars and cents. Eliminate those functions not essential for adequate use of the component, thus eliminating that portion of the cost; use the following outline in your evaluation:

What is it?
What does it do?
What does it cost?
What else will do the job?
What does that cost?

Value is measured by comparison. Compare the cost of an item with the cost of other familiar, commonplace products that perform similar functions. In a defense industry it is very easy to say, "We have never done anything like this before, so how can we make a comparison?" For example, a defense weapon may be unique, but Lockheed is not unique in defense weapon building. Many other companies have capable staffs and design specialists and are successfully established in the defense business. Some of them, most likely, have more stringent financial limitations than we have. Budget limitations have a tendency to force designers to become cost conscious. For comparison purposes, attempt to obtain design data produced by other companies or by other Lockheed divisions. A number of differences will exist, but a comparison of end product cost can be made.

7. Work on specifics, avoid generalities

This technique can be used effectively with "evaluate the function." You must work on each function individually before attempting to combine them into a single multifunctioning product. By using this techique, hidden costs can be more easily removed from the overall assembly. Recognize that if a generality exists, it has probably deferred effective action in the past. As an example, in value analyzing the engine control cable tension regulators for the C-130, each of the various functional parts was examined separately with respect to function, tolerances, and finish. As a result, it was found possible to make two major cost reduction changes. One involved removal of the viscous damper from the regulator used in the condition lever controls. The other permitted substitution of an extruded section for a very complicated machined cross-head. In addition, it was found possible to relax tolerances on spring tensions and surface finishes and to make other changes to procurement specifications which resulted in a saving of $466 per aircraft or 35 percent of the previous cost.

8. Think creatively

Use as many creative techniques as necessary to get a fresh point of view. One accepted technique has been aptly named "brainstorming." While applying this technique do not evaluate ideas. Turn the evaluation part of your brain off and become a dreamer. Make short statements to express your ideas. Don't attempt to develop your ideas. Once you have expressed the idea, record it, forget it, and go on to the next idea. Don't limit yourself to the conventional approach. The main purpose is to accumulate as many different approaches to the problem as possible before evaluating any of them.

9. Blast and create, then refine

When first attempting to remove costs from a product or process, you will find it helpful to blast away all thought of the existing concept. Attempt to remove 50 percent to 75 percent of the cost, as opposed to 5 to 10 percent. Removal of such a large percentage requires that you use new methods, possibly using a completely different design concept or fabrication procedure, but always without changing the primary function.

As an example, each of the four main wing tanks in the C-130 fuel system contains an electric booster pump. To ensure that the booster pump is adequately supplied in all flight attitudes, an electric scavenger pump was provided to transfer fuel continuously from the opposite side of the tank to the surge box surrounding the booster pump. By blasting away the concept of a "pump," it was suggested that an eductor, with no moving parts, would accomplish the transfer of fuel with high reliability. Bleed air is used as the motivating force. Additional savings resulted from simplified installation requirements and reduction of functional testing. Reliability was increased, weight was reduced 16 pounds per plane, maintenance was simplified, and the cost of spares was reduced. Production and installation costs were reduced $1000 per airplane or more than 85 percent.

Begin to refine only after creating ideas that promise to remove 50 percent or more of the cost. In the refining process, it may be necessary to add 10 to 15 percent to ensure that essential secondary requirements are met. The net gain should amount to a minimum of 30 percent. After using this technique, you will find that it is easier in the long run to go through this procedure and remove 30 percent of the cost than to refine the present component and remove 10 percent.

10. Put a dollar sign on each main idea

Prior to launching a thorough investigation into the whys and wherefores of your ideas, estimate their worth. Use a dollar sign in setting up a priority on which ideas merit your first and most serious consideration. Before evaluating these ideas, try to estimate the possible dividends in return for your invested time.

Following is an illustration of how a cost breakdown developed in value analyzing a filter circuit:

Item	Function	Cost
Diode #1	Clips Signal	$ 2.00
Diode #2	Clips Signal	2.00
Transistor	Isolates Inputs	4.00
Condenser	Holds Charge	3.00
Filter #1	Selects 60 cycles	27.00
Filter #2	Selects 400 cycles	30.00
Misc. (Case, Wires, Resistors, etc.)		15.00
	Total	$83.00

This quickly pointed up the fact that the two filters accounted for more than two-thirds of the total cost and therefore merited first consideration. In this case, it was possible to combine the functions of the two filters into a single filter that could be produced in the quantity required for $20.00 each, or a saving of 65 percent on this item.

11. Use company specialists and services

During the analysis and decision phases of your idea development, be sure to make full use of the many and varied company services available to you. Don't hesitate to consult company specialists or service groups. They are competent and readily available sources of information. Proposals by in-plant specialists made possible a saving of $125,000 on 35 main landing gear strut lock collars produced as part of the ground support equipment for the C-141. Originally designed to be fabricated by welding numerous hinge and latch fixtures to split sections of heavy tubing, unit cost was nearly $4000. Moreover, difficulty was experienced with warping of the split tubing. Company specialists recommended redesign to produce by casting with integral fittings. This approach made possible a unit cost of $375, including the engineering and tooling costs, and also solved the warping problem.

12. Use standards

Wherever possible use standard components, preferably those governed by military standards. Eventually all parts and materials will require government specifications prior to their acceptance in a weapon system. The use of standard hardware reduces costs by increasing competition, eliminating proprietary information or processes, eliminating tooling costs, and ensuring quality products. A little time spent searching for a standard item can pay big dividends. For example, a design engineer on the C-141 needed a two inch lanyard to prevent a push rod from dropping if the nut backed off. The shortest standard lanyard available was eight inches. He was on the verge of designing a special lanyard when Standards Engineering suggested using a standard electrical bonding jumper. This suggestion was accepted for an estimated saving of 80 percent, plus the cost of stocking an additional part.

13. Bring new information into each functional area

Use specialists when investigating fields unfamiliar to you. A theoretical approach may lead you to previously untried approaches which, when developed, can be great cost savers. Technical breakthroughs and financial breakthroughs usually go hand in hand.

14. Use industry and vendor-specialized knowledge

Many firms specialize in limited fields. Their ability to stay in business depends on their being well in the forefront of the technology in those fields. Approach appropriate specialty suppliers with your problem—not with a detailed drawing of your solution. Explain the function that must be achieved and ask for recommendations. Frequently the specialist will suggest solutions which are new to the design engineer and will offer to furnish the hardware at a greatly reduced price as compared to in-plant manufacture of the design engineer's solution. As an example, an appliance manufacturer used large quantities of a special screw, threaded for about one fourth of its length and with the shank undercut between the threads and the head. Made on a screw machine and then undercut, they cost $150 per thousand. When the problem was put before a specialty supplier, he devised a method of using the roll-threading process to remove the metal from the undercut portion. Using this process, he quoted a price of $15 per thousand, a 90 percent saving.

15. Use specialty processes

The old tried and proved processes are often overused because they require the least investigative work. They also give the least financial return. Using new methods can reduce costs. For example, precision forging is cutting the combined cost of forging and machining. Tape-indexed, three-dimensional machining is replacing forging, machining, welding, heat treating, final contouring, and stress relieving. Precision molding minimizes the high cost of machining, cuts rejection rates, and simplifies assembly procedures. As an illustration, Manufacturing Research and the

Plastics Department recently developed a rapid, economical method for hot-forming small polyester glass fabric parts which previously were produced by the wet-layup, oven-cure method. Direct labor costs, using the new method, are reduced by more than 80 percent, and tooling is inexpensive. Mold dies for the hot-form process are made of a plastic ceramic material, using as a model the layup block from the wet-layup process. The old method requires slow, painstaking hand layup of the impregnated fiberglass followed by oven curing for two to four hours. By the hot-forming method, impregnated fiberglass is placed in the female mold of a set of heated matched dies and is both formed under pressure and cured in about five minutes. Little or no hand finishing is required. A more uniform and lighter weight part results. Applications to the C-141 result in savings of more than $2000 per aircraft.

16. Use specialty products and materials

Specialty products are those that are not necessarily covered by a design or blueprint but could be covered by a specification, reliability requirement, or specification-controlled drawing. It could be an item that is unlike what you might design, but which would fit the part or assembly and perform the desired function with no sacrifice in quality or reliability, and in most cases at a fraction of the cost of a specially designed part.

$740 and 30 pounds weight were saved per aircraft by using specialty materials in the center section of the C-141 main landing gear fairing. Crushed honeycomb sandwich was substituted for the sheet metal skin. Its greater rigidity permitted elimination of the longitudinal stiffeners. At the same time, built-up frames were replaced by extruded frames. The entire structure was thus greatly simplified.

17. Put a dollar sign on key tolerances

Put dollar signs on key tolerances whether they be on dimensions, chemical constituents, weights, or surface variations. It is often difficult during development to relax initial tolerances because so little is known of their importance to the final assembly. A careful review of tolerances can lead to worthwhile cost reductions.

An example is found in the 25,000 pound tie-down receptacle which is typical in 92 places in the C-141. The design specified the outside dimension of the receptacle neck to be 1.8727–1.8719 inches. This required a grinding operation after it was turned on a lathe. By relaxing these tolerances to 1.8727–1.8700, cost was reduced $167 per aircraft, for a total saving of over $21,000 on aircraft under contract.

18. Use your own judgment

While you should ask the advice of specialists and other designers, do not jump to use the suggestions of others. Use your own judgment. After having come this far in your investigation, you are the expert on this particular project. You have most of the information, and your design sense and your common sense are your greatest aids.

19. Spend the company's money as you would your own

Your decisions commit the company's money and our country's money. Spend the company's money exactly the way you would your own. You would be surprised how easy this makes decisions. Many times you will be deciding whether to follow tradition or to do what you know full well is right. Ask yourself, "What would I do if it were my money?"—or—"If it were my money would I be willing to pay that much for it?" Applying this criterion can be very effective in eliminating overdesign.

20. Identify and overcome roadblocks

Roadblocks are considered to be anything that impedes progress or progressive thinking. They commonly evolve from negative thinking, fear —particularly of personal loss—ignorance, laziness, self-defense, or undesirable habits. Your first hint of danger in confronting one of these roadblocks will be when you hear phrases such as "We've always done it this way." "Why change it? It works." "It's company policy." "The Air Force doesn't like it." When your progress is impeded, clearly define the obstacle. Overcoming the obstacle then becomes the problem. To do this, more facts must be brought to bear.

21. Use better human relations

A high percentage of failures can be charged to poor human relations. Convince the people with whom you deal that you are asking, not demanding; suggesting, not criticizing; helping, not hindering; and interested, not bored with them. In this manner, you will not only enlist their voluntary aid but will make contacts that can be useful to both of you in future assignments. It is often difficult to see the other person's point of view and his associated problems. Put yourself in his shoes; take the time to investigate his problems. This makes it easier to understand and live with existing conditions. In a large company there are bound to be stumbling blocks that must be overcome regardless of the task. But by avoiding personal irritations, the majority of these can be removed. Sell yourself and you have sold your ideas.

The Value Engineering job plan

The first and perhaps the most important technique of value engineering is the organized approach—the Value Engineering Job Plan (see chart). If outstanding results are to be achieved in getting better value, and 30, 50 or even 75 percent of the original costs are to be removed, you must have a systematic plan of attack.

Session No.	1	2	3	4	5	6	7	8	9	10	Reporting
Hours	1 2	1 2	1 2	1 2	1 2	1 2	1 2	1 2	1 2	1 2	1

ORIENTATION

INFORMATION PHASE
What is it?
What does it do?
What does it cost?

SPECULATION PHASE
What else will do the job?

ANALYSIS PHASE
What does that cost?
Will it work?

(SUPPORT) INFORMATION

DECISION PHASE

EXECUTION PHASE

PRESENTATION TO MANAGEMENT

SELLING

Get All the Facts

Define the Function

Try Everything

Eliminate the Function

Simplify

Put $ Sign on Every Decision

Determine Suitability

Determine Feasibility

Use Your Own Judgment

Develop and finalize ideas.

Select first choice and alternate (s).

Gather convincing facts.

Translate facts into meaningful action terms.

Prepare material for presentation to management.
a. Oral with charts
b. Written

The job plan consists of five phases:

The information phase
The speculation phase
The analysis phase
The decision phase
The execution phase

The 21 techniques that were just presented are related to one another as well as to the job plan.

The information phase

Each problem requires a phase in which all the facts are clearly determined. By securing all the necessary information before attempting to solve problems, the solution is simplified and expedited.

Get complete information concerning costs, inventory, usage, specifications, development history, material, manufacturing methods and processes. Get drawings, manufacturing operation sheets, and actual samples. Define the primary function and secondary functions. This is a realistic hardboiled job. You frequently find that, when all the facts are supposed to be in, they're not! Unless you get more facts than anyone else has accumulated, you miss untold opportunities. You can't work properly without all the facts; for when you don't have them, you are forced to substitute personal opinions for facts. Many times a problem solves itself when you do get all of the facts. As an example, a mixing chamber with a complicated arrangement of internal tubes was fitted in the air conditioning system of the C-130. Its function was to mix hot and cold air thoroughly in order to get accurate and consistent readings at the controlling thermostat. Early in the program, this thermostat had been moved much farther downstream where the hot and cold air were thoroughly mixed by passing through the moisture separator and around several 90° and 180° bends. This knowledge made possible a saving of $160 per aircraft by eliminating the internal tubing and substituting a simple duct.

When making decisions, most successful people agree on these common sense practices:

Be certain you know what the problem is (define the function).
Collect too much rather than too little information.
Exhaust all possible sources of information.
Separate facts from opinions.
Collect all the facts, not just those that support the conclusion you hoped for. In short, don't "stack" the evidence.

Speculation phase

Here is where you put to use your creative ability and the creative approach. Once the problem is defined and you have all the facts, you are ready to find a solution. Try to answer the question, "What else will do the job?"

Blast away old concepts of existing hardware so as to leave your mind free to create many new ideas for achieving essential functions. Make use of the brainstorming method. Exclude negative thoughts. Avoid analysis of ideas at this stage. Record all ideas, then forget them for the time being. To start the ideas flowing try asking simple, suggestive questions such as:

In what form could this be?
How would I make it in my home workshop?
Should it slide instead of rotate?
What other layout might be better?
What if it were turned upside down? Inside out?

Record all ideas for achieving the function regardless of specifications, interchangeability, etc. Many times good ideas come from trying to develop others that obviously wouldn't work.

Set a target to take out at least one-half of the cost from functional areas and nine-tenths of the cost from some of the components. By so doing you will be forced into new areas—areas not previously explored. Consequently, you may find it easier to remove 50 to 75 percent of the cost than it would be to remove 5 to 10 percent by conventional cost-reduction methods.

The analysis phase

In the analysis phase the primary objective is to analyze and weigh the ideas generated during the speculation phase with regard to cost, function, and feasibility. Establish a dollar value of each idea. Challenge each idea by applying the following tests for value:

Does its use contribute value?
Is its cost proportionate to its usefulness?
Can it or some of its features be eliminated?
Can its required function be achieved in a simpler manner?
Can a usable standard product be found?
Is it made on proper tooling, considering quantities used?
Will another supplier provide it for less?
Is anyone buying it for less?

Refine all ideas that show promise of providing improved value. Evaluate these ideas by comparison. Select for further consideration those ideas that have weathered the storm of evaluation.

It is important to remember that you are *not* trying to eliminate ideas. You are trying to analyze ideas to see how they *can* be made to work. A positive approach must be used. It must be understood that ideas emanating from a brainstorming session are not going to spring to life correct in all details. They are concepts only. Don't let an obvious fault hide the merits in a proposal and thus prevent its thorough analysis. By making a small modification, it may become a promising idea.

The decision phase

In this phase take the best ideas and plan a program to obtain the information you need to develop these ideas into sound usable suggestions. You may feel here that you don't have enough knowledge to work on the ideas yourself. This is natural, since no one can ever know everything he needs to know. What must be done is to recognize the problem and search for the person who can help. There are many specialists in our company, and the services of every specialist in industry are available on request. In drawing help from outside the company, from suppliers or specialists, don't just hand them a drawing and specifications and say, "What can you do with this?" Instead, inform them of the function you want, draw out their ideas on the problem, give them some latitude to work in. By these means you can really benefit from their knowledge. They may know of a specialty process, product or material that can help you. Be sure to determine costs of these ideas.

Now you will see that certain ideas are really beginning to develop and have a future. Each idea should be reviewed with the thought, "Is this really the best idea?" "With this new information could a better job be done?" Now is the time to use your best judgment, select those ideas showing the most promise, and plan your campaign for selling your proposals to management.

The execution phase

In this phase you must sell your idea. You must be prepared to meet and triumph over considerable resistance. People who must make major decisions are a cautious lot. You must sell your idea to them. To do so, you must present a clear and concise picture of just what it is you are proposing and what your proposal will mean to them, their project, and the company. Always be prepared when making recommendations to give and take. Have an alternate plan ready in the event the primary proposal is rejected. Stress the technical capability of your proposal and use cost reduction as an incentive.

Discussion of functional evaluation

In Value Engineering we are attempting to relate the cost of each product, process, or procedure to its function. To accomplish this, we must divide the project into parts or groups of parts and determine the function or service which each achieves. Let us review the definitions.

Maximum Value—the lowest cost to reliably accomplish the essential function. The key points in this definition are "lowest cost" and "essential function." The term *essential function* is understood to include those attributes needed to satisfy the requirements for performance, maintainability, serviceability, and other essential qualities.

Cost will be discussed later. For now, what is a function and what are the types of functions? Function is that which makes a product work or sell. The primary or basic function is the most important essential function the part accomplishes; all other functions are secondary.

We must take care to discriminate between the value of the function and the consequences of failure. When evaluating the function of an airplane part, there is a strong tendency to equate its value to the worth of the plane or its passengers. This is a serious mistake in evaluation of a part of any product. The value of the part, according to the definition, is the lowest cost necessary to obtain a part that accomplishes the required function with the required degree of reliability.

As mentioned earlier, there are five steps in the systematic approach to evaluation of function: (1) What is it? (2) What does it do? (3) What does it cost? (4) What else will do the job? and (5) What will that cost? Let's take an example:

An assembly in the C-130 electrical system had eleven relays mounted on a single horizontal panel. Each relay was covered by a cup shaped plastic cover. The eleven covers cost $191. In defining the function it was found that the sole purpose of the covers was to exclude falling dirt. The question, "How else can falling dirt be excluded?" brought forth the suggestion that a single cover be used over all eleven relays. This was priced out at $19.80 per aircraft for a saving of almost 90 percent. Following the five questions, this information was developed as follows:

What is it?	Cover for 11 relays
What does it do?	Excludes falling dirt
What does it cost?	$191 per aircraft
What else will do the job?	A single cover
What does that cost?	$19.80 per aircraft

The functional approach in design

Before a drawing is made, the designer must decide how it will be made—for example by casting, forging, machining, stamping, or welding. The drawing takes on the characteristics of the process selected. The planner tends to plan the manufacturing operations based on this process. Similarly, the buyer calls in his sources on this process. Thus the attention is focused on a process or method visualized by the designer and sight of the function is lost. Everyone who makes a decision on the basis of a drawing must determine the function so he can determine the value. By determining the function rather than focusing attention upon the drawing, many opportunities for obtaining better value can be explored.

Usually it is a good approach to divide the costs into functional areas. By dividing costs into such areas as electrical, mechanical, appearance, protection, and assembly, we can see if any of these areas seem costly in relation to others. You may find a $25 cover on a $10 functional component. Or you may find that assembly costs are high compared to the cost of the parts. This also helps solve another problem; namely, "Where do we start our concentrated value effort?"

It is important to note that contrary to many cost-reduction techniques, the pressure in value engineering is to maintain quality and reliability while achieving the function at the lowest cost. In striving to obtain the best value we frequently find that quality and reliability are improved and weight is reduced as well.

In trying to achieve better value, it is important to have confidence that it *can* be done. The positive attitude that costs are too high and there is something that we can do about it must prevail if effective action is to be taken. Almost everything being produced today could be replaced by something that would perform the same function equally well or better and at lower cost. Techniques are only the tools to help achieve better value. No matter what the product—commercial or military, high or low volume, light or heavy—defining and evaluating the function is one of your most effective tools to use in developing a better, more reliable product that can be produced at lower cost.

Creativity

Most of us have been conditioned to regard creativity as the result of very special talent, the exclusive province of a select few. We apply the term "creative" to the arts and to those strokes of genius that produce a new invention or a major scientific discovery. There is a strong tendency to disregard the creativity aspect inherent in many phases of our own work, the day-to-day, step-by-step discovery of new methods, variations on old methods, new techniques, and improvements of existing inventions and products.

Creativity is not a rare commodity. Everyone has creative ability to some degree. In your own work, you are probably making creative contributions regularly; but like many creative people, you may be creating intuitively—without a knowledge of the creative process. Our education provides training mainly in analytical or deductive thinking, and in judicial or evaluative thinking, while synthetic or creative thought is often neglected. Thus, for most of us, there is a gap between creative potential and actual performance. The myth that creative ability belongs to a few has persisted.

Recently this myth has been exploded. A few deliberate training programs have shown that it is possible to develop latent creative ability. The General Electric program is a good example. Engineers who have attended their creative engineering program can produce three times as many worthwhile ideas as engineers who have not had this training. One of the most gratifying aspects of creativity is that when a beginning has been made, when the creative process is understood, and a person develops the habit of creating, there is no limit to the ever broadening area in which this creative ability can be used.

What is creativity? As Eugene Von Fonge defines it in his book *Professional Creativity,* "Creativity is obtaining a combination of things or attributes that is new or different as far as the creator or those about him are concerned." We were born with unlimited imagination and as children we had the ability to create untold numbers of fanciful illusions. We could make a stick our trusty rifle and, in the next minute, a prancing stallion.

From birth until a child enters our educational system, his creative ability is increasing in terms of imagination, ingenuity; and curiosity. As he goes through the educational system from grade school, high school, and on into college, his creative ability is suppressed. In college he has to pass three or four examinations a year; if he fails once he is out. There is no premium on creativity. A gifted or creative child has only of late been recognized; we are still trying to determine how to evaluate him.

Even our job experience may play a harmful role in our creative development. We have heard this remark, "The poor fool, he will learn by experience that it won't work." Failures stunt our initiative to strive forward. As we become experienced and gain more knowledge in the field of engineering or any other endeavor, we too say the same thing to our co-worker. When he comes up with a new idea, we discourage him and say, "That won't work," and give him reasons why it won't work—we block his creativity. We should help him develop his idea and thereby encourage his creative ability.

This then is the state of most of us. What can we do about it? In Kettering's book *Inventive Philosophy,* he says, "Creative people are those who don't take their education seriously." This suggests the possibility of a person recouping his losses and regaining part of his creative capability. A person can, if he chooses, be as imaginative as he was in childhood and yet later apply the knowledge gained through experience and education.

If we are to improve our creative capability, we need to know what these creative qualities are. First is an active and inquisitive mind. Curiosity, powers of observation, and a mental organization all tend to make the mind active and inquisitive. This quality is most often exhibited by the desire when seeing something new to take the lid off and find out what's inside. Inquisitiveness leads to creativeness simply because we ask ourselves, "Can't we do it better or at lower cost than that?" Then we say, "What if we do such and such, and suppose we do this?" Now we are on the road.

Secondly, coupled with the active and inquisitive mind, we should find a constructive discontent. Simply stated, this is seeing the need by itself. To illustrate, how many times have you scraped your white sidewall tires on the curb? Two fellows saw the need. One made a wire feeler to make noise as the car approaches the curb. The other put bumper rings on the sidewalls and marketed it under the name General Tire. Many modern devices, such as the electric dishwasher, resulted from the obvious discontent on someone's part with the status quo.

This brings us to a third quality—an inner drive to get something done. Once something is started, finish it; obstacles do not prevent the problem from being solved. To quote Mr. Kettering again, "One of the most difficult things to do when I get a new man is to teach him to fail intelligently." When something fails, analyze it. Why did it fail? What is wrong with it? How else can I do it? What is it trying to tell me? Failures can be like knives—if handled properly they are useful tools, otherwise they can be harmful. Mr. Kettering also said, "Another difficulty I have with young fellows, particularly the educated ones, is that they have a natural tendency when they get a problem to run for the textbook. They hasten to prove that it says right here on page 284 that it can't be done." It is this attitude that we are trying to discourage in Value Engineering. Most likely the problem is new and a different way is needed to solve it. If it is written in textbooks, the solution is obvious or too old.

The fourth quality necessary to be successful is a good background in fundamental knowledge. This you get in school and through experience on the job. It includes mathematics, physical law and effect, the new and unusual devices, as well as new materials and processes. You have the knowledge of how devices work, their limitations, and the problems associated with them.

The fifth quality you need is an approach to any problem. This can be nothing more than a deliberate and organized approach. More often than not, we find people taking what they might call the indirect approach, getting all snarled up in their own doing, missing the heart of the problem, taking months, then years, to find an answer. With deliberate and organized thinking, we can develop a direct approach to any problem. To outline briefly the creative approach:

Define the problem.
Search for methods.
Evaluate the ideas.
Select and develop the ideas.
Execute the solution.

If you will notice, each of these steps has its corresponding Value Engineering phase outlined as follows:

Information phase
Speculation phase
Analysis phase
Decision phase
Execution phase

In order to summarize, here is a quote from the preface of *Physical Laws and Effects* by Hix and Alley:

> There is an old Scotch tale about a teacher known for his wisdom and a student who decided to test it. The student caught a small bird and went to the teacher's home. I will ask him if the bird in my hand is alive, he thought. If he says it is, I will crush it. If he says it is dead, I will release it. But when he asked the teacher his question, the wise man said, "The choice is yours."
>
> Products and industry, men and nations grow not from one idea, but from many, and ideas in turn do not come as flashes from space, but as minute advances around an individual grain of experience or technical principle. By themselves, they are valuable improvements, but only that. When brought carefully together, sifted to remove the sound from the unsound, they become the basis for the kind of products upon which great industries are built. Ideas are fragile. At each step of development, they can die as easily as the bird in the student's hand—simply because the immediate possessor of them, or the person coming into contact with them, does not recognize the importance of his influence over them. It is at the point that industry becomes stronger or enters stagnancy through the value of the idea that is given or denied them; that careers advance or become static to the degree that a person has the ability to recognize progressive thinking and to see that it is applied most effectively. In other words, ideas and sound thinking can be stifled or poorly utilized, or they can be weighted carefully and passed on to strengthen the base of technical knowledge and human progress.[1]

The choice is yours.

[1] Reprinted with permission from C. F. Hix, Jr., and R. F. Alley, *Physical Laws and Effects* (New York: John Wiley & Sons, Inc., 1958).

12 | Creativity training: A testing program that became a sales training program

CLOYD S. STEINMETZ
Reynolds Metal Company

In Chapter 23 of this volume, Torrance will briefly describe the *Torrance Tests of Creative Thinking,* the most carefully developed and extensively evaluated of any tests or inventories attempting to measure "creativity." In the present article, Cloyd S. Steinmetz describes how their modification of Torrance's battery is used as a teaching device in a sales training program. In a very involving fashion, and in a short hour and a half, salesmen learn first-hand about the nature of a creative idea, analytic procedures for producing more ideas, the rut-avoiding value of seeking wild ideas, and other important factors related to creative salesmanship. The Torrance Tests could be used easily and profitably by teachers in the same fashion for the same purposes.

When my attention was called to Dr. Robert McMurry's article in the *Harvard Business Review* on "The Mystique of Super-Salesmanship," I was warned that there would more than likely be parts to which I would strongly react—some favorably and some unfavorably. That is exactly what happened.

In discussing "The Selling Spectrum," Dr. McMurry points out that the classification of salesmen into creative and maintenance type selling is not so black-and-white simple but, rather, ranges over a spectrum from one extreme to the other. He said, "Thus, thinking particularly of creative skill, I find it useful to array salesmen in terms of positions requiring increasing amounts of that ingredient, from the very simple to the highly complex." In his seven-point range from where the job is predominantly to deliver the product (milk, bread, fuel oil, etc.) to what he rates as the most difficult, requiring the creative sale of intangibles (insurance, advertising, education, etc.), he feels that the former requires only courtesy whereas the latter calls for salesmanship.

Here is where I differ with him. Every business wants to grow and I firmly believe that, properly motivated, every individual wants to grow. His greatest potential for growth is in the exercising of his creative capacity to think up new ideas, to take new approaches to life whether it be business or personal. Furthermore, I believe that people respond to this situation, for it is not a question of their being taught to be creative, it is a matter of getting them to feel their creativity power and develop it through exercise.

Why a lack of creativity?

Business literature is replete with the statements—yes, the pleadings —of key businessmen asking for more creativity, forecasting a tremendous future if that release of creativity does come about. Somehow or other people look upon it as a mystical something. When they stop to consider, it actually is not mystical at all, although it is certainly very much an almost minus quantity in the lives of most people. The question is why?

One of the conclusions that I've arrived at is that most people exercise a minimum of creativity because they have been "shushed to death." From the time they first exercised their innate curiosity as children, they started asking questions, questions which were usually sound, provocative and, also, embarrassing to parents and elders. Yes, and to teachers, too. The result is they were "shushed." "Children should be seen and not heard!" Unfortunately, they grew up into adults who still felt that they should be seen and not heard, that their ideas were wild or weird, that their questions were unfair or embarrassing. This is the type of person with whom sales trainers are forced to deal. Whether forced or not, we want to deal with them because, here again, our greatest opportunity for services lies in tapping this tremendous potential.

Some misleading ideas have developed. These we have to overcome or at least neutralize. For example, E. L. Stentz, vice president and general manager for Packaging Corporation's Eastern Region, said, "It has been wisely, and mistakenly, assumed that you merely analyze a problem. Ideas for improvement will come automatically." The great fallacy in this is that people frequently do not even know how to get started on possible solutions to a problem.

The anatomy of selling

Since back in the mid-forties when Alex Osborn's first book on creative thinking, *Your Creative Power,* came into being it has been our endeavor to utilize his approach in awakening the creative power within the people who have come into Reynolds sales training programs or who are in our sales and management organization. We were always haunted with the fact that nearly every successful idea requires two successful problem-solving efforts: (1) arriving at, or creating the idea, and (2) selling the idea. The minute we leave the realm of order taking and enter the realm of order making, we recognize that a successful sale starts with an idea. As Herbert Swope puts it, there are three *why's* of selling. First—why do it at all? Secondly—why do it now? Third—why do it this way?

For years we have had a constant consciousness of the necessity for cultivating within our people the habit of asking questions, the courage to have an idea and stick with it, and, equally important, the capacity to sell that idea to others. We have been ever seeking new information and inspiration to help promote this most worthy cause.

So frequently we meet the salesman whose philosophy is, "I'm trying." But the salesman who is most successful is rather easy to identify. He is the individual who tackles his problems by asking the question, "How many *other* ways might it be done?" Since the Reynolds Metals Company's motto is "He succeeds best who helps others succeed," it is natural for us to ask, "How can you help others succeed?" The answer, of course, is do more creative thinking in his behalf.

Mr. Robert Leander has said, "Where there is trouble, there is opportunity." Since every salesman seems to feel that he has an overdose of trouble, it is sales training's job to show him how to convert it into opportunity. Our task is to get their imaginations working. To give them a formula for creative thinking. Or, as Mr. Throgmorton said at the ASTD Conference in Dallas in 1962, we need to "turpentine their imaginations."

Testing for creativity

It was our good fortune to have our eye arrested by an article in *Look* magazine. It started our company on what some people call a testing program, but what I prefer to call one of the most successful sales training programs we have ever held.

The article was entitled, "The Creative Child." Dr. E. Paul Torrance, Psychologist at the University of Minnesota, said in this article, "If we were to identify children as gifted on the basis of intelligence or scholastic aptitude tests, we would eliminate from consideration approximately 70 percent of the most creative." He went on to point out that IQ tests do not measure the child's flexibility, originality, depth of thinking, or intuition. Creativity tests, however, do this thing. It takes no brilliant mind to be challenged by such a startling statement and wonder what the situation is in regards to adults.

Therefore, I wrote to Dr. Torrance and asked him, first—would the test he used on children be applicable or adaptable to adults. Secondly, could we get permission to use it. A prompt reply was received saying—

first, it was an adult test adapted to children—secondly, yes—we could use it. And, in the third place, that they had a doctoral candidate who would like to make a study of an industrial population to see what the creativity test might identify under such marketing circumstances. Would we be interested? After studying the information, reviewing the test, and talking with management, we wrote back and said indeed we would.

The result is that we have administered the test to approximately 500 of our field salesmen and supervisors, as well as quite a number of our headquarters marketing group.

We consider the program an unqualified success and don't care too much about the statistics that we may get later. The balance of this article explains why.

The test and its use

A copy of the test, as well as pictures of the two principal objects used in five of the six parts of the test (the sixth part is found in the test itself and has to do with the circles) is included at the end of this article.

It takes 41 minutes to administer the test. We usually administer it in groups of around 18 or 20 people. This is because it is the number of people who are usually available in a particular office or at a particular time.

At the conclusion of the test, we spend about 25 or 30 minutes in reviewing the tests and pointing out facts which, as a result, make this experience for our men as extremely meaningful as it was entertaining.

In a session following the test, we point out that creative thinking consists of: (1) fluency of ideas, (2) flexibility of ideas, (3) originality, and (4) elaboration, improving on your own or others' ideas. We explain that every answer is weighted on the basis of one to four, depending upon its originality or its complexity, and that there are no wrong answers, but better and poorer answers.

Having experienced the test, they are still filled with the sense of frustration which occurs in dealing with each of the six parts of the test. It is easy for us then to emphasize what five facets of creative thinking are or, should I say, what the tools of creative thinking are, namely, the asking of questions—particularly "w" questions—second, guessing causes—third, guessing consequences—fourth, suggesting improvements—and five, suggesting unusual uses.

"Horsie Hollow Candy Shops"

First let us consider the Dun & Bradstreet picture (Figure 1) which is used for the first three phases of the test. Five minutes are devoted to asking questions about facts that cannot be answered by looking at the picture. Since the picture we used was in color, such a question as "What is the color of the smallest boy's hair?" was answerable by examining the picture, therefore, not qualified. But, asking his age, where he lives, what

his father did, where they got the material, why they were building the shack, where they got the candy, etc., are all applicable questions.

The second part has to do with guessing causes for five minutes. These are the facts that led up to the present situation. The third portion of the test is a five-minute period in which they guess as many of the possible consequences as they can. In nearly every instance, people run out of questions long before they run out of time. On the other hand, when we point out to the participants that all they would have needed to have done would have been to ask questions about each piece of material, its source, each person, his future, etc., they would have far more questions than they could write in the allotted time.

In sales this is extremely important. A man needs to know who and what influences him and influences the people with whom he is dealing. They need to know the past history of the company as well as being able to foresee possible results if his prospect will follow his suggestions. As one or two people in each group usually expressed it, one of the lads in the picture might catch fire to the idea of creating Horsie Hollow Candy Stores all over the country. This man is thinking big, but most of them are unable even to foresee that the dog might grab the all-day-sucker in the hand of the small boy—dogs being dogs.

We show pictures of the first Reynolds Metals plant in Louisville and, also, a picture of J. L. Kraft's first wagon in which he delivered cheese. We pointed out that it took imagination to envision the large corporations that those pictures now represent.

The toy dog picture

Now let's take a look at the toy dog (Figure 2) and what it taught our salesmen about creative thinking. Quite likely, the most important single lesson they learned involved the dog. I can now report to you with sta-

tistical accuracy a finding that is startling but also a stimulus for constructive action. At the time that they were given the assignment (8 minutes is allotted for each part of the test concerning the dog) to suggest improvements for the dog as a toy (to make it more likable to children) we would carry the dog to the various tables and show it to the individuals.

And—here is the startling discovery! On an average, only 2 out of 20 would reach for the dog to handle it. They made no attempt to have physical contact or explore it through the sense of feel, no attempt to discover its operating features—or lack of them.

We then told them the story of the little boy and girl who were playing doctor. The little boy with the stethoscope was examining the little girl's doll. When she asked him, "What is her trouble, Doctor," he replied, "She has tired sawdust." This story usually produced smiles or laughs. But, this attitude quickly passed when we pointed out that 18 out of 20 of them did not know whether the little dog had tired sawdust or not. In fact, they had no idea what material was used as stuffing. How then could they make any suggestions in that phase of improvement?

We make it a point to remind them that they have not been restricted as to size, cost, materials, practicality, color, feel, smell, or taste—and, yet, they run out of ideas early.

It was also pointed out that in most instances people do not ask themselves how wild, weird, or unusual could it be made. Or, how could it be used by salesmen. Or, how could it be used by your wife. Or, how could it be used by a minister. Or an attorney. Or an astronaut. Or whomever— or, how could it be used to promote a product or a service. Here again we emphasized that creative thinking starts with curiosity . . . and curiosity has as its best food the asking of questions, especially the "w" questions and by the manual manipulation of an article. If our salesmen or your salesmen were to take apart the product; were to read and study the service or the material, the advertising; were to dig into the history of the company, the background of the people with whom they deal—all of these things and many more could change their whole approach. Such actions would develop the valuable quality of uniqueness. It tailors the proposition to the individual, making it more serviceable, more truthful, and, also, more pleasant.

The circles test

The test involving the circles demonstrates several very important facts about creative thinking. First of all it emphasizes the possibility of getting in a rut. It also points out how ruts can be helpful. For example, one man was caught allowing his eyes to rove all around the room trying to find something that was round. He couldn't find anything new, although the buttons on his coat and the door knob were round, they simply didn't register. At last he stuck his hand in his pocket and a bright light came to his eyes—coins. He started marking one circle one cent, another five cents, and then a dime, a quarter, a half dollar, and a dollar. Then he ran out of coins until he remembered his French coins. He started over again. Basically, he was in a rut. But here is an interesting fact. He had been looking for an opportunity to promote an idea inexpensively. The test reminded him that a certain South American country had a small copper coin which he could buy eight for a penny. This enabled him to cut his "gimmick" cost to one-eighth of a cent and add to it the romance of a foreign coin. Thus, thinking in a rut did have its value.

Another man was so distressed because he couldn't think of another use for any of the circles. He finally removed his glasses, laid them on the paper on top of the circles and rubbed his eyes. Finally he put the glasses back on just as time was called. I happened to have observed this performance and so I asked him, "Did you draw a pair of spectacles?" He looked very sheepish and acknowledged that he hadn't. Two circles in the form of two lenses, laying directly on top of the circles but he did not see the relationship between reality and an idea.

Summary

Now let's summarize. Why do we feel this testing program was an extremely successful training program? First of all, it *was* a training program. The people felt their involvement. They knew their limited performance. We didn't even have to grade the papers. They knew that they had not had as many ideas as they now knew they could have had. Secondly, they discovered the means for creating more ideas. They felt the importance of asking "w" questions. They sensed the significance of investigating causes and guessing consequences. The importance of suggesting ideas

. . . lots of ideas . . . weird ideas . . . ideas that other people would not be likely to think about took on reality. They learned that even getting in a rut can sometimes be helpful as long as you are endeavoring to think creatively about a problem. They learned that having ideas is frustrating and involves effort. Therefore, frustration *can* be an encouraging signal indicating progress toward creative-thinking success. And, most important of all, they learned and felt the vital fundamental that there is no one answer to any problem. Rather, there are a multitude of answers and it is well to try and think of as many answers as you can, as many suggestions as you can, before you exercise judicial judgment and determine what answer you are going to propose. It gives a man a great deal of confidence to know that if one idea doesn't work, he can come up with others, any one of which will be equally as successful as the one that didn't work and maybe a whole lot more successful.

There have already been some by-products showing up. For example, we learned that certain people give a high percentage of negative responses when they take such a test. Others have a preponderance of optimistic reactions, so we find that by this sampling people are revealing their personality tendencies.

We also found that some men tend to focus their responses on problems related to the business enterprise. For example, they will ask: How will they cool the drinks? How will they preserve the candy? Where will their customers come from? How can the boy handle the sign without touching wet paint? What time of day is it? Is it summer? What is the dog's name? It makes us wonder if there isn't some significance in an individual's choice of pertinent questions.

We also learned that there were a lot of common response items. Some gave fewer but nevertheless important, less common, or what we might call original items.

We also find that there seems to be a tendency which issues a warning —the more creative people tend to be less appreciated by the supervisors —at least, generally speaking. They are not conformists. They are more individualistic. They are not as easy to control. They do not give pat answers. They insist on additional facts. They require or request or insist upon additional services.

This has been one of the very shortest of our successful sales training programs. It required an hour and a half at the very outside, but was definitely a producer of specific identifiable changes in people—people who are now trying harder to get more ideas, to ask more questions, and to solve more problems.

And, we are also finding, as the months grind by, that by feeding them with additional creative-thinking material, by reminding them of what they experienced in taking the test, the initial experience is revived with a beneficial effect to all.

Creative Thinking Tasks

Cooperative Research Project
Reynolds Metals Company and the University of Minnesota

Introduction: These tasks are a test of your ability to use your curiosity and imagination, to think of new ideas. There are no "right" answers in the usual sense. You are asked to think of as many ideas as you can. Try to think of unusual, interesting, and clever ideas—ideas which no one else is likely to think of.

You will be given six tasks to do and you will be timed on each one, so do not waste time. Work as rapidly as you can with comfort. If you run out of ideas before time is called, wait until instructions are given before going on to the next task.

TASK 1. ASK AND GUESS. The first three tasks will be based on Figure 1. The first task will give you a chance to show how good you are at asking questions. In the spaces below, write down all of the questions you can think of about the things you see in the picture. Ask the questions you would need to know to understand what is happening. Do not ask questions which can be answered just by looking at the picture.

1. ....

2. ....

3. ....

4. ....

TASK 2. GUESS CAUSES. In the spaces below, list as many possible things as you can which might have caused the action shown in Figure 1. You may use things that might have happened just before the event in the picture, or something that happened a long time ago that had an influence on the present event. Make as many guesses as you can. Don't be afraid to guess.

1. ....

2. ....

3. ....

4. ....

TASK 3. GUESS CONSEQUENCES. In the spaces below, list as many possibilities as you can of what might happen as a result of what is happening in Figure 1. You may use things that might happen right afterwards or things that might happen as a result long afterwards in the future. Make as many guesses as you can. Don't be afraid to guess.

1. ....

2. ....

3. ....

4. ....

TASK 4. PRODUCT IMPROVEMENT. List below the cleverest, most interesting, and most unusual ways you can think of for changing the toy dog in Figure 2 so that children would have more fun playing with it.

1. ....

2. ....

3. ....

4. ....

13 | Understanding creativity for use in managerial planning

TOM COMELLA
Automation *staff*

Reprinted from Automation, *April 1966. Copyright 1966 by The Penton Publishing Co., Cleveland, Ohio.*

In provocative contrast with most articles in this volume, Comella de-emphasizes training for creativity, crediting heredity as the main determiner of creative ability. The most important implication of his viewpoint is that, rather than attempt to develop innovators through deliberate training programs or by providing a creative atmosphere, management must direct its main efforts to recruiting creative talent. Now while we must admit to profound individual differences in creativity, which in some proportion must be genetically determined, there is no doubt that creative *attitudes* and effective creative *techniques* can be learned (see Chapter 18 for further discussion). So much for our disagreement. On the positive side, Comella sheds light on many important facets of creative problem solving. Specifically, he explains a sequence of problem-solving steps, describes factors inhibiting creative growth in childhood, and identifies some important characteristics of creative personnel.

Originality of thought is the motive power of innovation. Innovation is essential to continued technological progress. Technology is the principal source of change in our modern world. From these observations, it is easy to recognize the primal significance of *ideas* in the hierarchy of human endeavor. Nowhere is this truer than in manufacturing engineering. Economic facts of life are continually pressing industry to create a greater variety of products with better quality and at lower cost. The result is an entire automation technology with an incessant yield of exotic equipment, complex processes, and powerful methods.

The problem of applying methods and mechanisms to do work is straightforward. But the application of the creative faculty in Man which gives birth to these tools of labor has proved very difficult indeed. This is because the creative process is not a problem in engineering analysis, as many management people have thought. It is a delicate and sometimes mysterious human response to challenge which involves the deepest recesses of the human psyche. If management and supervisory personnel would stop thinking about controlling creativity and seek, instead, to understand it, they will be better able to make use of its practical benefits.

The first step in solving a problem is to define it accurately. To understand the nature of the creative process and its relevance to managerial technique we must, first, establish what creativity is. Some people see creativity as an ability to generate new ideas. Others define it as a basic human faculty for solving problems. Both of these approaches have some truth in them, but neither tells the whole story.

Original thought certainly plays the central role in the creative process. But if this thinking is confined to the random notions of the thinker, it is useless. To be creative, original thought must have direction. It must be triggered by a specific problem and must result in a work which meets the requirements of that problem.

Ingenuity is not creativity

In this way, creativity *is* a faculty for solving problems. However, problems can be solved without creative ability. By simple trial and error or mechanical manipulation, a great variety of tasks can be accomplished. But to ascribe the quality of creativity to these functions would not be accurate. Ingenuity is not creativity! Creativity involves new ways of thinking about old problems. As such, it is a complex mental process which may or may not have a tangible result.

Ideas, therefore, are the main resource of creativity. The power of ideas over things and events stems from two qualities. First, ideas are vantage points which provide new perspectives. Second, being bound only by the knowledge and imagination of the thinker, ideas have the flexibility to be applied to greatly diverse situations. The power of ideas is concisely portrayed by this quotation of Robert Galvin, president of the Motorola Corp.

> If you take away all of Motorola's factories, all of our inventories, and leave me with ten scientists and engineers of ideas, we could rebuild our corporation in a few short years. But if you leave me all of our physical assets and take away all of our ideas, you leave me virtually nothing.

An excellent example of the flexibility of ideas is the concept of programming. Not only has this concept transformed manufacturing methods through the use of computer process control and numerical control, but it is finding extensive use in biology as well. Brain researchers are applying programming concepts in an effort to understand the function of the mind and geneticists are using the same basic principles in their quest to break the genetic code. Other manufacturing methods and equipment can be traced to basic ideas which were born in other, unrelated branches of pure or applied knowledge.

With these observations as background, a working definition of creativity can be derived. It must contain four elements: (1) Creativity is a mental activity. (2) It is triggered by specific problems. (3) It results in novel solutions. (4) These solutions usually have implications and/or applications beyond their immediate uses.

Creative process is art, not science

Far more is known about the products of human creation than about the process of creating. There are no formulas for creativity. Attempts to systematize it can be misleading. The most that can be safely done is to categorize the various mental functions which are observed to accompany the creative process. These functions include: (1) problem perception; (2) incubation; (3) insight; (4) elaboration, test, and evaluation; (5) application.

Problem perception

There can be no creative solutions without problems to solve. In this regard, it is important to realize that problems are not objective realities. They do not exist in themselves. They are only manifested in relation to specific human needs and goals. The fact that an assembly operation is accomplished manually, for example, is not problematical in itself. It only becomes a problem when company officials require greater production efficiency. In such a case, the search for methods and equipment to automate the assembly operation becomes an imperative necessity.

Being a subjective quality, problem perception varies between people. The creative person is more sensitive to problems than others. He "sees" them before others do, consequently, his efforts are more comprehensive and they yield more advanced results. It may even be said that the creative person invents problems as grist for his psychic mill. He enjoys being challenged. This psychological quality differentiates him from the ordinary person who has a relatively low tolerance for problematical situations.

Once the problem is perceived, it must be analyzed and formulated in the most meaningful terms. Only then can the search for a solution begin.

Incubation

The search for a solution to the perceived problem takes place on three levels simultaneously. On the physical level, data pertinent to the problem is sought out, accumulated, and evaluated. On the level of conscious thought, available facts, ideas, and experience are brought to bear on the problem. On the subconscious level, mysterious psychic processes work to synthesize all known information into a new and useful framework.

The net result of these three levels of activity is a development period in which a potential solution germinates, takes shape, and grows. Because subconscious processes are involved, the individual is not completely aware of the progress of this conceptual growth. He only knows the direction of his conscious thought, which is one reason the creative process is so difficult to pin down and analyze.

In this stage of the process, the creative person is characterized by an exceptional amount of mental stamina. He doesn't give up easily. He wrestles with his problem long after most people would have quit or sought outside help. Such intellectual persistence forces concern for the problem to ever deeper levels of consciousness where it can incubate and partake more fully of subconscious processes. This exceptionally active interplay between conscious and subconscious thought processes is essential to creativity. It manifests itself as *imagination*. But unlike the daydreamer or psychotic, the creative person possesses the will and intellectual capacity to apply his imagination to real situations.

Insight

Thomas Edison once said that "genius is 2 percent inspiration and 98 percent perspiration." Though the statement is true enough, it obscures the primary significance of that 2 percent! Without it, there is no creativity. Inspiration—or insight—is the key to the creative process. It follows no logical rules. It cannot be predicted or controlled. It emerges out of the sum total of conscious/subconscious activity as an answer or approach to the problem under consideration.

While psychologists do not know what goes on in the far reaches of the mind to produce insight, experiences of it consistently testify to these qualities.

1. Insight is sudden and dramatic.
2. It usually comes when the conscious mind is passive.
3. Insight is triggered by a specific experience, whether that experience is in the form of an actual event, a dream, or a vision.
4. Insight is a synthesis of many lines of thought which the individual could not consciously relate.
5. Elements in the triggering experience are transposed into the framework of the problem, providing what seems to be the last crucial link in the emerging concept.

It is no wonder that the creative person is frequently absent-minded. This quality signifies a certain preoccupation with his problem, sometimes to the detriment of other activities awaiting his attention. The creative individual is constantly "tuned in" on his problem. Therefore, his attention is almost always available for whatever relevant material his subconscious thought processes may be preparing.

Preoccupation, conscious or unconscious, is a prerequisite for insight. Understandably, then, insight can come at the most bizarre moments and in the most diverse ways. Science lore is replete with anecdotes about creative personalities which illustrate this point. Legend tells us, for example, that Newton was observing an apple fall from a tree when the last link in his chain of thought about gravity was forged. Archimedes was taking a bath when his famous "Eureka!" experience struck, giving him the key to the law of buoyancy. Nichola Tesla had waking visions which portrayed design principles he later applied in his electrical inventions. James Watt was watching his mother boil a kettle of water when he "saw" how his steam engine would work. Johannes Kepler's mystical inspirations were the genesis points of his history-making theorems of planetary motion.

Elaboration, test, and evaluation

Most of the "perspiration" Edison wrote about is spent during this stage in the creative activity. Insight may provide the key to a solution, but the solution itself still must be worked out in detail. Once it is systematically formulated, it is tested for how well it meets the problem's requirements and is evaluated in the light of feasibility, economic and time factors.

Application

The final step is the application of the solution, whether it be in the form of a concept, technique, or piece of equipment. Like any engineering debugging procedure, this stage in the creative process many times results in changing or adapting the new solution in some way. Practice has a way of humbling theory, and the results of creativity are no exception to this rule.

Though this sequential pattern of the creative process is consistently repeated, no time limits can be put on its various stages. And while this has been a rather schematic description, it is important to realize that these stages of mental activity are fluid aspects of the creative person's psychology. For him, the creative process becomes a live, incessant response to intellectual challenge. That response doesn't always result in a valid or useful product. But when it does, the product is likely to be of great value.

You can't teach people to be creative

How is creativity developed in people? Does everyone possess it? Can creativity be taught? Answers to these questions are of vital importance to manufacturing management. They are important because they provide the framework within which management should plan and staff those technical and managerial activities requiring creative abilities. Without this knowledge, management planning may actually inhibit, rather than promote, progressive innovation.

In ancient times, the extraordinary talents and abilities of men were explained in terms of supernatural powers. The Gods were thought to have bestowed special favors upon creative personalities. By explaining creative qualities as personal gifts, this primitive solution seems to portray the hereditary explanation of creativity which many present day psychologists endorse.

In direct contrast to this concept is the mechanistic approach of some twentieth-century environmentalists. They envision the creative process as the inevitable result of certain environmental conditions "operating" upon people. Establish a creative environment, they reason, and you shall have creative people!

Both heredity and environment can be demonstrated to have influences upon creative development. A clue to which of these factors plays the major role, however, is revealed from the many studies of creativity in children. These studies show that nearly everyone originally possesses the psychological qualities which creative personalities display. However, most of us either lose or inhibit the development of these qualities as we grow. Here are some of the forces causing this inhibition.

1. Desire to be accepted by others works toward the elimination of individualistic traits, promoting conformity.

2. Progressive encounter with civil laws and social rules prompts most people to adopt prescribed patterns of thought, as well as behavior.

3. Systematic methodology of educational systems inadvertently stifles curiosity and restricts intellectual activity to conventional techniques. Our institutes of learning are oriented more toward teaching *what* to think rather than *how* to think.

4. The learned axiom "the majority rules" is equated with "the majority is right" in the minds of many people. This error further restricts the thinking process. Majority opinions and approaches are heavily relied upon.

5. People develop habits of thought which are as resistant to change as behavioral habits. Newton's first law of motion—describing how an object's momentum resists changes in speed and direction unless acted upon by an external force—is equally descriptive of the mental ruts people dig for themselves.

To various degrees, these social forces are present in everyone's life. The fact that highly creative people react to them differently than the majority of people shows that they are "made of slightly different stuff." Heredity is responsible for an individual's basic capacities, emotions, and temperaments. These physio-psychic elements determine, to a great extent, how the individual will react to specific circumstances. Given the right physio-psychic structure, a planned environment can *spur* creativity. Environment, however, cannot supply what the person doesn't have.

What does this mean for management? It means, primarily, that management cannot think in terms of creating innovators out of whatever personnel may be hired at random. *Management must recruit for creativity!* Only then will efforts to stimulate creativity through environment and motivation pay off. You can tap creative potential, but you cannot create the potential itself. To accomplish the goal of recruiting for creativity, management people must learn to *identify* those individuals with greater than average creative abilities.

Many psychological tests for creativity have been developed. While being far from foolproof, these tests can be of help in a specially designed recruitment program. But the success of such a program will ultimately rest upon an understanding of the creative process and of the personality type which generates it. This understanding will not only enable management to recognize creative talent. It will also teach management how to appeal to the creative individual, thereby interesting him in company challenges.

Creativity is not free

Creative people have characteristic attitudes and traits which present unique problems for management. The price management must pay for creativity, then, is in the special planning for and handling of creative personnel. Any planning for creativity should consider these attributes of the creative personality.

Competence

Creative people are highly competent in their chosen field of endeavor. They have great pride in their work. They require respect first, and adequate compensation second. They believe that performance should be the sole standard for advancement.

Challenge

Creative qualities are stimulated by challenge. Creative people, therefore, should be presented with problems which tax their talents and intelligence. Routine work should be reduced to an absolute minimum. Nothing clogs the creative process more than routine.

Freedom

Creative people are "loners." They have a deep awareness of their intrinsic freedom. This sense of freedom manifests itself as a marked independence of thought and judgment. Enough latitude must be given them in their work to exercise this independence in the pursuit and development of new ideas, for therein lies the principal value of creativity. Unfortunately, independence of this nature can also show up as unsociable and argumentative behavior.

Interest

The creative mind responds best to problems it is naturally intrigued by. Therefore, managers would do well to match specific job challenges to personnel interests whenever possible. This may mean reorganizing those company programs which involve highly creative personnel. Company programs which periodically rotate job assignments, for example, are not conducive to creative interest. The creative individual wants progressive challenge and responsibility, but he wants them in areas of his special interest.

Nonconformity

All nonconformists are not creative. Yet, creative persons do display various degrees of nonconformity. They rely heavily on their own experience. They dare to be different in matters which make a difference to them. Creative persons, therefore, should be treated as individuals. Attempts to overregiment their work activity can result in determined resistance and/or sub-par work performance.

Discipline

Creative people are highly rigorous and flexible in their own thinking. They distrust "pat" answers and formulas. They strive to uncover assumptions. Creative people are not bound by categories. Their thought can move easily from one framework to another. They are very adept at breaking down information and reassembling it again in new data patterns. This discipline and flexibility of thought is sometimes displayed as an impatience, intolerance, or lack of interest in the ideas of others. Having a fierce confidence in their own ability to solve problems, they may not respond well to group work activities. For example, many creative people shun the various "brainstorming" techniques which have come into vogue during the last few years. These techniques are looked upon as substitutes for creativity rather than as methods to stimulate creativity.

Creative men will design the future

To the public, creativity is the latest in an endless series of status symbols. You aren't "in" if you're not creative. To industry, however, creative talent is an imperative resource for continued production improvement. That improvement takes the form of new approaches to traditional manufacturing problems which, in turn, open up new avenues of economic growth.

The occurrence of creativity in people is a random phenomenon which cannot be controlled. But the recognition, development, and effective utilization of creative ability can and must be controlled. This is the challenge and the hope for future progress in manufacturing.

14 | An eye more fantastical

FRANK BARRON

University of California, Santa Cruz

From Frank Barron, "An Eye More Fantastical," Research Monograph No. 3, 1967. *Published by the National Art Education Association. Reprinted by permission of the author and publisher.*

As a leader in the Institute of Personality Assessment and Research (along with Donald W. MacKinnon, Chapter 15, and Richard S. Crutchfield, Chapter 20), Frank Barron has examined personality characteristics associated with artistic and scientific creativity for many years. In the present selection, taken from his Viktor Lowenfeld Memorial Lecture which was given at the 1967 NAEA National Conference in San Francisco, Barron proposed that mature, adult creativity is determined not by IQ, but by perceptual and attitudinal styles of using the mind. Stylistic variables characteristic of the highly creative individual are (1) a *perceptually* open and flexible attitude, instead of a *judgmental* one; (2) an *intuitive,* sometimes "transliminal" awareness of deeper meanings, rather than a *sense-perceptive,* reality-based attitude; and (3) a preference for the complex, even chaotic and disordered, in contrast with the less creative tendency towards balance, simplicity, and predictability. Quoting from his fine book, *Creativity and Psychological Health,* Barron sketches the personality of individuals who, deliberately or not, make the perceptual decision for creative disorder—which includes, at worst, the real danger of personal disintegration. The thoughtful reader will reap many insights into the nature of creativity from Barron's own perceptiveness.

In this monograph I shall attempt to develop further a general thesis that I first set forth in my 1965 paper, "Creativity in Children." My essential claim is that a genuine, pervasive innocence or naiveté of perception underlies mature, productive originality, but that the creative process in maturity is not based, as psychoanalytic theorists have argued, upon "regression in the service of the ego" (Ernst Kris' phrase), but upon progression, without loss, from the sense of awe and wonder and the natural spontaneity of childhood into integrated adult functioning with fine command of ways and means acquired through discipline and technique.

This thesis is one that I think Viktor Lowenfeld would find quite of a piece with his own formulation of the nature of creative activity. I am grateful for the opportunity to present my reflections on these matters in a publication honoring the memory of Lowenfeld.

Viktor Lowenfeld was fascinated by the problem of how visual forms are seen and represented by children whose eyesight is not normal. He was convinced that his own investigations had shown that in the evolution of individual vision each of us passes through a stage of "naturalistic perception" that characterizes also the evolution of vision from primitive man to modern man. In creative activity, he held, the visual sense "relinquishes its primacy," and universal symbols come to dominate the very process of seeing. The weak-sighted are thus strangely compensated for their inability to perceive the visual world "just as it is." Though their perception is primitive in the sense that their discrimination of form permits only a low level of differentiation of visual phenomena, it is closer to the archetypal and symbolic and is suffused with a sense of mystery which is the natural stuff of poetry and art.

Providentially, Viktor Lowenfeld left us, in his germinal work, *The Nature of Creative Activity,* dozens of photographic reproductions of the art work of the weak-sighted children whom he studied, and so we can go to his book and see at a glance what he means. I think of such examples as Plate 4, "Jacob's Dream," Plate 5a, "Drowning Man," Plate 8, "Being Throttled," and the incomparably expressive sculpted head titled "Longing for Sight," done by a congenitally blind boy.

Yet it would be misleading if I were to seem to suggest that Lowenfeld put primary stress on this theme, or dealt with it alone. His approach to the art of the weak-sighted was not sentimental, but scientific, and his main interest was in the relative predominance of "haptic" as opposed to "visual" tendencies in his subjects. The concluding paragraph of *The Nature of Creative Activity* expresses well not only the substantive result of his work but the spirit in which he approached it. I quote:

> As has frequently happened before, the study of an extreme case has resulted in the clarification of a certain field. In this case, an analysis of the phenomena of shape and form at the physiological frontiers of blindness demonstrated that it is the psychological attitude itself which determines to what creative type (haptic or visual) an artist belongs. The battle of the two impulses towards orientation in the world of appearances could have been nowhere better demonstrated than in this region, where, in order to possess a world of his own, man has himself to create its foundations.

I shall seek to enlarge upon this statement of Lowenfeld's by relating what the world gives to what the eye takes and makes of it. That is to say, I shall treat of the experiential fundaments of the ego, and its reaches. In doing so, I shall take as point of departure a trio of findings that have emerged from the researches of myself and my colleagues at the Institute of Personality Assessment and Research on the personality and intellectual characteristics of outstandingly creative persons. Let me begin by reviewing the most solidly established of our findings.

A result of fundamental importance came from our investigation into the relationship of creativity to intelligence quotient, taking the latter in its commonly accepted meaning as an index of performance on "intelligence tests."

Two statements must be made here, which at first may seem mutually incompatible:

1. Persons of a high order of creative ability are usually in the upper 10 percent, or perhaps upper 5 percent, of the general population in terms of IQ.
2. Within groups of such persons, and even when highly creative persons are compared with merely representative persons in a profession which calls intrinsically for creative ability, there is usually zero correlation between creativity and measured IQ.

A clearcut example of these findings is provided by the study of creative architects, carried out by Donald W. MacKinnon, director of the Institute, and Wallace B. Hall. MacKinnon and Hall compared 40 architects (who were drawn from the sample of 66 architects judged by the panel of experts to be the most creative) with two control groups: one selected at random from the Directory of American Architects, and the other selected so as to match the highly creative group in certain characteristics, such as age, geographical location of their offices, and similarity of background in training and professional experience. They found that the high-level test of general intelligence we had employed because it is considered to provide accurately differential measurement in the high IQ ranges (the Terman Concept Mastery Test) failed to differentiate among the three groups. In order to counter objections that the test was too much limited to verbal reasoning, and that it was perhaps subject to errors of measurement because its administration was not individually monitored, they called upon their subjects some time after the original study to take another test: the Wechsler Adult Intelligence Scale, which is the most widely used and generally considered the most valid, factorially variegated, and comprehensive individually administered intelligence test. Again, the group averages proved to be virtually identical, all within one point of 130 IQ. While similar retesting has not yet been completed for other groups studied, the findings with the Terman Concept Mastery Test for those groups have been quite similar. Creative writers score significantly higher than architects, and their estimated IQ is greater than 140. So too with mathematicians and scientists, and only in the mathematicians' sample is there a positive relationship between rated creativity and measured general intelligence. That relationship is small though significant. Among student painters who took part in one of our research projects at the Rhode Island School of Design, the correlation between their Scholastic Aptitude Test scores and faculty ratings of their creativity at the end of the three years was − .09.

The generalization suggested by these findings is that for certain activities a specifiable minimum IQ is probably necessary in order to engage in the activity at all, but that beyond the minimum, which often is surprisingly low, creativity is uncorrelated with IQ.

If creativity is not a function of IQ, what then is it a function of?

Most of all, our findings suggest, it is a function of *style or modes of experiencing,* or stylistic ways of using the mind. There are three distinct stylistic variables that we have found consistently to mark the highly creative person. Two of these are drawn from C. G. Jung's theory of psychological types, and the third rests upon the polar opposition between *preference for phenomenal complexity and asymmetry* and *preference for simplicity and symmetry* that some of my own work has established. Let us now consider this trio of findings.

I. The perceptual versus the judgmental attitude

According to Jung, whenever a person uses his mind for any purpose, he performs either an act of perception (i.e., he becomes aware of something) or an act of judgment (i.e., he comes to a conclusion, often an evaluative conclusion, about something). If one of these attitudes is strong in a person, the other is correspondingly weak. The judging attitude is said to lead to an orderly, carefully planned life based on relatively closed principles and categories, whereas the perceptual attitude leads to more openness to experience, including experience of the inner world of self as well as experience from without. The perceptual attitude facilitates spontaneity and flexibility.

In our studies, every group but scientists is predominantly perceptual rather than judgmental, and in every group, including scientists, the more creative individuals are more perceptually oriented and the less creative are more judgmentally oriented.

II. The intuitive versus the sense-perceptive attitude

The act of perception itself, according to Jung, may be of two kinds: *sense-perceptive* or *intuitive*. The sense-perceptive attitude emphasizes simple realism, and is a direct awareness of things as they most objectively are in terms of the evidence of the senses. Intuition, by contrast, is an indirect awareness of deeper meanings and possibilities. Creative individuals are characteristically intuitive. This is shown in test results on the Myers-Briggs Jungian Type Indicator, where scores on the Intuition Scale show more than 90 percent of the creative individuals we have studied to be predominantly intuitive. It has shown also in experiments and interviews devoted to what MacKinnon in 1965 called "transliminal experience," which on close examination proves quite similar to the Jungian definition of intuition. One such interview was devoted especially to the fantasy life, ranging from day dreams to night dreams and hypnagogic experiences to transcendental experiences in full and acute consciousness. An unusually high percentage of creative persons claim to have had experiences either of mystic communion with the universe or of feelings of utter desolation and horror. The prologues to these experiences were frequently described with considerable vividness in the interview, and this statistic does not represent a checking of "yes" or "no" to a question such as "Have you ever had a mystical experience?" Other experiences of an unusual sort were also described, such as being barraged by disconnected words as though one were caught in a hailstorm, with accompanying acute discomfort, or seeing the world suddenly take on a new brightness. A high frequency of dreaming was also reported, as well as a high frequency of dreaming in color, as compared with control groups we have studied.

William Blake, a great artist both in writing and in painting, has made transliminal perception the basis of his interpretation of artistic experience. He spoke of *"four*fold vision." Single vision, for him, is simply what ordinary physical eyesight enables us to see: the world that the consensus of opinion, based on a limited use of the senses, would affirm as real. A tree is a tree, an inkblot is an inkblot, the sky is blue, and so on. Twofold vision is the still-limited act of imagination; a cloud formation looks like two lions fighting, or an elephant pushing a Mack truck; an inkblot "might be" two dancers, or a bird in flight, or a monk kneeling in prayer. In threefold vision, we do not see the mean thing-in-itself as in a single vision, nor the thing as it might be if it were a little, or even a lot different, as in twofold vision, but we see the thing as symbol. Recall the heavenly chorus at the conclusion of *Faust:*

> All things transitory
> But as symbols are sent;
> Earth's insufficiency
> *Here* grows to event.

The symbol presents a reality transcended. It is the medium through which a superior vision of reality is sought; it amplifies the poor real world by an act of imagination. The symbol, the play, the dream: these are the manifestations of threefold vision.

Fourfold vision is still a step beyond. It is the vision of the mystic, the seer, the prophet; it is vision suffused with the most intense feeling: horror, awe, ecstasy, desolation. A passage from Blake himself illustrates it well:

> I assert for myself that I do not behold the outward creation, and that to me it is hindrance and not Action . . . "What," it will be Questioned, "When the Sun rises, do you not see a round disk of fire somewhat like a Guinea?" Oh, no, no, I see an Innumerable Company of the Heavenly host crying, "Holy, holy, holy is the Lord God Almighty." I question not my corporeal or Vegetarian Eye any more than I would Question a Window concerning a Sight. I look through it and not with it.

I will leave the finding regarding this aspect of perception by quoting part of a poem by William Butler Yeats that I think apposite. To the finding and the poem we shall return later.

> Some few remembered still when I was young
> A peasant girl commended by a song,
> Who'd lived somewhere upon that rocky place,
> And praised the colour of her face,
> And had the greater joy in praising her,
> Remembering that, if walked she there
> Farmers jostled at the fair
> So great a glory did the song confer.
>
> And certain men, being maddened by those rhymes,
> Or else by toasting her a score of times,
> Rose from the table and declared it right
> To test their fancy by their sight;
> But they mistook the brightness of the moon
> For the prosaic light of day—
> Music had driven their wits astray—
> And one was drowned in the great bog of Cloone.
>
> Strange, but the man who made the song was blind;
> Yet, now I have considered it, I find
> That nothing strange; the tragedy began
> With Homer that was a blind man,
> And Helen has all living hearts betrayed.
> O may the moon and sunlight seem
> One inextricable beam,
> For if I triumph I must make men mad.[1]

In this poem, illusion becomes part of the theme. Intuitive perception can lead one far astray if it goes unchecked. When light plays, it may play tricks. Yeats asks: Must the poet control the light to produce his effects? Will he indeed "drive men mad" if he can make fact and fancy seem one? These are important questions to consider if we are to arrive at an understanding of creative vision, "the eye more phantastical."

[1] Reprinted with permission of the Macmillan Company from W. B. Yeats, "The Tower," *Collected Poems.* Copyright 1928 by The Macmillan Company, renewed 1956 by Georgie Yeats.

III. Complexity versus simplicity

One of our main findings, probably the one most solidly supported by diverse kinds of evidence, has to do with the relationship of complexity to simplicity, and of order to disorder. We have observed consistently that individuals identified as more highly creative seem to be able to discern and to prefer more complexity in whatever it is that they attend to. They prefer displays that are not readily ordered, or that present perplexing contradictions which cannot immediately be resolved. On the Rorschach Inkblot Test, for example, creative individuals show a marked tendency to strive for a single synthesizing image in the inkblot which brings together many elements. This tendency shows itself in other tests as well. One such test is our "Symbol Equivalence" test. We present a stimulus image, such as leaves being blown along in the wind. Then we ask the respondent to create other images somehow equivalent to the stimulus. For example, leaves in the wind could be "clothes in a Bendix dryer, being tossed up and down, seen through the window," or "a civilian population fleeing before armed aggression," (i.e., scattered like untreed leaves before the winds of war). The responses of creative individuals to this test are marked by a finely differentiated complexity of symbolic equivalence.

Another test that we developed, not intended to be a measurement of this factor, but relevant to it, is called the Barron-Welsh Art Scale. This consisted originally of 400 line drawings in black ink on 3 in. × 5 in. white cards. We asked some 80 painters throughout the United States to take this test. We asked them to say which ones they liked and which ones they disliked. We compared their likes and dislikes with those of people in general and then we picked out those figures which showed a big percentage difference of like and dislike between painters and others. Those were cast into a scale to yield a score representing one's degree of resemblance to painters in such preferences. Painters prefer figures that are more challenging, in the sense that they are more complex then the other figures, and less obviously balanced. The kinds of figures disliked by painters are generally static rather than dynamic, and constructed by a geometric principle easily deduced at a glance. They are generally cleaner. The other figures are frequently described as messy, or even chaotic in some cases. Our finding has been that creative individuals, whether artists, scientists, architects, or writers prefer the kinds of figures that the painters in the original standardization group preferred.

I have interpreted these and related findings elsewhere (in my book, *Creativity and Psychological Health* [2]) as follows:

"We are dealing with two types of perceptual preferences, one of them being a choice of what is stable, regular, balanced, predictable, clear-cut, traditional, and following some general abstract principle; the

[2] From *Creativity and Psychological Health* by Frank Barron. Copyright © 1963, by Litton Educational Publishing, Inc., by permission of Van Nostrand Reinhold Company.

other a choice of what is unstable, asymmetrical, unbalanced, whimsical, rebellious against tradition, and at times seemingly irrational, disordered, and chaotic.

"We suggest that the types of perceptual preferences we have observed are related basically to a *choice of what to attend to* in the complex of phenomena which make up the world we experience; for the world *is* both stable and unstable, predictable and unpredictable, ordered and chaotic. To see it predominantly as one or the other is a sort of *perceptual decision;* one may attend to its ordered aspect, to regular sequences of events, to a stable center of the universe (the sun, the church, the state, the home, the parent, God, eternity, etc.), or one may instead attend primarily to the eccentric, the relative, and the arbitrary aspect of the world (the briefness of the individual life, the blind uncaringness of matter, the sometime hypocrisy of authority, accidents of circumstance, the presence of evil, tragic fate, the impossibility of freedom for the only organism capable of conceiving freedom, and so on).

"Either of these alternative perceptual decisions may be associated with a high degree of personal effectiveness. It is as though there is an effective and an ineffective aspect of each alternative. Our thinking about these various aspects is as yet based only upon clinical impressions of our subjects, but it is perhaps worth recording while we go on with the business of gathering more objective evidence.

"At its best, the decision in favor of order makes for personal stability and balance, a sort of easy-going optimism combined with religious faith, a friendliness towards tradition, custom, and ceremony, and respect for authority without subservience to it. This sort of decision will be made by persons who from an early age had good reason to trust the stability and equilibrium of the world and who derived an inner sense of comfort and balance from their perception of an outer certainty.

"At its worst, the decision in favor of order makes for categorical rejection of all that threatens disorder, a fear of anything which might bring disequilibrium. Optimism becomes a matter of policy, religion a prescription and a ritual. Such a decision is associated with stereotyped thinking, rigid and compulsive morality, and hatred of instinctual aggressive and erotic forces which might upset the precariously maintained balance. Equilibrium depends essentially upon exclusion, a kind of perceptual distortion which consists in refusing to see parts of reality which cannot be assimilated to some preconceived system.

"The decision in favor of complexity, at its best, makes for originality and creativeness, a greater tolerance for unusual ideas and formulations. The sometimes disordered and unstable world has its counterpart in the person's inner discord, but the crucial ameliorative factor is a constant effort to integrate the inner and outer complexity in a higher-order synthesis. The goal is to achieve the psychological analogue of mathematical elegance: to allow into the perceptual system the greatest possible richness of experience, while yet finding in this complexity some overall pattern. Such a person is not immobilized by anxiety in the face of great uncertainty, but is at once perturbed and challenged. For such an individual, optimism is impossible, but pessimism is lifted from the personal to the tragic level, resulting not in apathy but in participation in the business of life.

"At its worst, such a perceptual attitude leads to grossly disorganized behavior, to a surrender to chaos. It results in nihilism, despair, and disintegration. The personal life itself becomes simply an acting out of the meaninglessness of the universe, a bitter joke directed against its own maker. The individual is overwhelmed by the apparent insolubility of the problem, and finds the disorder of life disgusting and hateful. His essential world view is thus depreciative and hostile.

"We have not hesitated to refer here to perceptual *decision,* to an act of choice on the part of the individual. That is to say, we conceive this as a matter not simply of capacity, but of preference. Such a choice does of course involve perceptual capacity, but beyond capacity it is a matter of orientation towards experience; in a sense, perceptual attitude."

I have given here a somewhat sketchy overview of some of our best established results. Those who are interested in a much fuller picture and in the psychometric details may find them in my forthcoming (fall 1967) book, *Creativity and Personal Freedom,* to be published by D. Van Nostrand Co., and in *Creativity: Its Diversity and Development,* to be published in the spring of 1968 by Holt, Rinehart and Winston. These results I have elected to emphasize because of their importance to the problem of ego development in persons whose orientation to its experience is a creative one. Let me turn now to my interpretation of what I have earlier referred to as "the experiential fundaments of the ego."

These fundaments are given, I believe, in our own physical and psychical structure and in the furniture and the motion picture of the firmament, which itself has generated both the viewer and the viewed, the eye that looks and the interior and exterior realities that are reflected and that are changed in the perceiving. Though the mind may balk at the idea, cosmological reconstruction of the history of the physical universe tells us that at some point the universe itself generated the structure with which it could view itself. In a sense, it opened an eye upon itself, the prototype of the reflective act.

The rudiments of consciousness proceed from the function of the eye itself in discrimination of outside and inside, opening and shutting, letting in light or excluding it. Whether a thing moves or does not move is of primitive importance, and in lower forms this is expressed simply as reaction to the presence or absence of light.

The human infant, upon opening his eyes, in those first days of establishing place and person, will fixate upon the eyes of the mother, there to find assurance of stability and "looking after" in the face of the unfamiliar. Not to be able to establish an outside is the condition of selflessness, to be taken in both its negative and positive possibilities. "The idiot greens the meadow with his eyes" is a poetic statement, by Allen Tate, of the failure in this fundamental discrimination, although it suggests also a potentiality in this lack of ability to discriminate outer from inner.

The sensory nonvisual world comes to help, of course. There is wet and dry, and hot and cold, and up and down, and pressure ("it hurts") and nonpressure. Even going and staying are not entirely visual. "There goes the BM," or "here it comes," or, much later, "here I come," or "here I go" are rudimentary kinesthetic discriminations of self and the world. They may later have to have words to go with them; and words, through the importance they take on because of their efficiency in getting us life-sustaining information, are a weighty part of our equipment. Yet the primitive kinesthetically experienced goings and comings may not only precede the verbal developmentally but, with the purely visual, may come to occupy permanently the interstices of the conceptual framework of mind. They remain there, effective though unnoticed and largely unverbalizable. To restore them to attention is surely one of the functions of the arts of sculpture, architecture, and painting.

The baby, then, notices mostly whether things are here or there, moving or being still, outside or inside, wet or dry, warm or cold, pleasing or displeasing, serving or disserving, producible by action on the part of the self or simply autonomous or the result of chance.

Perhaps the chief internal structures in these rudimentary analogues of the psychic basis of reflection, repression, and production are the orifices of the body and its integument—boundaries and portals. The production of self-initiated effects, especially in their developing reciprocal relationship with autonomous external forces, and especially also as they involve objective mastery and an internal sense or feeling of competence, serve to define the self in terms of process and structure *as reflected*. There is more to this than simple competence, however; there is fitness, or a sort of symbolic aptness or equivalence, between the self-initiated act and the *delighting* effect, which in turn serves as a fundament of ego and a motive towards creation of effects at a much later stage of development.

After these early discriminations come others which emphasize more the content and process of the firmament. Fundamental to process are rhythms: periodicities such as the gross ones of night and day and the turning of the seasons, or the more internally signaled ones of the beating of the heart or the taking in and letting out of breath. These periodicities are reinforced by the social practices that arrange themselves around physical rhythms: habitual times for taking meals, for example, or, at a more complex and symbolic level, the observation of holidays with their freight of religious meaning.

Sun and moon, stars, the wind, rocks, flowers, water, fire—these give us the colored and moving, or uncolored and stationary world. In the childhood of philosophy, earth and fire and air and water were thought the stuff of life, and they are the universal early experiences of children. The moon is said to be the eye of night, and the sun the warming yet sometimes fierce eye of day. Not to look at the sun directly is one of the earliest adaptations, and indeed may be the prototype of the act of repression.

The seasons in their turning go sometimes in simple doubles, sometimes in double doubles; like hot and cold, we have summer and winter, and like our bodily wets and drys we have the rains and the dry spells. The moon, unlike the sun, changes shape and appears at what may seem whimsy of position and time—the moon is fickle—the moon also is definer of month, and of menses, and of mind (mens, mensis), and of mensuration. The eggs of females go by the moon, and so do the tides, and some think even that madness or lunacy does. The moon gives us numbers to go by: 28, 14, multiples of 2 and 4 and 7. Through the sun and the moon and the seasons we learn of the wheel—gyres—the turning around and around of the great orbs. Gyration is the most forcible of the periodicities that the universe shows us in showing its face to us.

Facedness itself is one of the fundamentals of structure out of which many processes grow. We face forward in time, and we look ahead in space. What we may yet experience lies ahead of us. How we see ourselves in a mirror tells us of ourselves. Other faces too can mirror us. We may use our face to mask ourselves as well as to express or assert—and unused at all it seems to *be* ourselves.

Very early in life we learn of growth. There are bigger ones of the same shape, and we may even see photos that show they were once small. We can see ourselves growing. Near this realization comes also the realization of death—"What would happen if I became bigger and bigger and bigger?" The rule is that whatever grows must die, and that there is a limit to growth. Cancer is consequent upon the failure of tissue to enforce the normal inherent restraint upon growth.

The central fact of fate for everyone is death, and the ego marshals all its resources to accommodate itself to this fact. Culture is replete with the most elegant of symbolic constructions aimed at denying the finality of death. Christianity and Buddhism, while they are at opposite poles in their interpretation of the sources and governance of the cosmos, are identical in the mission assigned their archetypal personage: both Christ and the Buddha are to conquer death. The Judaic-Christian monotheistic account of the Creation, the Fall, and the Redemption is a story of God the Father's enmity towards man, God the Son's love and pity for him, and God the Holy Spirit's gift of grace; the Father establishes the law from of old, and punishes; the Son dies for all, and so redeems; the Holy Spirit comes with a saving gift, something free, and so blesses. A well-rounded tale, whether "true" or not. Some of the greatest minds of Western culture have been at pains to elaborate the metaphysics and theology of this account of the universe and man's fate, and in many cases the story has used elements of pre-Christian myths from Greece and the Middle East to establish the character of the personages of the drama. The study of myth and symbol is one of the most fascinating branches of the psychology of the ego, and it tells us over and over again that the questions of children about their origins and their fate are original religion and poetry.

The end of innocence and the beginning of experience (to use again the terms of William Blake) has as point of passage the recognition that one is fated. Death is not all of fate, of course; being a woman or a man, with all that the differentiation of sexual function entails, is one of the most powerful aspects of fate, and behind it lies the fact of permanent division of the two generative principles. Plato in "The Symposium" has given us a most beautiful statement of various human thoughts on the subject of love, and one of the most striking of these is the theory he puts into the mouth of Anaximander: that male and female were once one but in time beyond memory were divided into two parts that continually seek one another. Herman Melville expressed this thought in a poem, which emphasizes that this aspect of fate is a bitter one:

> What cosmic jest or anarch blunder
> The human integral clove asunder
> And shied the fractions through life's gate.
> And such the dicing of blind fate
> Few matching halves here meet and mate.

Changes are rung on this theme in all the love stories and the love lyrics of the world, and a nostalgia for the condition of unseparatedness must be counted among the most primitive of feelings, a response to the counterpart of death in human fate.

There are of course many common but less universal aspects of individual fate that enter into consciousness at nearly the same time in the child's development (differences from others in race, strength, health, beauty, status, and so on). The general point is that the recognition of the fact that fate has things in store for one, and that the individual has no choice in the matter, is significant in ego formation; this marks the end of innocence and the beginning of the development of "persona."

I believe that it is at this point that a decisive bifurcation may occur, one psychic path leading to a way of being that remains open to experience and the other leading to a personal adjustment that is "normal" but that is achieved at the cost of repression of the spontaneity and wonder of childhood. The person who is open to experience does not separate himself from the process of life by repression but rather gives himself over to the life processes within him. Because the childhood experiences are thus retained in consciousness and integrated into the personality, "regression in the service of the ego" is in fact not necessary; rather, a progression has occurred that keeps the best of innocence while moving ahead to the command and control that experience brings. I have elsewhere described creative architects whom we studied in our researches as "practical transcendentalists," and this phrase I think captures something of what I have been trying here to elucidate in terms of ego development. One might also say that in creativity we have a love-marriage of innocence and experience, thus implying that they need not be separated. Or, to put it another way, the creative individual retains his innocence in the face of fate. I am reminded of a passage from the great Indian poet Rabindranath Tagore, who wrote of children: "They build their houses with sand, and they play with empty shells. With withered leaves they weave their boats and smilingly float them on the vast deep. Children have their play on the seashore of worlds. They know not how to swim, they know not how to cast nets. Pearl-fishers dive for pearls, merchants sail in their ships, while children gather pebbles and scatter them again. They seek not for hidden treasures, they know not how to cast nets."

In the creative adult, the child remains fully alive.

15 | Educating for creativity: A modern myth?

DONALD W. MacKINNON
University of California, Berkeley

Reprinted with the permission of the author and the publisher from the article of the same title, in P. Heist (Ed.), Education for Creativity. *Berkeley: Center for Research and Development in Higher Education, 1967, Pp. 1–20.*

Developing creativity at the university level is described by Donald W. MacKinnon as a dual problem: (1) selecting the creative—not just intelligent—student, and (2) providing experiences for increasing creative potential. Regarding the former, MacKinnon states that it simply is not known if creative students are systematically denied admission to IQ- and GPA-oriented colleges, undergraduate and graduate; his Berkeley Institute of Personality Assessment and Research (IPAR) studies with architects, mathematicians, and research scientists showed little or no relationship of either IQ or GPA to later creative eminence, a fact which suggests a long second look at college admission requirements. Indeed, MacKinnon noted that one characteristic of creative individuals is a lack of strong motivation in conformity-requiring situations—for instance, the classroom. In response to the problem of developing creativity, then, MacKinnon recommends independent study and research to allow the creative student to bloom and to provide a creativity-stimulating environment for the grade getter. Further extrapolating from his IPAR research, MacKinnon proposes the use of creative teachers as models to encourage more abstract and theoretical thinking. Finally, the author observes that a liberal education, including the arts, humanities, social sciences, and history, is much more likely to increase self-awareness, esthetic sensitivity, and imagination than strictly professional training.

The topic to which I was asked to address myself was originally cast as a simple declarative statement: "Educating for Creativity: A Modern Myth."

It was I who added the question mark, recasting it in the form of an inquiry. I doubt very much whether we are doing all that we can by way of fostering the creative potential of our students. However, I also question whether we have any firm evidence that other forms of education being proposed in such great numbers today would succeed any better than our present practices, simply because they have not been tried and tested in any systematic study of their effectiveness.

The field of education is strikingly like that of psychotherapy, not only in that both take as their goal the improvement of the objects of their efforts—students in one case, patients in the other—but that in the past both have not been especially concerned to test the effectiveness of their theories or their practices. The reasons for such strange neglect have been mainly the same in both fields.

Educators and therapists are alike in their concern for others. All too often, they feel that this concern makes whatever they do or propose to do for their charges right. Their missionary zeal for their theories and their practices makes them impervious to the demands for proof of their efficacy. One or two striking positive observations far outweigh in their thinking a host of negative instances, many of which are probably not even observed by them. Thus the need for rigorous checking of their claims is often not even recognized. When, several years ago, a colleague of mine sent to Freud reprints of papers which reported controlled laboratory investigations of the Freudian concept of repression, Freud responded: "I have examined your experimental studies for the verification of the psychoanalytic assertions with interest. I cannot put much value on these confirmations because the wealth of reliable observations on which these assertions rest make them independent of experimental verification" (MacKinnon and Dukes, 1962, p. 703). The attitude of educational reformers toward the innovations which they have proposed or instituted has, in general, not been much different.

The second reason why both educators and psychotherapists have traditionally been disinclined to test the adequacy of their theories and their practices has been the enormous difficulties that any valid test would impose upon the investigator. Such studies obviously must deal with a great complex of variables over extended periods of time. It is a brave, or foolhardy, researcher who undertakes such difficult studies when other simpler experiments are at hand of shorter duration with the possibility of neater research design and certain to yield unequivocal findings. And so, over the years we have repeatedly witnessed new theories and practices, both of education and of psychotherapy, proposed with exorbitant claims made for their effectiveness, which subsequently seem never to be quite fulfilled although never submitted to adequate systematic check. And in the course of time they are shoved aside for the new theories and practices which come upon the scene only to experience, sooner or later, the same fate.

Education for creativity at the college level

One reason for questioning whether colleges are educating for creativity is that colleges, until the last few years, have not concerned themselves with creativity. In this they were merely reflecting the values and interests of society at large. Even within psychology, creativity was a long neglected topic. The present concern with creativity—which at times appears to have become a fad—was stimulated by J. P. Guilford's presidential address to the American Psychological Association in 1950 entitled "Creativity." But it was not until the late 1950s and the early 1960s that the implications for education of the findings of research on creativity began to appear in print, and almost without exception the conclusions seemed to be that those with creative potential were forgotten if not discriminated against at all levels of American education.

All of the studies from which such conclusions so critical of the American educational system were drawn leave something to be desired. Both Torrance's (1959) study of elementary school children and Getzel's and Jackson's (1962) investigation of students in the sixth year through high school took as a measure of their subjects' creativeness their performance on so-called tests of creativity, a highly questionable procedure since the relation of test performance to demonstrated creative behavior was not known. My own studies and those of my colleagues in the Institute of Personality Assessment and Research with mature, practicing members of several professions—research scientists in industry, mathematicians, architects, and writers—had the advantage of a much more acceptable criterion of creativity. We used the judgment of their peers, who evaluated the demonstrated creativeness with which our subjects practiced their professions.

Our studies, however, suffered from the fact that whatever conclusions we drew about the earlier educational experiences of our subjects were drawn from their retrospective descriptions of their experiences at home, in school, and in college, and of the forces, persons, and situations which, as they saw it, nurtured their creativeness. We must remind ourselves that these self-reports are subject to the misperceptions and self-deceptions of all self-reports. Even assuming that the testimony of these creative persons is essentially accurate, this is no assurance that the conditions in the home, school, and society, the qualities of interpersonal relations between instructor and student, and the aspects of the teaching-learning process which would appear to have contributed to creative development a generation ago would facilitate rather than inhibit creativity if these same factors were created in today's quite different world and far different educational climate. It just may be that if there is any myth about the role of colleges and universities in nurturing creative potential, the modern myth may be that we are *not* educating for creativity. If that should turn out to be the case, I should have to take my share of responsibility for having fostered it.

The problems of selecting for creative potential

If colleges are, indeed, to educate effectively for creativity, two basic conditions must be met: (1) They must admit as students those who have creative potential, and (2) they must provide such students with experiences which will serve to develop whatever creative potential they possess.

What are the facts, first with regard to admissions, and second, with regard to the educational experiences offered undergraduate and graduate students?

Are colleges and universities indeed refusing admission to large numbers of students who are especially creative or likely to become creative if they are privileged to have a college education? The truth is that we do not know nor do we have reliable data from which firm conclusions can be drawn. We do have the continuing concern that admissions practices may be working an injustice in individual cases and a mounting fear that the number of cases in which injustice is done may well be on the increase. If we do not have the facts about the number of students with creative potential who are not admitted to college, we, nevertheless, have an increasing body of research data that suggests that highly creative youths are not always those whose academic records are such as to insure their admission to college. It is, then, not surprising that college admissions officers are questioning their policies as never before.

It is fair to say that the general practice has been to select and admit students on the basis of their academic record, performance on aptitude and achievement tests, good citizenship, and leadership potential, with certain notable exceptions, of course. In some large state university and college systems, the only criterion for admission has been graduation from high school or graduation with some minimum grade point average or a specified level of performance on a scholastic aptitude test. Private institutions, especially the smaller ones, have paid more attention to individual cases, with the possibility of greater flexibility in applying the rules. Sons and daughters of important alumni and outstanding high school athletes who do not meet the usual standards have been welcomed in the past by many colleges and, in many instances, recruited.

If exceptions are to be made in admissions practices, however, some would ask: Wouldn't it be better to make them for students who, although their academic records and measured aptitudes and achievements leave something to be desired, have already manifested creative behavior or shown signs of creative potential? But, the skeptic might ask: *How* can one justify the admission of a student who has shown some creative promise if he cannot or will not measure up to the academic requirements of the college which admits him, at the expense of some other student whose record leaves nothing to be desired in terms of academic achievement? Or he might ask: *What,* if any, are the reliable signs of creative potential in a student applying for admission to college? *What* guarantee is there that such creative potential, provided it can be identified, will ever be realized? And finally the skeptic might well be led to question whether colleges, considering their present shockingly high rates of attrition, can afford to admit students who, regardless of their creative potential or demonstrated creativity, have shown neither an interest in nor motivation for conventional academic achievement?

These are questions of policy which every college and university must answer for itself. The basic question is, of course, for what purpose does the college wish to select a student? In line with this conference, I shall assume the answer to be that many students are selected to encourage creativity and to develop creative potential.

Predictors of creativity

There is substantial evidence garnered from many studies that the best predictors of academic achievement in college are high school grades and scores on tests of scholastic aptitude. If, on the other hand, one wishes to predict creative achievement in college in both artistic and scientific fields of endeavor, the best predictor is creative achievement—either artistic or scientific—during the high school years or even earlier. Our own studies of highly creative persons in a variety of fields have yielded congruent findings: As students they were, in general, not distinguished for the grades which they received, and in none of the samples did the high school grade point average of the subjects show any significant correlation with their subsequently achieved and recognized creativeness. Further, the productive achievement of our highly creative subjects was not something first manifested in college or after college; rather earlier accomplishments prepared for and in a sense predicted it.

If high school grades and scholastic aptitude scores are not good predictors of nonacademic creative accomplishment during the undergraduate years, are they any better as predictors of creative achievement after college? By now there is plenty of evidence that college grades are generally poor predictors of achievement or success in later life (Price, Taylor, and Richards, 1964; Taylor, Smith, and Ghiselin, 1963; Richards, Taylor, and Price, 1962) or are at best only inefficient predictors (Taylor, 1963). In our own investigations, college grades, in general, have not been predictive of later manifest creativeness. Indeed, in a group of research scientists, college grade point average correlated low and negatively ($-.19$) with their later rated creativity as scientists. Only in the case of architects did college grades predict significantly ($+.27$) their subsequently rated creativeness, probably because so much of their graded work in college—the solution of design problems and the like—is exactly what they do as architects. But, even in this sample, the most creative architects were not generally A students. They averaged about B. They were not poor students or lazy. Rather, they were extraordinarily independent as students, turning in an A performance in work and courses that caught their interest, but doing little or no work at all in courses which failed to stir their imagination. This suggests that if we really wish to select for creative potential we should pay more attention to patterns of low and high grades or grade records that improve as the student advances in his major field, as well as nonacademic creative achievements during the undergraduate years. Also, we should give somewhat less credence to mere grade point average when selecting students for advanced graduate work.

However, with even more students applying for admission to graduate schools, increasing emphasis is being placed on undergraduate grade point average and scholastic aptitude in selecting students. This is true despite the considerable evidence that undergraduate grades are generally poor predictors of success in life and the lack of evidence as to just what, if anything, the scholastic aptitude test scores predict. The most widely used tests of scholastic aptitude for graduate work are those of the Graduate Record Examination. But a reviewer of these tests in the *Sixth Mental Measurement Yearbook* of 1965 writes: "The paucity of validity information is especially unfortunate. In the present atmosphere, critics of testing are bound to ask whether an aptitude test is appropriate or necessary for applicants who have recorded 16 years or so of school achievement and taken a number of similar tests in the process. Other more sympathetic critics may well wonder at the lack of continuing exploration and appraisal of a variety of factors in graduate performance, some of which they might suspect are more accessible and more important than scholastic aptitude for differentiating applicants" (French, 1965, rev. 461).

Reviewing findings similar to those I have presented, John Holland concludes:

> . . . [such data] imply a need to examine grading practices, since a college education should be largely a preparation for life, both in the community and in a vocation. Under current grading practices a college education is mainly preparation for more education in graduate school.
> . . . If a sponsor is interested only in finding students who will do well in the classroom in college, then high school grades and tests of academic potential are the best techniques available. On the other hand, if the sponsor wishes to find college students who will do outstanding things outside the classroom and in later life, then he should continue to make an effort to secure a better record of the student's competencies and achievement in high school.
> . . . national surveys concerned with the conservation of talent, since they use tests of academic potential almost exclusively, probably present a grossly inaccurate picture of the loss of talent for "real life"— that is, non-classroom—accomplishment (Holland, 1965, pp. 22–23).

In seeking to correct the imbalance in past and still current admissions practices, it is important that we not simply substitute a new imbalance for the old. Holland cautions, ". . . we should not make the same mistake that purveyors of aptitude and intelligence have made in the past; that is, to rely on only one kind of measure and to exclude others" (Holland, 1965, p. 21). We should not assume that nonintellective factors solely determine creative performance.

In earlier institute studies of the relation of intelligence to creativity, we found essentially no relationship between these variables. Taking scores on the Terman Concept Mastery Test as measures of intelligence, the correlation of intelligence with creativity in a sample of architects was $-.08$ and $-.07$ in a sample of research scientists. In view of this, I suggested that we may have overestimated in our educational system the role of intelligence in creative achievement (MacKinnon, 1962 b, p. 493). However, I pointed out that no feeble-minded subjects had shown up in any of our creative groups.

Over the whole range of intelligence and creativity there is undoubtedly a positive relationship between the two variables. But, of course, no college population represents the whole range of intelligence, and, within that limited range, how crucial are differences in intelligence for differences in creativity? My conclusion was that, above a certain minimum level required for mastery of a field, being more intelligent does not guarantee a corresponding increase in creativeness. It simply is not true that the more intelligent person is necessarily the more creative one. We would be foolish to select students for admission to college who have the lowest scores on intelligence tests, but, on the other hand, we clearly are deluding ourselves when we favor one student over another solely on the grounds that he scores some 10 to 20 points higher on some measure of intelligence.

Whereas, in 1962 I was cautioning against "setting the cutting point for selection on the intellective dimension too high," today I would caution against setting it too low, for in some quarters there has been a misunderstanding of my earlier writing. The range of Terman Concept Mastery Test scores for creative architects was, to be sure, a low of 39 to a high of 179, and in another place I reported that in a study of independent inventors the inventor who held more patents than anyone else in the group and, indeed, held more patents than any of our creative research scientists working in industry, earned a score of 6 (MacKinnon, 1962a)! Although I hastened to point out that these were arbitrary or raw scores on the test and not IQ's, that fact, I am afraid, sometimes has been ignored.

One difficulty with Terman Concept Mastery scores has been the impossibility of converting them to IQ's. To fill this gap in our knowledge we have returned subsequently to our architects, mathematicians, and research scientists and administered to as many as were willing the Wechsler Adult

Intelligence Scale (WAIS), the most thoroughly standardized test of adult intelligence which yields three measures of the IQ: a verbal IQ, a performance IQ, and an overall or full-scale IQ. This study is still in progress, but the results to date confirm the earlier finding in our samples of no relationship between intelligence and manifest creativity. I shall report here only on the full-scale IQ measures.

The samples of architects and research scientists were divided into three subsamples, ranging from most creative to least creative. Each sample of mathematicians, one male and one female, was divided into two groups, a creative group and a control group. The most striking finding is the lack of any significant difference in IQ among the subsamples characterized by different levels of creativeness. The mean IQ's for the three groups of architects are 132, 131, and 130; for the research scientists, 132, 132, and 132; for the male mathematicians, 135 and 133; and for the female mathematicians, 129 and 133. The ranges of IQ's are similarly comparable from subsample to subsample: for architects, 120–145, 117–142, and 119–143; for research scientists, 120–141, 121–142, and 114–142; for male mathematicians, 118–152 and 126–138; and for female mathematicians, 118–140 and 118–145.

The findings are clear: careers in demanding fields, such as architecture, mathematics, and scientific research, would seem to require an IQ level approaching 120. Although the range of IQ for 140 persons in these professions is from 114 to 152, only one has an IQ above 145 and only two have IQ's below 118. In other words, 98 percent have IQ's in the range of 118 to 140. The range of IQ's and the mean level of IQ are not significantly different for subgroups whose levels of creative performance vary markedly. Further evidence that, above a certain minimum level, having a higher IQ does not guarantee a corresponding increase in creativeness is found again in the sample of architects. In this group, WAIS IQ's correlate with creativity + .19 (not quite significant at the 10 percent level of confidence).

While many vocations may require less intelligence than architecture, mathematics, and scientific research, I believe our findings should make us think twice before concluding that by markedly lowering the level of intelligence required for college admission we shall be admitting large numbers of students with outstanding creative potential. We can, I believe, maximize the probability of admitting students with creative potential to college and to graduate training, but not if we merely replace intellective requirements by nonintellective demands. We must supplement tests of intellective functioning and aptitude with independent measures of extracurricular achievement and originality.

However, I am not proposing that we administer to our applicants a battery of so-called tests of creativity. In recent years, Guilford (1959) has worked on the structure of intellect and identification, by factor analysis, of several dimensions of creative thinking. The work on the latter dimensions, including adaptive flexibility, originality, and sensitivity to problems, has led to a widespread hope and expectation that his tests of creative ability would provide us with reliable means for identifying creative persons. So far, however, this hope has not been realized.

In an intensive study of research scientists in the U.S. Air Force (Taylor, Smith, Ghiselin, and Ellison, 1961), Guilford's tests of creativity failed to predict the criterion. In our own studies, these same tests likewise have shown essentially a zero correlation with the criterion. In view of such negative findings, the use of Guilford's battery of tests of creativity potential would be questionable, to say the least.

It is not that tests of this sort fail to tap the kind of psychological processes involved in creative thought, requiring, as they do, that the subject think of unusual uses for common objects or the consequences of unusual events. It is rather that they fail to reveal the extent to which a person faced with a real life problem is likely to come up with solutions that are novel and adaptive and which he will be motivated to apply in all of their ramifications. Much more promising as self-report predictors of future creative performance are autobiographical questions concerning past and present manifest activities, competencies, and achievements, as are found, for example, in the American College Testing Program.

Essential experiences for creative development

The second condition colleges must meet if they are indeed to educate for creativity is that they must provide their students experiences that develop whatever creative potential they possess. The difficulties in discussing this topic are several. Although our findings concerning the characteristics of highly creative persons seem to be reasonably well established now, their implications for the nurturing of creative talent are far from clear. Even if we think we know what kinds of experiences a college should provide, there is no guarantee that providing such experiences will have the same consequences and effects for all students. The wide range of individual differences surely must mean that there is no single method for the nurturing of creativity; ideally the experiences which we provide would be tailor-made, if not for individual students, at least for different types of students. We should remember that the same fire that melts the butter hardens the egg.

Just as grades and the academic record have been emphasized in determining admission to college, all too often a continuing stress in college on academic achievement is the prerequisite for admission to special programs, honors seminars, independent study, and research projects. At least an overall B average is the usual requirement for such educational experiences. There is reason to believe, however, that independent students frequently are denied those very educational experiences from which they would profit most because as independent students they are not always among the grade getters. College programs for the talented in the past have been invariably programs for the *academically* talented.

Our research has shown that creative persons are independent and that this independence, already manifest in high school, tends to increase in college and thereafter. Since it is a fundamental characteristic of creative persons that they are not strongly motivated to achieve in situations which demand conforming behavior, they would seem to be the ideal candidates for independent study and research. I have never been successful in petitioning for exceptions to be made for just such students. I would not want to suggest that the academic achievers with high grade point average be excluded from opportunities for independent work, for clearly they need this, too, and perhaps especially so since their independence of spirit needs particularly to be fostered.

The independence of our creative subjects appears to have been fostered by parents who, very early, showed an extraordinary respect for the child and confidence in his ability to do what was appropriate. The expectation of the parent that the child would act independently but reasonably and responsibly appears to have contributed much to the latter's sense of personal autonomy which was to develop later to such a marked degree.

Let it be noted, however, that these parents did not leave the life space of the child unstructured. Within the family there existed clear standards of conduct and ideas as to what was right and wrong, but at the same time there was an expectation, if not requirement, of active exploration by the child and the internalization of a framework of personal conduct. Discipline was almost always consistent and predictable. In most cases there were rules, family standards, and parental injunctions which were known explicitly by the children and seldom infringed. Thus there appear to have been both structure and freedom which carried with it expectations of reasonable and responsible action.

This parental policy, I submit, is a far different thing from the kind of permissiveness which is so often granted by parents and also demanded by children today. Extreme permissiveness means the absence of standards and a lack of structure of the child's life space with the consequence that he does not know who he is, where he stands, or what he can or should do. Small wonder then that alienation and anxiety are so often his fate.

I am inclined to believe that the college or the university that can create an atmosphere similar to that of the homes of those who were to become so highly creative would, by that alone, contribute importantly to nurturing the creative potential of its students. And this, I would note, is different from the kind of unstructured campus which some seek today, a campus on which no rules regulate the manner, time, and place for the activities appropriate to college life.

There is another aspect of the early life space of our creative subjects that is especially worthy of notice. In addition to the mother and father, the larger familial sphere also provided a plentiful supply of diverse and effective models with whom the child could make important identifications —grandfathers, uncles, aunts, and others who occupied prominent and responsible positions within their community. Whatever the emotional relation between father and son, whether distant, harmonious, or turbulent, the father generally presented a model of effective and resourceful behavior in an exceptionally demanding career. What is perhaps more significant, however, is the high incidence of distinctly autonomous mothers who had active lives and interests and sometimes careers of their own apart from their husbands.

The college might similarly foster the creative potential of its students by offering a plentiful supply of diverse and effective models—teachers who are themselves effectively creative persons.

But, more specifically, what is it that the instructor—models can offer that will nurture the creative potential of their students? For one thing, they can offer a deep appreciation of the theoretical and esthetic ways of thinking, for these, we find, are the two values most highly prized by outstandingly creative persons. A student is on firmer ground in dealing with facts and things than in grappling with theoretical concepts and issues, and many will be tempted to remain in such safe territory. But if their creative potential is to be realized they must be encouraged to think abstractly and to concern themselves with concepts and issues construed in abstract and symbolic terms. In research, and especially in basic research, one must venture into the realm of abstract thinking. Thus, one of the great advantages in participating in research as an undergraduate is that the student is encouraged to develop theoretical interests.

Of course, there is nothing magical about mere participation in research; its consequences for the student depend upon the conditions under which it occurs. If the professor treats the student largely as a laboratory assistant or technician, as someone to do "the dirty work" in handling objects and things, while he reserves the thinking for himself, the gain to the student will be minimal and the student's time might be better spent in more conventional course work.

On the other hand, the professor can greatly encourage the development of the student's theoretical interests if he treats the student as a full collaborator in all phases of the research and most importantly in its conceptualization and planning or, even better, encourages the student to formulate his own problem and to design his own research. A professor of this type, one who places high value on theoretical issues, provides the student with a model with which he can identify, and, thus, gives him confidence to develop his own theoretical interests.

From association with such a professor, more appropriately designated a guide or mentor or a true exemplar, the student experiences something of the delight and joy and fresh insights which come from confidence in thinking abstractly and in exercising one's skills. He is motivated to acquire through study and hard work the theoretical know-how, knowledge, and competencies which, alone, provide grounds for confidence in setting for himself ever more challenging problems in the field of his interest.

Although some have stressed the incompatibility and conflict of theoretical and esthetic interests, it would appear that he who would nurture creativity must foster a rich development of both, for the truly creative person is not satisfied with the solutions to his problems unless they are also esthetically pleasing, unless, to use the mathematician's term, they are elegant. He demands of his work that it be simultaneously true and beautiful. The esthetic viewpoint permeates much of the work of the creative person, and it should find expression in the teaching of all skills, disciplines, and professions if creativity is to be nurtured.

Among the more salient characteristics of the creative person are a breadth of cultural and intellectual interests, an openness to his own feelings and emotions, a sensitive intellect, and an understanding self-awareness.

The implications of these findings for the nurturing of creativity are rather clear, it seems to me, and especially so for vocational training. We should not seek to train our students too narrowly, or only for the practice of a profession, although tradition distinguishes between the liberal arts colleges which do not prepare their students for any particular career and the professional schools which train their students for the practice of a particular vocation. John Arnold might have said that liberal arts colleges seek to produce generalists, professional schools specialists. We find that regardless of whether our creative subjects were educated in liberal arts colleges or trained in professional schools or had the benefits of both kinds of learning they, more than their less creative peers, reveal an awareness both of the inner self and outer world and an inclination to give expression to most aspects of inner experience and character, admitting into consciousness and behavior much which others would repress, integrating reason and passion, and reconciling the rational and irrational.

I believe we would all agree that most professionl training is not designed to foster such liberation of the human spirit as characterizes our creative subjects. And I think we would also agree that just because a course is taught in a liberal arts curriculum does not guarantee it will have a liberating influence on the student. Any course, no matter what its content, can be taught in a rigid and stultifying manner, or it can be designed to encourage awareness of one's impulses and a freeing of one's imagination. I would argue, however, that increased esthetic sensitivity, self-awareness, and imaginativeness are more likely to be engendered by a study of the arts, humanities, and the social and behavioral sciences, by courses in literature, history, poetry and drama, in the psychology of personality, and the sociology of ideas than by professional training. In such areas of human experience the student most easily can be brought to an awareness of the meaning and uses of analogy, simile, and metaphor, or the symbolic equivalents of varied experience, the delights and possibilities in imaginative play, and of the place of human experience in the cosmic scheme.

Considering this, I would suggest that in professional education, the creative potential of students perhaps can be fostered best by broadening their experience in fields far beyond their specialties. Instead of viewing such wanderings as distractions, we would do better to think of them as providing the student with that variety and richness of experience without which the highest levels of creative achievement are unlikely to be reached.

Although especially perceptive and open to experience, the creative person, like everyone else, must also judge and evaluate his experience, but it is clear that his preferred mode is that of perceiving rather than judging. The difficulty with judging is that one may come to prejudge, thus excluding from perception large areas of experience. Since critical judgment is emphasized so much in higher education, we need to emphasize the opposite, if we are to foster creativity. We will do well to discuss with our students, at least occasionally, the most fantastic ideas and possibilities. Discipline and self-control are also necessary. One must learn to exercise them to be truly creative, but it is important that they not be overlearned. Furthermore, there is a time and place for the learning and use of discipline and self-control, but having been learned, they should be used flexibly not rigidly or compulsively.

In our research we have found that creative persons not only are open to experience but are intuitive about it. We can train students to be accurate in their perceptions and logical in their reasoning, and these, too, are characteristics of the creative person. But can we train students to be intuitive, and if so, how? I suggest that we can do so by emphasizing the transfer of training from one subject to another, by searching for common principles, by seeking relations among quite different domains of knowledge, stressing thinking in terms of analogies, similes, and metaphors, seeking symbolic equivalents of experience in the widest possible number of sensory and imaginal modalities, engaging in imaginative play, and by training in retreating from the facts in order to see them in larger perspective and in relation to more aspects of this larger context.

You will note that in the latter part of this presentation I have discussed the implications of our studies for the education of students as though they are rather obvious. These suggestions seem reasonable to me, but I would remind you that they are only questionable hypotheses to be tested. I have not so much described new practices as I have pointed to a few out of many more which I believe should be more extensively employed. They surely have been used by some instructors, at least part of the time, with some students in some colleges—but how widely or how consistently or how effectively nobody knows. For that reason it remains a question in my mind whether educating for creativity is or is not a modern myth.

REFERENCES

French, R. L. Review of the graduate record examinations aptitude test. In O. K. Buros (Ed.), *Sixth Mental Measurement Yearbook*. Highland Park, N. J.: Gryphon Press, 1965. Pp. 728–730.

Getzels, J. W., & Jackson, P. W. *Creativity and intelligence*. New York: Wiley, 1962.

Guilford, J. P. Creativity. *American Psychologist,* 1950, 5, 444–454.

Guilford, J. P. Three faces of intellect. *American Psychologist,* 1959, 14, 469–479.

Holland, J. L. Academic and non-academic accomplishment: Correlated or uncorrelated. *ACT Research Report,* April, 1965, No. 2.

MacKinnon, D. W. Intellect and motive in scientific inventors: Implications for supply. In *The rate and direction of inventive activity: Economic and social factors*. A conference of the universities—National Bureau Committee for Economic Research and the Committee on Economic Growth of the Social Science Research Council. Princeton: Princeton University Press, 1962. Pp. 361–378. (a)

MacKinnon, D. W. The nature and nurture of creative talent. *American Psychologist,* 1962, 17, 484–495. (b)

MacKinnon, D. W., & Dukes, W. F. Repression. In L. Postman (Ed.), *Psychology in the making*. New York: Knopf, 1962. Pp. 662–774.

Price, P. B., Taylor, C. W., Richards, J. M., Jr., & Jacobsen, T. L. Measurement of physician performance. *Journal of Medical Education,* 1964, 39, 203–211.

Richards, J. M., Jr., Taylor, C. W., & Price, P. B. The prediction of medical intern performance. *Journal of Applied Psychology,* 1962, 46, 142–146.

Taylor, C. W., Smith, W. R., Ghiselin, B., & Ellison, R. Explorations in the measurement and prediction of contributions of one sample of scientists. *Report ASD-TR-61-96,* Aeronautical Systems Divisions, Personnel Laboratory. Lackland Air Force Base, Texas: April, 1961.

Taylor, C. W., Smith, W. R., & Ghiselin, B. The creative and other contributions of one sample of research scientists. In C. W. Taylor & F. Barron (Eds.), *Scientific creativity: Its recognition and development*. New York: Wiley, 1963. Pp. 53–76.

Taylor, D. W. Variables related to creativity and productivity among men in two research laboratories. In C. W. Taylor & F. Barron (Eds.), *Scientific creativity: Its recognition and development*. New York: Wiley, 1963. Pp. 228–250.

Torrance, E. P. Highly intelligent and highly creative children in a laboratory school (Explorations in creative thinking in the early school years, No. 6). *Research Memo* BER-59-7. Minneapolis: Bureau of Educational Research, University of Minnesota, 1959.

16 | Nurture of creative talents

E. PAUL TORRANCE
University of Georgia

Reprinted with the permission of the author and the publisher from the article of the same title, Theory Into Practice, *1967, 5, 168–173, 201–202.*

Probably no single individual has contributed as much to creativity—its nature, measurement, and training—as has E. Paul Torrance. In this article, Torrance summarizes some important cultural-historical differences in fostering creative development and then sketches a number of American inhibitors to creative behavior. (The thoughtful reader may wish to compare these "barriers" with those described by Simberg in Chapter 9.) As a prescription for some of these ills, Torrance outlines a series of in-service teacher workshops designed to improve skills which are crucial for nurturing creative talents.

Plato said, "What is honored in a country will be cultivated there." He surely must have included creative talents among those nurtured by honoring them in a culture. The prevailing concept now some twenty-four centuries later, however, is that creativity must be left to chance and that outstanding creative talent will somehow flourish in spite of neglect and abuse. This erroneous idea has dominated thinking even among educators, despite contrary evidence.

No one would argue that heredity does not place limits upon creative development and achievement. Creative abilities are inherited to the extent that a person inherits his sense organs, peripheral nervous system, and brain. How these abilities develop and function, however, is strongly influenced by the way the environment responds to a person's curiosity and creative needs.

Historical evidence is compelling. How can one otherwise account for the great number of creative musicians in the period of a single century in Europe? There were Handel, Mozart, Chopin, Liszt, Verdi, Schubert, Mendelssohn, Debussy, Dvorak, Berlioz, and Wagner. How can one account for the preponderance of great artists and sculptors during the Renaissance? Why were there so many inventors in the late nineteenth century? Why does Australia produce so many good tennis players, the United States so many good basketball and baseball players, and Russia so many good women athletes? Why has the past ten years produced so many outstanding Negro athletes? As Reynolds (1958) pointed out, it is doubtful that the basic potentialities of people vary greatly from one century to another. It seems that many kinds of talent, including creative talents, exist in most populations at any given time. Reynolds explains this by suggesting the principle that "talents will develop most frequently and to the highest level in the fields that are given heroic character"—essentially what Plato said in ancient Greece.

   Further evidence of the power of cultural influences in the nurture of creative development and functioning is indicated through cross-cultural studies (Johnson, 1963; Prakash, 1963; Torrance, 1963; Torrance and Goldman, 1966). For example, in the United States, after about age ten, girls consistently perform better than boys on almost every kind of verbal test for creative thinking. In India, however, two investigators using independently collected data from different parts of the country and about five years apart, found that boys excelled girls in practically all of the same verbal tests (Prakash, 1963; Raina, 1966). It was also found that children in India perform disproportionately better on verbal than on figural tests of creativity. Children in Western Samoa, Negro children in Georgia, and lower class children in Pittsburgh, Pennsylvania, performed better on figural than on verbal tests. It is difficult to believe that children in India are born with better verbal than figural creative thinking abilities and that the reverse is true in Western Samoa, among Negro children in Georgia, and among lower-class children in Pittsburgh (Smith, 1965). It is also difficult to believe that in the United States girls are born superior to boys in verbal creativity and that the reverse is true in India. Differences in the nurturing influences of the cultures involved help explain these differences. In Indian cities like Delhi where data was collected, one has to know several languages. Verbal abilities are given heavy emphasis. Western Samoa has had an alphabet for only a short time and verbal skills are even now not greatly honored. In the United States, schools and middle-class culture reward verbal skills. This has not been true, however, in the Negro and lower socioeconomic class subcultures. Patterns of the developmental curves and levels of creative functioning from one culture to another can be explained logically on the basis of the nurturing influences of the cultures (Torrance, 1965a).

   If cultural and historical influences are so powerful, is it possible for teachers, educational methods and materials, and parents to make real differences in the creative development and functioning of children? Evidence calls for a definite "Yes."

In previous works, I have summarized a variety of laboratory and field experiments indicating that the behavior of teachers can make differences in creative functioning (Torrance, 1965a). In field experiments, instructional materials, designed to provide experiences in creative thinking and containing information about the nature and value of the creative process, proved powerful enough to make differences in creative development (Torrance and Gupta, 1964). Dozens of experiments from kindergarten through graduate level tell the same story. The history of medical and scientific discovery tells a similar story. How else can one explain why certain teachers produced so many students who made outstanding discoveries (Gibson, 1958; Peterson, 1946)?

I shall now attempt to review some cultural influences that seem important in nurturing creative talents in the United States and to propose a program for helping teachers gain the insights and skills necessary if teaching is to make a difference.

Cultural influences

Success orientation

The United States has frequently been characterized as the most success-oriented culture in the world. American education is said to prepare only for success, not frustration and failure. These must be avoided either by succeeding or in not attempting ventures where failure is a possibility. This inhibition to creative thinking occurs repeatedly in the testing of children with creative thinking tests. Many children refuse to think of what Mother Hubbard could have done when she found the cupboard bare, because "it never should have happened."

Success orientation, when greatly overemphasized, is detrimental to creative growth because creative learning involves experimenting, taking risks, making mistakes, and correcting them. If making errors is forbidden and they are severely punished, children soon give up all hope of success and stop trying to learn. To nurture creativity, teachers may have to modify their concepts of classroom success and permit children to succeed first in ways possible to them and use the resulting growth to motivate them to higher levels of creative functioning. There is a strong need for more ways in which children can succeed in school.

Peer orientation

The United States has also been characterized as a culture in which children and young people are more concerned about the evaluations of classmates than of parents, teachers, and other authorities. Evidences of the inhibiting effects of pressures from classmates to conform emerge when we conduct sociometric studies, creative writing studies, and the like. It is likely that this powerful group orientation is largely responsible for the sharp drops in curves of creative development at about the fourth and seventh grades in most United States schools. Original ideas are common targets of pressures to conform.

The distressing thing is that many youngsters seem so concerned about these pressures that they "give up" all efforts to learn and to think. In an unpublished study I did concerning 45 seventh-graders nominated by their teachers as likely dropouts, 95 percent indicated they did not think anyone would take seriously their ideas and suggestions.

Schools can do much to lighten the tyranny of the group pressures that inhibit creative development. In creative problem-solving experiences, respect can be developed for unusual, minority ideas. Ability and interest groupings can lighten these pressures for many children. Arranging for appropriate sponsors or patrons for promising youngsters can be very powerful. Historical evidences seems to indicate that the child who starts earliest in his special efforts has the best chance of developing to the highest level in his field (Reynolds, 1958). Sponsors can give promising youngsters a chance to develop in creative ways at an early age.

Sanctions against questioning and exploration

Although teachers generally recognize the need for children to ask questions and inquire about the wonders and mysteries about them, such tendencies frequently are squelched. Forty-three percent of those potential dropouts indicated that they were afraid to ask questions. Only 17 percent of a large sample of fourth-graders indicated they were afraid to ask questions (Torrance and Gupta, 1964).

Misplaced emphasis on sex roles

Boys and girls in different ways suffer in creative development from society's misplaced emphasis on sex role differences. Pressures resulting from this misplaced emphasis needlessly make vast areas taboo for experiencing. Creative behavior, by its very nature, requires both sensitivity and independent thinking. In the United States, sensitivity and receptiveness are feminine virtues while independence in thinking is a masculine one. Again, there is much that schools can do to reduce the tyranny of this misplaced emphasis. One way is through activities that approve independence in thinking and judgment as well as sensitivity and receptiveness. Training in the arts for boys and in science for girls through science and art camps and various kinds of cocurricular and curricular activities is one approach.

Divergency equated with abnormality

"Genius" and "madness" have long been associated with one another. Almost all inventors, composers, creative scientists, and other creative persons have been regarded as insane. Although this belief was discredited long ago, the idea has persisted that any divergence from behavioral norms is unhealthy, immoral, and must be corrected. Teachers should be alert to look at behavior disapproved by the norm group for signs of creative potential. Such potentialities may not occur in the kinds of behavior valued by the school, at least not until recognized and given intelligent guidance and direction.

Other inhibiting influences

The foregoing are only a few of the cultural influences that seem to affect the creative development of children in the United States. We might have included emphasis upon a work-play dichotomy, a clock orientation with emphasis on speed, emphasis on appearing to be rather than actually being, and overemphasis on a limited number of talents rather than on the diversity needed. Instead of discussing these influences, I shall sketch briefly a proposed in-service education program to help teachers achieve the necessary skills and concepts to soften the tyranny of these cultural forces.

Crucial teacher skills

Almost any penetrating analysis of what is required for successful nurturance of creative talent leads to a recognition of the need for helping teachers improve certain skills. Through a series of articles in the *Instructor,* I proposed and outlined a series of learning experiences through which I believe teachers can improve the crucial skills.[1] This series of experiences is based on an analysis of skills necessary for nurturing creative talents and the status of these skills among most teachers. I have suggested that school faculties, groups of interested teachers, or individual teachers work on a different skill or set of skills each month. Participants would deliberately try to practice and improve one skill at a time, gradually integrating all of them into their behavior repertoire. For this purpose, I have suggested a number of workshops:

Workshop 1. Recognizing and acknowledging potentialities

One of the most important teacher skills needed in nurturing creative talents is the recognition and acknowledgment of potentialities. This skill is difficult to acquire, because recognizing potentialities of another is somehow threatening and requires imagination. One has to see a child—even one who misbehaves—not as he is, but as he could be.

There is little likelihood that teachers will do much to nurture creative talents until they become aware of these potentialities. Standardized tests are useful in becoming aware of abilities that might otherwise remain unnoticed. Teachers need not depend upon tests, however. Through the natural learning and problem-solving activities of children, there are many

[1] See the issues in *Instructor,* 1964–1965, 74 (September–June).

opportunities for observing creative potentialities. Teachers can also plan experiences that call for creative thinking and motivate children to participate in them. One of my classes compiled a list of 230 different observable signs of creative classroom behavior. One workshop experience might be to see how many of the following signs abstracted from this list can be observed in a given classroom and how these signs can be used in furthering creative development:

Intense absorption in listening, observing, doing
Intense animation and physical involvement
Challenging ideas of authorities
Checking many sources of information
Taking a close look at things
Eagerly telling others about one's discoveries
Continuing a creative activity after the scheduled time for quitting
Showing relationships among apparently unrelated ideas
Following through on ideas set in motion
Manifesting curiosity, wanting to know, digging deeper
Guessing or predicting outcomes and then testing them
Honestly and intensely searching for the truth
Resisting distractions
Losing awareness of time
Penetrating observations and questions
Seeking alternatives and exploring new possibilities

Workshop 2. Being respectful of questions and ideas

A major requirement for creative behavior is the capacity to wonder, to puzzle, to see gaps in knowledge, and to respond constructively. Children have this capacity, and it impels them to ask questions and seek answers. Being respectful of children's questions is not always easy for teachers. It requires responding with interest and curiosity rather than with threat and punishment.

To develop the skill of respecting questions and ideas, I propose that teachers begin with the exercise sketched below:

1. Think about what it really means to be respectful of the questions and ideas of children. Make a list of the common ways teachers respect or fail to respect them.

2. Try deliberately to be respectful of the questions and ideas of youngsters.

3. Write detailed descriptions of one incident in which an effort was made to be respectful of an unusual vexing question and one incident involving an original idea by a child or young person.

4. Discuss descriptions with one another, with a friend, or with a

supervisor, trying to decide how well the effort succeeded and producing a variety of alternatives the teacher could have used.

In workshops, success depends upon the extent that the participants feel psychologically comfortable and are willing to expose their values and behavior patterns so that perceptions and reactions can be analyzed and changed.

Workshop 3. Asking provocative questions

Several studies have shown that over 90 percent of the questions teachers ask call for the reproduction of information in the textbook or presented by the teacher (Sanders, 1966; Torrance and Hansen, 1965; Boesen, 1966). To improve skills in asking provocative questions, teachers need to know the different kinds of questions. Several available schemes lend themselves to this purpose. One is presented in the paperback, *Classroom Questions: What Kinds?*, by a curriculum researcher who discovered that teachers in his school system rarely asked anything except memory questions (Sanders, 1966). This book offers suggestions for improving memory questions—questions that emphasize the truly important facts, generalizations, and values. In addition, there are ideas for improving skills in asking questions that call for translation, interpretation, applications of information, analysis, synthesis, and evaluation. This book could be the focus of a series of workshop experiences. One week, practice could be given in making up and trying out translation questions that ask the learner to translate what he has learned from one abstraction level to another and go beyond the information to determine implications, consequences, and effects. The next week, emphasis could be given to practice with other kinds of questions. Finally, practice could be given in combining and integrating all of the different kinds of questions into a sequence of experiences.

This is one example of a scheme that could be used. Other, perhaps, equally useful schemes would be Guilford's (1959, 1966) *Structure of Intellect Model,* Bloom's (1956) *Taxonomy of Educational Objectives,* and Burkhart's *Divergent Power Model* (Burkhart and Bernheim, 1963).

After trying for a few days to ask more provocative questions, it would be useful to check progress. A class session might be taped and analyzed. Immediately after a session, the teacher could write down all of the questions he remembers asking. One member of a workshop group might write down the questions that another workshop member asks in a classroom. In classes of older children or adults, the teacher can have a student record the questions he asks. The skill has to be practiced, progress evaluated, and improvements made. Workshop members can analyze one another's questions and discuss possible alternatives.

Workshop 4. Recognizing and valuing originality

Teachers should make deliberate efforts to recognize and value original ideas and solutions because there is a strong tendency to ignore or discredit all unfamiliar ideas. One good way of helping teachers develop this skill is to involve them in production of original ideas and assess the degree of originality of a standard set of responses. Then participants can find out why certain responses are obvious and commonplace. The mind has not paused long enough to make the mental leap necessary for producing original responses. Such responses are not surprising, do not ring of the essence of the truth, and do not break away from the safe, easy, and ineffective.

In a series of experiences, teachers might deliberately try to recognize and encourage originality. One useful experience would be to write detailed descriptions of attempts and have them analyzed by the group. The following questions might be used as a guide:

1. In what form did the original idea occur?
2. What was the immediate reaction of the teacher?
3. What were the reactions of other pupils?
4. How was the original idea recognized and respected?
5. What were the immediate consequences of respecting the idea?
6. What do you predict that the long-range consequences will be?

Workshop 5. Developing elaboration ability

No idea or solution will make much difference unless some one elaborates and works out the necessary plans for its execution. Several current studies indicate that the single characteristic most differentiating the mental functioning of the juvenile delinquent and the school dropout is the inability to elaborate. Important scientific breakthroughs have frequently been postponed because the person producing the idea failed to elaborate. There is, of course, the danger of too much elaboration.

Workshop participants might focus on encouraging elaboration of some common, specific activity: a reading lesson, a plan for a classroom or playground activity, or the like. A workshop group might see how many different and original ideas it can produce to encourage elaboration within a particular curriculum task or area.

Workshop 6. Unevaluated practice and experimentation

Periods of unevaluated practice and experimentation have tremendously changed what happens to students in my classes. They make far greater progress in applying course content to the solution of personal and professional problems.

Workshop participants could try at least once a week to arrange a time for some kind of unevaluated experience. They should record their experiences by trying to answer the following set of questions and discuss them with another person. They should perhaps try to avoid correcting and evaluating what was done:

1. What was the initial assignment and the nature of the situation in which it was given?
2. How did you communicate that there was freedom to experiment without being evaluated?
3. What happened during the practice period?
4. What happened immediately after the practice period?
5. What was the nature of the similar follow-up task in which the new insights or skills were applied?
6. If rewarded, how?
7. What were the immediate outcomes?
8. What do you predict will be the long-range outcomes?

Workshop 7. Developing creative readers

It is easier to remember and use information read creatively than things read passively or critically. When a person reads creatively, he is sensitive to problems and possibilities. He searches for new relationships, synthesizes unrelated elements, redefines or transforms known information into new uses, and builds onto what he knows. Thus, he produces multiple alternatives, looks at information in different ways and in greater depth, and fills in the gaps.

It takes effort to change from a passive, absorbent, or critical reader into a creative one. A person can become a creative reader by heightening expectations and anticipations or by doing something with what is read. These two approaches are discussed in some detail elsewhere and prove as powerful with adults as with children (Torrance, 1965b).

Heightening expectations involves the creation of tension or warming up. Doing something with what has been read can occur at any one of four different levels:

1. Reproducing with imagination what is read, making things sound as if they're actually happening
2. Elaborating what is read
3. Transforming and rearranging what is read
4. Going beyond what is read

In workshop groups, the first week might be spent helping participants become more creative readers, heightening their expectations, and doing things with what they read. Subsequent weeks could be devoted to helping participants teach their pupils to become creative readers.

Workshop 8. Predicting behavior

The work of Ligon (1965) has demonstrated the value of improving the accuracy of one's ability to predict the behavior of others and the practicality of doing so. He has suggested the formation of "Co-Scientist Skills Clubs" and has provided the first edition of a manual for such clubs. The basic skills that would be cultivated are accuracy of observation and prediction of the behavior of others. He suggests three principles for developing improved skills in this area and a workshop program could be built around them:

1. The desire to be accurate
2. Prediction of what the child will do in a given situation and then observation
3. Use of the child's own words as much as possible in recording observations

Workshop 9. Guided planned experiences

Investigators such as Ojemann and his associates (Ojemann, 1948; Ojemann, Maxey, and Snider, 1965; Ojemann and Pritchett, 1963) are finding that mental development is quite different when children are provided with planned sequences of learning experiences rather than when they encounter only what the environment provides. Application of the concept of guided learning experiences represents a deliberate attempt to assist a child in learning by developing, from an analysis of the learning task and the nature of the learner, a planned sequence of experiences for mastering the learning task by motivating him to participate in these experiences.

Workshop 10. Searching for the truth with methods of research

Since the very essence of creativity is "searching for the truth," it is important that there be a series of workshops on the development of the basic concepts and skills necessary for this search. Without these skills, there will be a lack of depth in creative thinking. Attention should be given to the skills and concepts involved in different kinds of research: historical, descriptive, and experimental. For each of these kinds of research, a profitable workshop experience would be the development of at least one lesson through which a deliberate attempt would be made to develop relevant skills.

Workshop 11. Creative problem-solving skills

No program to improve the teaching skills needed to nurture creative talents would be complete without deliberate efforts to improve skills in creative problem solving. There are a variety of approaches that might be used. One of the most productive and widely used of these approaches is one formulated by Osborn (1963) and Parnes (Parnes and Harding, 1962) and their associates. It has been demonstrated that the basic concepts and skills can be developed to a useful degree through a series of workshop experiences as brief as two or three days. Such skills, of course, have to be practiced and improved.

REFERENCES

Bloom, B. S. (Ed.) *Taxonomy of educational objectives: The classification of educational goals. Handbook I: Cognitive domain.* New York: McKay, 1956.

Boesen, M. T. An analysis of the question-asking behavior of teachers in a parochial school. Unpublished research paper, University of Minnesota, Minneapolis, 1966.

Burkhart, R. C., & Bernheim, G. Object question test manual. Unpublished ditto, Pennsylvania State University, Department of Art Education Research, 1963.

Gibson, W. C. *Young endeavor.* Springfield, Ill.: Charles C Thomas, 1958.

Guilford, J. P. Three faces of intellect. *American Psychologist,* 1959, 14, 469–479.

Guilford, J. P. Basic problems in teaching for creativity. In C. W. Taylor & F. E. Williams (Eds.), *Instructional media and creativity.* New York: Wiley, 1966. Pp. 71–103.

Johnson, R. T. The growth of creative thinking abilities in Western Samoa. Unpublished doctoral dissertation, University of Minnesota, 1963.

Ligon, E. M. The co-scientist and his potential. *Character Potential,* 1965, 3(10), 1–26.

Ojemann, R. H. Research in planned learning programs and the science of behavior. *Journal of Educational Research,* 1948, 42(10), 96–104.

Ojemann, R. H., Maxey, E. J., & Snider, B. C. F. The effect of a program of guided learning experiences in developing probability concepts at the third grade level. *Journal of Experimental Education,* 1965, 33, 321–330.

Ojemann, R. H., & Pritchett, K. Piaget and the role of guided experiences in human development. *Perceptual and Motor Skills,* 1963, 17, 927–940.

Osborn, A. F. *Applied imagination* (3d ed.). New York: Scribner, 1963.

Parnes, S. J., & Harding, H. F. (Eds.) *A source book for creative thinking.* New York: Scribner, 1962.

Peterson, H. (Ed.) *Great teachers.* New Brunswick: Rutgers University Press, 1946.

Prakash, A. O. Understanding the fourth grade slump: A study of the creative thinking abilities of Indian children. Unpublished master's thesis, University of Minnesota, 1963.

Raina, M. K. A study of sex differences in creativity. Research paper, Regional College of Education, Ajmer, India, 1966.

Reynolds, M. C. Nurturing talents. Paper presented at Elementary Leaders Conference, Iowa State Teachers College, January, 1958.

Sanders, N. M. *Classroom questions: What kinds?* New York: Harper & Row, 1966.

Smith, R. M. The relationship of creativity to social class. U. S. Office of Education Cooperative Research Project 2250, University of Pittsburgh, 1965.

Torrance, E. P. *Education and the creative potential.* Minneapolis: University of Minnesota Press, 1963.

Torrance, E. P. *Rewarding creative behavior.* Englewood Cliffs, N.J.: Prentice-Hall, 1965. (a)

Torrance, E. P. *Gifted children in the classroom.* New York: Macmillan, 1965. (b)

Torrance, E. P., & Goldman, R. J. Creative development in a segregated Negro school. Minneapolis: University of Minnesota, Department of Educational Psychology, 1966.

Torrance, E. P., & Gupta, R. Development and evaluation of recorded programmed experiences of creative thinking in the fourth grade. University of Minnesota, Bureau of Educational Research, 1964.

Torrance, E. P., & Hansen, E. The question-asking behavior of highly creative and less creative basic business teachers identified by a paper-and-pencil test. *Psychological Reports,* 1965, 17, 815–818.

17 | Techniques of creative teaching

RALPH J. HALLMAN
Pasadena City College

From Ralph J. Hallman, "Techniques of Creative Teaching," Journal of Creative Behavior, *1967, 1, 325–330. Reprinted by permission of publisher, Creative Education Foundation, Inc., and author.*

Examining closely the relationship between current educational values and procedures on one hand and creative behavior on the other, Ralph J. Hallman identifies nine common barriers to creative imagination— appropriately described as "things to be avoided." Following this analysis, he proposes some concrete recommendations for more creative teaching. For example, the teacher can provide for self-initiated learning, create a nonauthoritarian environment, encourage creative thought processes and intellectual flexibility, and provide opportunities for the manipulation of objects and ideas. Hallman's recommendations are clearly intended to counter at least some creativity-stifling practices.

During the last decade research projects have turned up evidence that creativity can be taught, and at the same time have suggested that certain techniques are more effective than others in eliciting creative responses from pupils. There may be some value to the classroom teacher as well as to the research specialist in bringing together the findings of these otherwise isolated inquiries.

Obstacles to creativity

Because creative capacities cannot be deliberately controlled, but only encouraged, they can easily be inhibited. The following list of things to be avoided appears in the research literature.

First, the *pressure to conform* is perhaps the major inhibiter of creative responses. These pressures may take the form of teacher-chosen goals and activities, standardized routines and tests, or an inflexible curriculum.

Second, *authoritarian attitudes* and environments repress the creative potential of young people. They inhibit learning to be free, learning to be self-directive and self-responsible. Education by authority directs students to learn what others have already discovered, what others believe, what others have organized. Authoritarian education places emphasis on following directions, doing what one is told, and on solving problems which have fixed and predetermined answers.

Third, *ridicule* and similar attitudes destroy feelings of self-worth in students and therefore have a tendency to block off creative efforts. Domination of pupils for any reason, threats of any kind, fears which may be engendered for failure to obtain right answers or to know the proper information dissipate any creative tendencies which may be latent.

Fourth, those traits which make for *rigidity of personality* inhibit creative expressions. These traits may vary from psychopathic conditions to the unconsciously learned habits which simply annoy others. Inflexible defense mechanisms and compulsive fears on the part of teachers are common offenders. The facades which we erect in order to shield our true selves and our ego-centered interests dampen the exploratory and often risky ventures which characterize creative activities.

Fifth, an overemphasis on such *rewards* as grades arouses defensive attitudes on the part of pupils and to that extent threatens inventiveness. Perhaps all forms of evaluation which are external to a given situation deter the productive tendency, including even laudatory criticisms.

Sixth, an excessive *quest for certainty* stills the creative urge. This habit is instilled by teachers who demand the right answers, who insist on what they themselves want in the way of responses, who demand the predetermined solutions. These attitudes are extended by students into other affairs and express themselves in the form of demands to know what is right with respect to dress, what clubs to join, and what otherwise will be socially acceptable.

Seventh, an overemphasis on *success* drains off energies from creative processes and focuses them upon outcomes, perhaps upon some status symbol, or on the merely instrumentally valuable goals which might have been achieved. Such overemphasis blocks creativeness because it has the tendency to direct attention away from growth and from continual improvement.

Eighth, *hostility toward the divergent personality,* either on the part of teachers or peers, may serve as a cultural block. Every creative act is unique, idiosyncratic, and novel. For this reason alone creative persons tend to be individualistic, nonconforming, and often curiously onesided. This is not to say, of course, that all off-beat personalities are creative. The divergent attitudes can as easily become a pose and a sham and a rigid defense mechanism. The task of the teacher is to penetrate such shams and to discriminate between them and the genuinely inventive personality.

Finally, an *intolerance of the "play" attitude* in connection with school work characterizes the environments which stifle creativeness. Innovation requires freedom to toy with ideas and materials, encouragement to deal with irrelevancies, and permission to dip into fantasy and make-believe. This attitude allows the ideas and other materials under consideration to take on plastic qualities and so to lend themselves to rearrangements and fusions which mark the creative act. Creativity is profound fun.

Aids to creative teaching

Research literature supports the position that creativity indeed can be taught, but that it cannot be taught by the traditional, authoritarian methods. Creative procedures cannot be prescribed nor can they be written into lesson plans; yet creative teaching is the best way, perhaps the only way, to promote creative behavior on the part of pupils.

The effective teacher must invent his own creative techniques as a part of the specific, ongoing teaching operations in the classroom. The procedures which he invents will appear in the given situation as having been unforeseeable and unexpected. Because they come to him, and to the pupils, as a surprise, their effectiveness will be enhanced. It remains to be investigated whether the principles of creative teaching are identical with the principles of all *good* teaching. There certainly will be overlapping for the simple reason that good teaching *is* creative teaching. The following specific suggestions seem appropriate.

First, the creative teacher provides for *self-initiated learning* on the part of pupils. This time-honored principle applies to all good teaching, but it is indispensable in inducing creative responses. Self-activity encourages students to explore, to engage in experimentation, to hypothesize. It maintains the spontaneous, self-starting quality of learning; it keeps the motivational forces for learning within the individual learner.

Second, the creative teacher sets up *nonauthoritarian learning environments*. Conditions of freedom facilitate creativeness. The kind of freedom which is requisite to creativity is psychological freedom, symbolic freedom, the freedom experienced in a spontaneous expression and not an overt, aggressive freedom, not license. Freedom to engage in full and unimpeded symbolic expression promotes creativeness because it softens our defensive, rigid attitudes and creates an openness to experience. Freedom to explore within the limits of one's own interests and abilities places the responsibility for growth in one's own hands. But every authoritarian act performed by the teacher discourages decision-making and the learning of responsibility on the part of students.

Third, the creative teacher encourages pupils to *overlearn;* to saturate themselves with information, imagery, and meanings. The student must learn to accept the fact that this kind of teaching and learning involves a rather rigorous self-discipline. It is a kind of discipline which only the pupil can impose upon himself as he comes to enjoy the drudgery and hard work which are required for self-initiated discoveries. Overlearning functions creatively by allowing the pupil to detach himself from the materials so that the materials can become plastic and subject to restructuring.

Fourth, the creative teacher encourages *creative thought processes*. He stimulates pupils to seek for new connections among data, to associate, imagine, think up tentative solutions to problems at hand, make wild guesses, hitchhike ideas, build on the ideas of others and to point these ideas in new directions. He encourages students to juggle improbably related elements, to express theories which *appear* to be ridiculous, to shape theories which are far-out and unbelievable, to combine materials and notions into new and unexpected patterns. The good teacher allows students to take intellectual risks, to speculate on the basis of inconclusive information, to probe for structural and spatial relationships among things.

Fifth, the creative teacher *defers judgment*. He does not block off an exploratory effort by announcing outcomes or by providing solutions. Rather, he postpones the finalizing of solutions; he defers the closure of issues and inquiries and exhibits a willingness to reopen previously closed issues. He maintains a flexibility in the rounding out of a conclusion or in the structuring of an investigation. More important, the creative teacher minimizes the importance of errors. He makes clear that mistakes are both expected and necessary.

Sixth, the creative teacher *promotes intellectual flexibility* among the students. He encourages students to shift their positions of observation, to vary their approaches to problems, to consciously move away from their own preconceptions about the material at hand, and to avoid fixing upon a single track in attacking an issue. He asks students to change the functions of commonplace objects, to redefine problems in categories other than those with which he is currently working, to spurn the "coloring book" approach. He encourages them to look for new meanings in familiar materials, to employ old meanings in new contexts.

Seventh, the creative teacher *encourages self-evaluation* of individual progress and achievement. He rejects group norms and standardized tests on the grounds that they are both inappropriate and harmful to creative learning. Learning to become creative, to become self-active and self-responsible, requires constant practice in self-evaluation. This in turn depends upon the feelings of self-worth which we can build up within ourselves. In its turn, the feeling of self-worth supplies the criteria for making choices of the means and the materials which are used during the process of actual creating. This means that the criteria for evaluating novelty are personal and aesthetic and that the individual's own powers to judge values serve as the final standard in determining the worth of newly created objects.

Eighth, the creative teacher helps the student *to become a more sensi-*

tive person—to become more sensitive to the moods and feelings of other people, to all external stimuli, to social and personal problems as well as academic ones, to public issues, and even to the commonplace and the unknown.

Ninth, the creative teacher knows how to *make use of the question.* Every creative act begins with questions, but the questions must be operational and open-ended, questions which are meaningful to students, questions which have no predetermined answers, and especially questions which are not settled by a recitation of facts. Operational questions initiate the creative endeavor because they lead to exploration; they foster curiosity and stimulate connotative tendencies. Questions which are settled by citing already known facts hinder creativeness and restrict discussion. They hinder creative efforts because they make information a tool by which the teacher dominates rather than one which makes for inquiry and discovery.

Tenth, the creative teacher *provides opportunities for students to manipulate materials, ideas, concepts, tools, and structures.* Craftsmanship is an essential ingredient in the creative personality whether it be craftsmanship with words, with colors, tones, or lumber. The active handling of things facilitates creativeness, for it aids the student in understanding ongoing processes.

Eleventh, the creative teacher assists the student in *coping with frustration and failure.* The creative personality differs from the less creative in respect to his ability to accept and to live with uncertainties and ambiguities. Creative endeavors arise out of unsettled conditions, out of trying circumstances, and the students who can best handle such situations have an advantage in creative potential.

Finally, the creative teacher urges pupils to *consider problems as wholes,* to emphasize total stuctures rather than the piecemeal, additive elements. Directional cues for the actual creative process are supplied by the construction as an integrated whole. Understandings of problems occur with greatest insight when priority is given to structural patterns and to principles.

18 | Be creative!

WILLIAM S. HANKS
State University College, Oswego, New York

From William S. Hanks, "Be Creative," The Journal of Industrial Arts Education, *1968, 27 (March–April), pp. 19–20. Reprinted by permission of publisher and author.*

Focusing specifically upon developing creativity in the industrial arts class, William S. Hanks summarizes briefly a number of classroom/shop experiences which should contribute to a student's problem sensitivity and idea-generating capabilities. Hanks specifies that his exercises are intended to strengthen several of Guilford's primary abilities, particularly sensitivity to problems, associational fluency, ideational fluency, adaptive flexibility, spontaneous flexibility, originality, synthesis and closure, and redefinition. It is interesting to observe that Guilford himself has suggested that these abilities could be improved by giving students exercises similar to the tests measuring those abilities—which is precisely Hanks' strategy. [See Guilford, J. P. Creativity: Its measurement and development. In S. J. Parnes & H. F. Harding (Eds.), *A source book for creative thinking.* New York: Scribner's, 1962. Pp. 151–168.]

Much has been written of creativity and its relationship to national economic goals, personal accomplishment, mental health, and contributions to society in general. However, little has been done to explore and interpret measures found to enhance factors of creativity in the industrial arts laboratory. This article proceeds on the premise that creativity can, and should, be fostered wherever and whenever possible in the school program.

Industrial arts is not usually the first subject area that comes to mind when educators consider creative experiences in the curriculum. In fact, A. P. Meinz (1960) reports instances where industrial arts can do serious harm to the development of creative potential. It is doubtful that our content and method operate to the detriment of creativity more than any other subject area. However, with a basic understanding of what is known, positive action may be taken in the day-to-day routine to enrich the individual course or program with experiences found to foster creativity.

J. P. Guilford (1952) and W. L. Brittain (1952) have contributed greatly to the present understanding of creativity and the factors associated with it. It is with the factors of creativity that this article is most concerned, because industrial arts is in a unique position to provide many experiences implied by the Guilford-Brittain studies.

In completely independent investigations—one in search of creative scientific talent, the other looking for creativity in the visual arts—Guilford and Brittain found almost identical attributes related to persons believed to be creative. The Guilford listing reports sensitivity to problems, associational fluency, ideational fluency, adaptive flexibility, spontaneous flexibility, originality, synthesis, and closure and redefinition. It is not suggested that if one has these attributes he is notably creative. However, circumstances, interaction, and hard work do imply that the above contribute to general creativity.

An examination of the Guilford factors suggests certain categories of experience. These would be (1) finding problems, (2) generating ideas and alternatives, (3) developing ideas into tangible products, and (4) rethinking a problem, redesign, and improvement. If an individual's creative potential can be enhanced by engaging in such experiences, then the contributions of industrial arts to the development of creativity could be highly significant indeed. For the listing, as suggested, literally outlines the process of product development. Preliminary studies which investigate the possibility of encouraging creativity in the industrial arts laboratory have been conducted. Other promising experiments are in progress. A brief review of the completed studies follows.

In the Stout State Study, Dr. Wesley Sommers (1961) introduced a drafting class to concepts of creativity, brainstorming, sketch-storming, alphabet design, and group problem techniques. He found such experiences improved the performance significantly for students on measures of creativity when compared to those taught by more traditional means.

The Mankato State College Study, through a general education industrial arts course taught by Dr. Donald Anderson (1963), found a significant enhancement of creativity by lending descriptive material concerning creativity to students, and by brief group discussions.

The study at the Oswego campus of the State Univerity of New York (Hanks, 1966) encouraged the generation of ideas in an industrial arts design course. Considerable freedom was permitted in the selection of design problems, and a blend of experiences for problem discovery and refinement was introduced into the regular course work. The results clearly indicated that ideational fluency (idea productivity) was aided significantly by such experiences.

These studies show strong evidence that creativity can be encouraged in the industrial arts setting. Operational procedures for encouraging creativity, as suggested by the factors listed by Guilford and Brittain, would be many and diverse. A sampling is suggested here in the hope of inspiring still others:

1. Have the student list all the utilitarian objects with which he might come into contact during a twenty-four-hour period. Have him select for further exploration those items which pose considerable friction in terms of function or appearance.

2. Have the student list all the possible utilitarian items associated with areas of work, study, transportation, recreation, relaxation, eating, agriculture, etc. Allow him to elaborate on the more promising articles or problems found.

3. Pose a class problem and seek as many alternatives as possible. For example, why did a certain manufacturer extend paid vacations for employees from one to two weeks?

4. Present a common article, such as a plastic freezer lid, to the class and request alternative functions it might serve.

5. Have students guess the purpose of an object from a minimum of verbal or graphic clues. For instance, when a cup might be the unknown object, draw an incomplete handle on the chalkboard, adding parts, such as the remainder of the handle or a side, until the student guesses the correct item.

6. Allow the student to redefine, or redesign, articles by examining the characteristics of the object. For a wall calendar (representative of graphic arts) the list of attributes generated by the students might include numbers, months, cover, horizontal, vertical, sheets, paper texture, hanging device, illustrations, poems, sayings, advertising, descriptions, artists' names, color, fold-over, phases of the moon, important dates, typography, etc. Particular attention would then be given to the various attributes in terms of improvement or innovation. The reader will find a detailed description of this technique in Crawford (1954).

7. Have the student make associations between rather unrelated ideas or articles. The associations would serve as a point of departure in developing ideas for storage, units of combined function and other relationships that suggest continued development. The reader may wish to consult Whiting (1958) for further operational details of this method.

8. With students, lead a discussion which might indirectly offer refinement of an unannounced problem. If a discussion of "learning" as an "educational game" is to be developed, for example, as a favorable listing of possible attributes develops, announce the specific problem and

limitations and continue elaboration sessions until possibilities have been exhausted. Further implications are to be found in Gordon (1961).

9. Have students suggest (orally or graphically) improvements for an object of everyday use (e.g., a rubber band).

10. Encourage students to be open-minded to the ideas of others. Have students seek out instances where the "wild" idea has been very successful.

We are in a unique position to encourage creative potential in the industrial arts laboratory.

Investigations should continue to search for operational procedures which give a maximum of exposure to finding problems, generating ideas and alternatives, and developing and redesigning products.

REFERENCES

Anderson, D. W. An experimental evaluation of two methods for developing creative problem solving abilities in an industrial arts course. Unpublished doctoral thesis, University of Minnesota, 1963.

Brittain, W. L. Experiments for a possible test to determine some aspects of creativity in the visual arts. Unpublished doctoral dissertation, Pennsylvania State University, 1952.

Crawford, R. P. *The techniques of creative thinking.* New York: Hawthorn, 1954.

Gordon, W. J. J. *Synectics.* New York: Harper & Row, 1961.

Guilford, J. P. A factor-analytic study of creative thinking. II. Administration of tests and analytical results. Reports from the Psychological Laboratories, University of Southern California, No. 8, July, 1952.

Hanks, W. S. A comparison of methods for encouraging ideational fluency. Unpublished doctoral dissertation, Pennsylvania State University, 1966.

Meinz, A. P. General creativity of elementary education majors as influenced by courses in industrial arts and art education. Unpublished doctoral dissertation, Pennsylvania State University, 1960.

Sommers, W. S. The influence of selected teaching methods on the development of creative thinking. Unpublished doctoral dissertation, University of Minnesota, 1961.

Whiting, C. S. *Creative thinking.* New York: Reinhold, 1958.

19 | Creative and productive thinking in the classroom

Granite School District, Salt Lake City, Utah

Reprinted with permission of the author and publisher from the article of the same title, Journal of Creative Behavior, *1967, 1, 419–427.*

In order to improve creative thinking in the classroom, schools can initiate courses devoted to thinking and problem solving, perhaps built around such materials as the *Productive Thinking Program* of Covington, Crutchfield, and Davies (Chapter 20), *Thinking Creatively* by Davis and Houtman (Chapter 21), the *Idea Books* of Myers and Torrance (described in Chapter 21), or the *Creative Behavior Guidebook* by Parnes (Chapter 22). Alternatively, teachers can incorporate creative problem-solving principles and procedures into existing curriculum areas. Following the latter strategy, Hutchinson describes one fifteen-day study in which modified instructional methods, which treated social studies students as *thinkers,* resulted in improved activity test scores and increased productive thinking in the classroom, with no loss in subject-matter comprehension. Furthermore, the training made productive stars out of several "low ability" students emphasizing the failure of the schools to foster creative development. One important contribution of Hutchinson's experiment is his measure of actual creative behavior in the classroom. Working from transcripts of tape-recorded classroom sessions, judges categorized verbal responses as *convergent thinking, divergent thinking, evaluative thinking, cognitive-memory,* or *routine.* The first three categories combine into a *total productive thinking* score. Such an interesting criterion of creative behavior certainly merits further attention by researchers in the field of creativity, all of whom are plagued with the problem of finding dependable and valid measures of creativity.

Neglected abilities

All the abilities of all our children must be developed fully if education is to do its job. Recent research suggests that some important abilities are not being developed by current classroom methods. This study reports some experimental evidence on the feasibility of developing these neglected abilities; it is based on Guilford's (1956) *Structure-of-the-Intellect* model, and recent study of the intellectual processes (Guilford, 1959, 1961). As developed by Calvin W. Taylor (1962), the crux of the theory is that students should and can use a variety of thought processes, while simultaneously learning a variety of subjects. This study will thus consider the student as a thinker, not just as a learner. My primary source of data is the student in the classroom as he verbalizes and reacts to the teacher and his classmates. I have tried to relate this data to current research in psychology.

Purpose

My major objective was to determine what learning and thinking processes (cognitive, memory, divergent, convergent, or evaluative) would be elicited in students by certain modifications of current teaching methods. The method of making naturalistic classroom observations for this report was based on that of Hughes (unpublished), and of Aschner and Gallagher (unpublished). Terminology, the *Structure-of-the-Intellect* model, and the mechanical operations of classifications were derived from Guilford, whose work has considerably extended our concept of intelligence. Traditional intelligence tests, for example, cover relatively few of the discrete factors in Guilford's model. Students should be given an opportunity in their total education to use all of Guilford's factors, but experimental work needs to be done in revising current curricula before this will be possible.

Rationale

As a framework for such experimentation, Taylor has suggested a three-dimensional model for analyzing educational programs. The dimensions are (1) the teaching methods, (2) the subject matters, and (3) the student's thought processes. I am concerned here primarily with the third dimension since it offers the greatest opportunity for improvement. It can be analyzed in the classroom with Guilford's "operation" categories. I am concerned particularly with classroom creative thinking at the verbal level.

The experimental design

The experimental and control groups were drawn from 417 students comprising the total seventh-grade (1961–1962) population of Valley Junior High School, Granite School District, Salt Lake City, Utah. Each of four teachers taught the same unit of social studies to an experimental group and to a control group of 32 students (16 boys and 16 girls), for a total of 256 (128 experimental and 128 control). All eight groups were matched for mental age and sex. The California Mental Maturity Test was administered to all seventh-grade students. The groups were then randomly designated as experimental or control. The mean mental age for the total group was 156.93 months; the mean for the control group was 156.60 and for the experimental group 157.27.

Tests

The seven creativity tests used (Hidden Shapes, Gestalt Transformation, Apparatus Test, Planning Elaboration, Plot Titles, Clip Uses, and Meaningful Statements) were taken from Guilford, Carroll (1941), and Getzels (Getzels and Jackson, 1959). All groups were given identical pre- and post-tests with a nine-week interval which included a fifteen-day instructional sequence, plus a final subject-matter test.

Treatment

The control group studied the subject-matter unit on transportation and communication first. Teachers were instructed to use their current methods. Both the control and the experimental groups were administered identical subject-matter achievement tests at the beginning and (three weeks later) the end of the transportation and communication unit. During the four days preceding experimental group instruction, an in-service training program was conducted for both experimental teachers and students. The purpose of the training program was two-fold: first, to acquaint the teacher with the experimental procedures, and secondly, to acquaint the students with group methods, "brainstorming," and concepts such as ideational fluency, originality, and planning elaboration. Students were told that they were going to be treated as "thinkers" rather than just as learners. A suggested outline of content, sequence, and teaching method was developed for the fifteen days of instruction. Each teacher was given some leeway in interpreting the outline (as needed) to facilitate class interaction. Methodology was the primary consideration; recall of the subject matter was secondary.

Data

Tape recordings were made of all eight groups during the fifteen sessions. Two observers took running notes, identified speakers, and recorded nonspoken behavior that occurred during the sessions. My basic data was taken from five fifty-minute, consecutive tape records from each of the eight groups. They were transcribed verbatim, audited for accuracy, and analyzed. In order to arrive at a method for classifying the verbal responses of children in the classroom, it was necessary to turn to the work of Aschner and Gallagher. The Aschner-Gallagher System was used for classifying students' verbal responses. It consists of five primary categories. Four of the categories—Cognitive-Memory, Convergent Thinking, Evaluative Thinking, and Divergent Thinking—are adaptations of factors from Guilford's *Structure-of-the-Intellect*. The fifth category is called Routine.

Categories

COGNITIVE-MEMORY operations are taken to involve only such thought processes as recognition, rote memory, and selective recall. CONVERGENT THINKING is both analytic and integrative, and operates within a closely structured framework. Because the information sought is so definitely specified, these questions or problems are "data rich." EVALUATIVE THINKING deals with matters of value rather than matters of fact and is characterized in verbal performance by its judgmental quality.

Problems and questions which elicit DIVERGENT THINKING provide for its operation within a definite but somewhat "data poor" framework. The respondent is put "on his own" within the structure, free to range broadly and flexibly in his thinking to select and/or construct a large number of possible ideas, associations, and implications, of which no single one could be predetermined as the unique right answer. The individual thus generates his own further data (ideas, associations, *etc.*) in producing his response(s) to the question or problem at hand, often taking a new direction or perspective (Carroll, 1941).

ROUTINE includes the variety of performances—both verbal and nonverbal—representing typical aspects of the day-to-day direction, conduct, and/or personal reaction to what is said and done in class.

I. Summary of findings

Modifying instructional methods produced a distinct change in the ratios of verbal response categories. Routine responses in the control groups were twenty-nine percent; cognitive-memory responses were thirty-seven percent; total productive thinking responses totaled thirty-four percent. Routine responses in the experimental groups were ten percent; cognitive-memory responses were forty-six percent; and total productive thinking responses forty-four percent. Most noticeable was the comparatively marked decrease in the number of responses, as well as percent of responses, found in the experimental group routine category. In every case this reduction was statistically significant. There was a sharp increase in total productive thinking, particularly in evaluative thinking (for the experimental group) which is considered to be last in the sequence of mental operations.

Twenty boys and ten girls were rated as creative stars, and forty-two boys and twenty-nine girls as productive stars. There were two boys to every girl rated as creative stars, and a third more boys who were rated as productive stars. There was, however, a statistically significant correlation between mental age and total productive thinking. There was also a statistically significant correlation between mental age and divergent (creative) thinking.

When teachers utilized experimental methods more nearly geared to the full range of thinking abilities found in the normal classroom and not merely in the high MA (mental age) students, new productive and creative stars emerged and the correlation between mental age and productive and creative thinking responses tended to decrease. It was not necessarily the high MA student who became the productive and creative star. In one experimental group three students out of ten in the lowest quartile were productive stars, and the correlation between the actual classroom responses and the measures of creativity increased significantly.

Correlation between mental age and increases on the subject-matter tests for the control groups was significant. In contrast, at the .01 level there was no correlation between mental age and the increase on the subject-matter tests for the experimental groups. By changing methods of instruction, the normal correlation between MA and subject-matter increase for high MA students was reduced to zero. Normal methods are apparently designed only for the high MA student. Gains for the high MA students were not as great in the experimental groups as in the control groups.

Although the total experimental group gained more on the subject-matter post-test than did the control groups, the difference was not statistically significant.

The experimental group had significant gains over the control group on four of the ten measures of creativity, with one other measure approaching significance. The measures showing significant growth for the experimental group were apparatus fluency, plot titles fluency, clip uses flexibility, and clip uses ideational fluency. The measure approaching significance was apparatus originality. The control group had no significant gains on creativity measures over the experimental group.

II. Conclusions

Hypothesis: In the typical seventh-grade social studies classroom using current teaching practices, verbal responses of the students are found primarily in the cognitive-memory classification, and productive thinking is primarily convergent.

Study of the control groups indicates this hypothesis to be true for three of the four groups. Since teaching methods in the fourth control group (D) more closely resembled that of the experimental groups than those of the other control groups, this hypothesis should be accepted. Analysis of the classifications of the control group clearly shows that the traditional classroom was teacher-centered, thereby limiting students' divergent and evaluative thinking responses. When traditional methods were used, an excessive amount of time was consumed in routine responses. Traditional methods are geared to the high MA students. The high correlation between mental age and the gain made on subject-matter tests in the control group is consistent with this conclusion.

Hypothesis: Modifying instructional procedures in seventh-grade social studies so as to treat students as thinkers rather than only as learners, elicits wider ranges of verbal responses, *i.e.,* a greater percent of responses in the productive, convergent, divergent, and evaluative thinking categories.

Modification of the teaching procedures increased productive thinking and reduced routine thinking responses significantly. The evaluative thinking category showed a marked increase. Observation indicated that students would often proceed mentally through divergent as well as convergent operations and then respond at the evaluative level. For this reason, it appears that the explicit divergent thinking responses remained relatively the same throughout the experiment. Analysis of the tapescripts and the classification of the verbal responses support this hypothesis.

In contrast to the control groups, experimental group instruction was not geared to the student with the high MA but, as far as possible, to the full range of mental abilities. The lack of correlation between growth on the subject-matter tests and the mental age for experimental groups is consistent with this difference in method.

Hypothesis: Modifying the instructional methods should make no difference in measured growth of the subject-matter knowledge between the current and experimental teaching practices. In other words, it is expected that both the experimental and control groups will show equivalent growth in subject matter on post-tests, if the tests are based upon subject-matter concepts and facts.

This hypothesis is accepted. Three of the four experimental groups not only showed no loss but actually showed greater growth than the control groups. The gain of experimental over the control group C was statistically significant at the .01 level. In the total combined groups, application of the t-test for significant differences produced a t-ratio of 1.56 in favor of the experimental group. While this was not large enough to be significant statistically, at the .05 level it was approaching significance. Control group D showed a slightly greater but nonsignificant gain over experimental group D. It was clearly demonstrated that students can experience a wider range of intellectual activities with no loss in subject-matter growth.

Hypothesis: Through practice in the use of a wider range of mental processes over a short period of time, students in the experimental groups will show a greater growth on tests of creativity than students in control groups.

This hypothesis is true for four of ten measures and of no significant difference for the other six. The experimental group achieved four statistically significant gains on the measures of creativity over the control group. The control groups had no significant gains over the experimental group. In every measure involving ideational fluency, the experimental group made statistically significant gains over the control group. The factor of originality was approaching significance.

There is no question that students can be placed in a classroom situation that will release and foster their creative ability. The increase in the correlations between the verbal responses and creativity points to the real opportunity of releasing creative and productive potential in students as opposed to the continued depression of creativity by the traditional classroom methods. Much work now needs to be done in revising curricula. One of the main objectives of the in-service training period was to increase ideational fluency through new methods over a short period of time. This objective was achieved. Yet the explicit divergent thinking responses did not increase as much as was anticipated.

Hypothesis: Students who measure high on the creativity tests do not have much of an opportunity to use their creative potential in the typical control classroom.

This hypothesis is accepted. The control group was literally controlled. The high correlations between the verbal response categories and mental age for the control groups is a strong indication of the fact that traditional classroom instruction is designed for the student with the high MA and not the productive and creative students. In the experimental groups, in contrast, correlations between the verbal responses and mental age decreased. The number of significant correlations between the tests of creativity and the verbal response categories was greater for the experimental groups than for the control groups. When the opportunity to be more creative and productive in the classroom was present, the number of significant correlations between creativity and verbal response increased two to one in favor of the experimental group.

When instructional methods favored the high MA students, as they do in the traditional classroom, there was little correlation between the measures of creativity and the verbal responses produced in the classroom. When methods favored the full range of mental abilities found in the classroom, there was a high correlation between the measures of creativity and the verbal responses produced in the classroom. The method, then, was the controlling factor in determining who would respond. Student growth in subject matter depended greatly upon the role the student was allowed or encouraged to play in the classroom situation. When the low MA student was allowed to contribute and his contribution was accepted, his growth was often as great as that of the high MA student. There was evidence, in fact, that when new stars from the lower MA range started to emerge, the high MA students started to lose ground. It is quite possible that the creative and productive change in the role of the low MA student produced a threat to the traditional status and efficiency of the high MA.

Hypothesis: There is a positive correlation between creativity test scores and the total productive thinking in live educational situations.

This hypothesis can be accepted. Every measure of creativity produced a significant correlation between the test and total productivity for the combined experimental group, while six of the ten measures produced significant correlations for the combined control groups. Creativity scores are thus as good as IQ or MA scores in determining which students will be the verbally productive and creative. The more that control class instruction approached the experimental procedures, the more indicative were the measures of creativity. The more traditional the class instruction, the less indicative were the measures of creativity in predicting the students who would be creative and productive.

Hypothesis: When provision is made in the classroom for permitting productive thinking, children who measure high in the creativity tests will tend to produce more verbal responses in the productive and evaluative thinking categories.

Although this hypothesis was not proven to be correct from a statistically supported standpoint, it could not be rejected. High creative students produced a greater number of responses (raw scores and percentages) in the total productive category. Students did tend to produce more verbal productive responses in the experimental climate. However, only in evaluative thinking was the number of responses as statistically significant.

We do not yet know how to increase divergent and convergent thinking significantly.

Some additional conclusions are not directly related to any of the major hypotheses. It is evident that there is a positive relationship between mental age and creativity. Yet there are many students who have high mental ability, but do not produce creatively. Conversely, there are many students who produce creatively but do not necessarily have a high MA. Productive thinking follows a similar pattern. High MA and creativity do not necessarily go hand in hand, and neither do high MA and productivity. Productivity and creativity are more likely to correlate than either is to match MA. The student may be productive in convergent and evaluative ability and not in divergent ability. A student high in divergent verbal responses was likely to be high in total productive verbal responses. Every student who was rated as a creative star was also rated as a productive star. The evidence suggests that some students may be fortunate in having a high total profile, *i.e.,* a high MA, high creative ability, and high productive ability. Such a high profile student may easily dominate the entire classroom situation.

Traditionally girls have been rated as better students than boys and tend to have better grades. However, boys are more likely to produce creative responses than girls. Boys are also more likely to be productive thinkers than girls. It is possible that our social values make girls more likely to conform, and less exploratory. This seems true in the traditional classroom. The boy's role is traditionally more exploratory and searching and thus more creative. This tendency increases as classroom methods approach those used for experimental groups in this project.

REFERENCES

Carroll, J. B. A factor analysis of verbal abilities. *Psychometrika,* 1941, 6, 279–307.

Getzels, J. W., & Jackson, P. W. The highly intelligent and the highly creative adolescent: A summary of some research findings. In C. W. Taylor (Ed.), *The third research conference on the identification of creative scientific talent.* Salt Lake City: University of Utah Press, 1959. Pp. 46–57.

Guilford, J. P. Factorial angles to psychology. *Psychological Review,* 1961, 68, 1–20.

Guilford, J. P. Intellectual resources and their values as seen by creative scientists. In C. W. Taylor (Ed.), *The third research conference on the identification of creative scientific talent.* Salt Lake City: University of Utah Press, 1959. Pp. 128–149.

Guilford, J. P. The structure of intellect. *Psychological Bulletin,* 1956, 53, 267–293.

Taylor, C. E. Development of a theory of education from psychological and other research findings. U. S. Office of Education, Research Project 621, 1962.

20 | Developing the skills of productive thinking[1]

ROBERT M. OLTON
RICHARD S. CRUTCHFIELD
University of California, Berkeley

From Trends and Issues in Developmental Psychology *edited by Paul Mussen, Jonas Langer, and Martin Covington. Copyright © 1969 by Holt, Rinehart and Winston, Inc. Reprinted by permission of Holt, Rinehart and Winston, Inc.*

The *Productive Thinking Program* is one of the very few sets of materials designed to improve creative-problem-solving skills in the schools. After sketching the critical need for such training, Olton and Crutchfield summarize the purposes and content of the materials and describe the outcome of one of their most recent field tests. They convincingly argue that in the 16 hours necessary for fifth- and sixth-grade students to complete the program, most students become more systematic and more imaginative problem solvers. Furthermore, students' attitudes related to creative thinking (such as open-mindedness and appreciation for novel ideas) are noticeably enhanced, and their perceptions of themselves as capable thinkers are improved.

Cognitive development of the individual proceeds in gradual, sequential stages—from the emergence of the most elementary perceptual functions in the young child through the elaboration of the most complex processes of productive thinking in the adult. Whether or not this cognitive growth

[1] The study reported here was made possible by a grant from the Carnegie Corporation of New York to the Institute of Personality Assessment and Research in support of a project directed by Dr. Richard S. Crutchfield and Dr. Martin V. Covington. This study was carried out at Cragmont School in the Berkeley (California) Unified School District. We wish to express our great appreciation to those whose cooperation made this study possible—Dr. Harold J. Maves, Assistant Superintendent for Instruction; Miss Glena Crumal, Principal of Cragmont School; and particularly the fifth- and sixth-grade teachers at Cragmont, who played an indispensable role.

can be accelerated appreciably by providing specific training of the various functions at appropriate stages is still a moot question. Most of the research on this issue has dealt with attempts to train the simpler processes in the young child, such as efforts to produce earlier acquisition of the concept of conservation. Relatively little has been done with the training of the more complex thought processes as these develop in the older child.

However, regardless of whether or not specific training can significantly speed up the time at which the various cognitive capacities *emerge,* it seems clear to us that the ability and readiness to *use* these capacities efficiently and effectively at any given stage of development can benefit substantially from direct training. This appears to be particularly true of the higher-level functions central to productive thinking and problem solving —our observations convince us that, for most individuals and at all age levels from the child to the adult, there exists a pronounced gap between productive thinking *potential* and productive thinking *performance.* To close this gap and to achieve a level of highly skilled productive thinking, the simpler cognitive functions must first be organized and integrated into appropriate skills. Since the development of any kind of skills (motor or mental) requires specific training, we believe that appropriate training can produce significant increments in the skills of productive thinking. In this article results from a recent school study are presented to confirm this view. Such results have both theoretical importance for the light they shed on the developmental stages of high-level cognitive processes, and practical significance in their implications for educational aims and methods.

The need to end "thoughtless" education

Systematic programs for teaching the student how to think should be one of the central concerns of education at all levels and for all types of pupils. An education without such instruction will produce adults who are destined eventually to become crippled by their own obsolete patterns of thought and by knowledge that is no longer relevant, to become confused and then overwhelmed by a vastly changed future society in which they will no longer know how to participate.

Since today's education emphasizes mastery of the *known,* it does very little to prepare an individual to cope effectively with the *unknown.* Yet many of today's school children will be spending more than half their lifetime in the unknown world of the twenty-first century. To cope effectively with the unknown, an individual must have a well-developed ability to think. Thus, an education that will prepare today's student for a useful, fulfilling life in the twenty-first century must provide him with extensive, systematic instruction in the skills required for original, independent thinking and problem solving.

This coming century will present man with enormously complex and urgent problems: how to limit population size, so that the "human" qualities of life will not be suffocated by the cruelly impersonal demands of life in an overcrowded world; how to cope in the coming computer age so that man, and not the machine, will be the master; how to find fulfillment, rather than an aimless boredom, in the leisure that will result from a three-day (or shorter) work week; how to deal with the consequences of man's awesome ability to change his capabilities and perhaps his very nature through the use of powerful new biochemical techniques; how to construct an urban environment that will bring out the best rather than the worst qualities of its citizens and make urban life a source of profound human satisfaction rather than of destructive frustration.

It is sobering to realize that it is *today's* students—not some comfortably distant generation—who are going to have to deal with these staggering problems. It is today's students who must be prepared for a world in which their ability to function will not depend on their mastery of the facts and principles now taught in school, but rather on their ability to deal with new facts and principles that have not yet even been imagined. It is today's students whose search for personal satisfaction and fulfillment will require them to reevaluate and restructure their beliefs and actions in accord with a vastly different and constantly changing world where many of today's beliefs and customs will seem irrelevant or even absurd. Thus it is today's students who should be receiving extensive, systematic instruction in how to think. This should be the very center of their education, for a "thoughtless" education makes the student an ultimate prisoner—rather than master—of his own knowledge and beliefs.

Fortunately, recognition of the need for teaching the student *how* to think, rather than *what* to think, is one of the central themes of the innovative movements now taking place in American education. Several recent noteworthy books by educators and researchers have stressed the importance of productive thinking in the schools (Aschner and Bish, 1965; Torrance, 1965; Fair and Shaftel, 1967) and this emphasis is reflected in the new curricula in mathematics, science, and social studies.

When parents in a recent nationwide Gallup survey were asked to rate the importance of some 48 possible goals of public school education, they gave a particularly high rating to "the ability to figure things out for oneself" as contrasted with relatively low ratings for many of the traditional educational goals. A similar note was recently sounded by a blue-ribbon citizens' committee in California which made the following recommendation to that state's Board of Education: "Let the schools concentrate on the heart of the matter, which is training pupils to think for themselves. Education should center around the ability to solve problems."

It seems clear that the kind of probem solving that these educators and citizens are talking about is not that of the cut-and-dried arithmetic problem or the exercise in formal logic. Their concern is with the kind of problem solving that requires the individual to do independent thinking and to strive to achieve his own solutions to complex problems. Such productive thinking involves generating original ideas, looking at a problem in a new or different way if one gets "stuck," asking insightful questions, and seeing the implications of crucial facts or events. It involves working in an organized, planned manner on problems that seem to resist solution, formulating and evaluating new possibilities, and developing a sensitivity to odd or unusual circumstances that may lead to a discovery or fresh insight.

This is the kind of thinking that will better equip an individual to cope with the unknowns of life in the year 2000. This is the kind of thinking that enables a person to deal intelligently and effectively with his own problems and opportunities, and that will provide him with an increasing sense of enjoyment in the use of his mind. And it is this kind of thinking in which today's student should (but does not) receive extensive, systematic instruction.

A program for the development of productive thinking skills

In order to help meet the need for instructional materials that will increase the student's ability to do this kind of thinking, *The Productive Thinking Program* (Covington, Crutchfield, and Davies, 1966) has recently been developed. This set of booklet materials, designed primarily for fifth- and sixth-grade students, provides systematic instruction and carefully guided practice in the skills of productive thinking and problem solving. The 16 programmed booklets are individually self-administered and self-paced, each requiring approximately one hour.

These materials have been used in a series of school studies (e.g., Covington and Crutchfield, 1965; Crutchfield, 1966; Olton, Wardrop, et al., 1967) and have consistently been found to produce significant gains in student performance on a variety of tests of productive thinking. Specifically, the trained students have demonstrated strengthened skills in such cognitive functions as generating ideas of high quality, asking relevant questions, being sensitive to crucial clues, making effective use of information, and achieving solutions to problems. These gains have been found to occur across a wide spectrum of ability levels—among low achievers as well as high, among the culturally disadvantaged as well as the advantaged.

These consistently positive outcomes support our view that properly directed training can bring about a measurable improvement in the individual's skilled *use* of his gradually developing capacities for productive thought. It is noteworthy that the amount of training we have employed in these studies is relatively modest (16 hours total) and that the conditions of training have been far short of optimal. For example, in the largest of the studies, that of 47 fifth-grade classes in Racine, Wisconsin (Olton, Wardrop, et al., 1967), the training was severely compressed into a four-week period, thus losing the advantages of distributed practice, and the materials were taken by each student entirely alone, without the support of teacher help or class discussion. Yet even under these restrictive conditions, the training produced an appreciable improvement in the students' thinking ability.

The present study

The school study reported in this article was carried out under conditions designed to maximize the impact of the training and hence to prove the upper limits of effectiveness of this instructional program.

This study went beyond the previous ones in four principal ways. First, the training period was extended from four weeks to eight weeks. Second, the teacher was brought into an active role in the instructional program, stimulating and guiding class discussions of the materials. Third, the basic 16-lesson series was augmented by a set of supplementary problem exercises that gave the student considerably more practice in using the productive thinking skills and strategies taught in the basic lessons. Finally, to enhance the transfer of these skills and strategies to a broad spectrum of problems representative of the several main school curriculum areas, the contents of these supplementary practice exercises were widely diversified, touching on social studies, science, human relations, and current affairs. A comparable variety of educationally relevant thinking tasks was included in the criterion battery of tests used to assess the effectiveness of the instructional program.

A total of 280 students, comprising five fifth-grade and five sixth-grade classes, participated in this study. These students were generally above average in intellectual ability. The mean IQ of the group was 115, with a range of IQ's from 80 to 150. The mean level of performance on six subtests of the Stanford Achievement Battery was approximately one and one-half school years ahead of the students' current grade level.

Most of the detailed results reported in this paper will focus on a comparison of two groups of fifth-grade students drawn from the total group, for whom the fullest test information is available. In order to equate these two groups for the influence of a particular teacher and a particular classroom climate, a split-class technique was used. Half the students from each of two fifth-grade classrooms were selected to receive instruction in productive thinking (Instruction group), while the other half of each class served as a noninstructed Control group. These two groups, of 25 students each, were matched as closely as possible with respect to IQ and achievement. Although the Instruction group showed a slight superiority and somewhat greater variance on both measures, these differences were far short of statistical significance (Table 1).

Both groups were given a pretest battery of productive thinking problems to determine the extent to which any differences in productive thinking proficiency existed before instruction began. Then during the next

Table 1   IQ and Achievement Scores of Instruction and Control Groups.

Measure	Instruction		Control	
	Mean	S.D.	Mean	S.D.
IQ	117.50	17.00	113.50	14.00
Achievement	6.88	1.64	6.60	1.36

eight weeks the Instruction group devoted approximately one hour per school day to instruction in productive thinking, while the Control group spent this same daily hour in an activities program consisting of stories, movies, and various projects chosen to interest the children and to have general educational value, but not to relate to productive thinking. At the end of the eight-week period, performance of the two groups was compared on an extensive post-test battery of thinking problems. Six months later their performance was again compared on a follow-up battery of thinking tests.

The instructional materials

The augmented version of *The Productive Thinking Program* used in this study contained two types of self-instructional material: (a) a set of 16 programmed lessons that provided direct instruction and a certain amount of guided practice in productive thinking and problem solving; (b) a set of supplementary exercises intended to strengthen the skills taught in the programmed lessons by giving the student extensive practice in using these general skills on productive thinking tasks representative of a variety of subject-matter areas.

The basic lessons

Each of the 16 programmed lessons is an individual booklet that features an engaging detective-type mystery problem that the student is called on to solve. As the mystery unfolds, the student is given instruction in appropriate productive thinking skills: how to generate many ideas, particularly clever and unusual ones; how to evaluate his ideas with respect to relevant facts and conditions of the problem; how to look at the problem in a different and more fruitful way if he gets "stuck"; how to clarify the essentials of a problem and work on it in an organized and planful way. At various points in the booklet lessons, the student practices using such skills and writes down his ideas, questions, or suggestions for what should be done next. Feedback or confirmation of his efforts is then provided on the succeeding pages in the form of a set of responses illustrative of those that would be appropriate at that point in the problem. Through such repeated guided practice of basic thinking skills in a variety of problem contexts, the student is led to understand what constitute relevant and original ideas, how to proceed fruitfully when faced with a challenging problem, and what effective strategies to use when one encounters difficulties.

Each of these lessons is self-administering, permitting the student to progress through the problem at his own pace and in accord with his particular reading level and intellectual capacity. The major points taught in each lesson are summarized for the student at the end of the booklet.

Student interest is readily engaged by the mystery theme and cartoon-text format of the lessons, and also by a continuous storyline that features two children of the student's age, Jim and Lila Cannon. Jim and Lila are intended to serve as stimulating "companions" for the reader as he pursues these intellectual adventures, and they are presented as typical children with whom the reader can identify—likable, human, and quite capable of making mistakes. As the series develops, a number of constructive changes occur in Jim's and Lila's attitudes toward thinking and in their sense of confidence in their own abilities. At the same time, a subtle but sustained attempt is made to increase the student's own interest in and liking for activities that involve the use of the mind, and to build up his willingness to work on thinking tasks in a persistent and concentrated way. Each lesson is so designed that, as the student works through the problem, he is led eventually to discover the solution for himself, thus giving him the thrill of discovery and helping him develop a sense of confidence in his ability to cope with difficult and challenging intellectual tasks. A brief segment of one of these lessons is illustrated on pages 246 through 248.

The detective-mystery content of these programmed lessons captures student interest and serves as an excellent vehicle for teaching productive thinking skills, but such content does not give the student direct practice in applying these skills to the types of problems found in the subject matter of the usual school curriculum. That function is fulfilled by the supplementary exercises.

The supplementary exercises

These exercises reinforce and strengthen the skills taught by the basic lessons and give the student repeated, guided practice in using these skills on curriculum-relevant tasks.

One of the exercises, shown in Figure 1, concerns the currently pressing problem of how to dispose of the ever-growing quantities of waste materials produced by our society—a problem clearly relevant to social studies and science. This exercise was administered to the student the day after he had worked on a lesson that showed him how to *look at a problem in a new and different way if one approach to solving it does not work.*

The students first worked on this exercise individually and then

Thinking about waste is not wasted thinking:

All cities and towns today are faced with the problem of what to do about the huge and constantly increasing amounts of trash, garbage, and other waste materials produced in homes and industries.

Experts have been working on various ways of destroying this waste material. They have thought of many methods for doing this—such as burning it so it makes little smoke, dissolving it with special chemicals, crushing it under high pressure, etc. But they are still searching for better methods of destroying the waste materials, and they need more ideas.

Now you try to look *in a new and different way* at this problem of what the cities can do about the huge and constantly increasing amounts of waste material. The experts have been asking themselves, "How can we *destroy* the waste material?" But a new way to look at the problem would be to ask the question:

_____
_____
_____
_____
_____

Another new and different way of looking at this problem would be to ask the question:

_____
_____
_____
_____
_____
_____

Figure 1   Sample page from a supplementary exercise of *The Productive Thinking Program.*

shared their ideas in a class discussion. During this discussion, the teacher sought to guide and clarify the students' understanding of what it means to look at a problem in a new and different way (as opposed to thinking only of new variations of a single approach). The teacher was assisted by a Teacher's Guide that suggested some new ways of looking at the waste disposal problem. One new way might be to ask the question: "What could be done to *produce less waste in the first place?*" (For example, packaging foods by spraying them with a specially developed plastic coating that would dissolve in warm water, thus eliminating the trash produced by containers.)

Another way of looking at the problem might be to ask: "What could be done to *transform waste materials into useful products?*" (For example, chemically converting the waste into fertilizers, fuel, insulation, or other building materials.) Yet another way of looking at the problem is to ask: "How could the waste materials be *used as a filler material?*" (For example, filling in gullies in eroded land and swamps.) These suggestions are, of course, by no means exhaustive, and the class discussions that took place in our study yielded additional ways of looking at this problem.

The basic lessons and the supplementary exercises were used in a carefully coordinated instructional schedule occupying approximately one hour per day for four days of each school week (the fifth day was used for individual make-ups) over a period of eight weeks. Typically, a basic lesson was given one day, followed on the next day by a brief class discussion and by a set of supplementary exercises related to that prior lesson. Two basic lessons and two sessions of supplementary exercises plus discussions were covered each week; thus the total instructional program occupied approximately 32 hours.

The intent was to give the student the materials under practical conditions approaching those of regular, large-scale school use, yet without pro-

Here's another thinking guide that will give you a method for discovering many of the different ideas about this problem.

What is it?

Pick out each of the important things in the story—each object and person. Then take each of these things one at a time, and try to figure out how it might have had something to do with the disappearance of the water.

This method will make sure that you don't miss any important part of the problem that could give you ideas.

Now, what will happen as Jim and Lila take Uncle John's advice? Turn the page to find out.

viding any special teacher training in productive thinking. Accordingly, the only preparation for the teacher was that supplied by a Teacher's Guide, which gave background information on the pedagogical aims and methods of *The Productive Thinking Program* and suggestions for administering the materials and conducting class discussions.

Criterion measures of productive thinking

The effects of the eight-week instructional program were assessed by comparing the performance of Instruction and Control groups on three batteries of specially created productive thinking tasks. These tasks are unlike most regular school tests in that they are not primarily concerned with how much the student *knows,* but rather with how well he *thinks.* In the construction of these tasks, particular effort was made to minimize the importance of specific knowledge, and to design tasks that the student would find novel and challenging and that would tap his ability to perform a variety of productive thinking functions on problems having educational relevance.

For example, in one task the student read an account of the migratory behavior of a hypothetical flock of birds, including facts about variations

in the size of the flock at different points on the route. Embedded in the account were several puzzling and unexplained circumstances in the birds' behavior (such as the fact that the size of the flock dropped sharply during one portion of the flight and never recovered). The student was asked to

A problem of poverty in a land of plenty:

When Americans travel abroad, they are sometimes asked how can it be that the United States, the richest nation in the world, is faced with such a great problem of poverty among many of its people.

Some people in other nations say they are puzzled by the fact that in spite of the great wealth of our nation, many of our cities have great slum areas, many of our people are dependent for their support on relief and welfare funds, and many of our people do not share in the American dream of enjoying a high standard of living.

Now, suppose that you and your family are visiting a foreign country this summer. Some children your age in that country ask you about why the United States is faced with such a problem of poverty. What would you say?

Take time to think about this; then write below what you would say to them about this puzzling problem of poverty in a land of plenty. (There are several additional blank pages attached to this page, so you may write as much as you wish.)

Figure 2   A sample productive thinking test item.

write down anything about the behavior of this flock that struck him as odd or puzzling, and later, after having had the several puzzling facts pointed out to him, to try to devise an explanation that could account for these facts. The student's responses were scored for the total number of puzzling facts noticed and for the total number of puzzling facts satisfactorily explained.

In another of the tasks, the student was told that during his lifetime, medical science will have made it possible to transplant various organs of the body from one person to another. He was then asked to consider the many possible consequences of such a technological advance and to list as many different such consequences as he could, both medical and nonmedical.[2] The student's responses were scored on three variables: number of acceptable ideas generated; number of main categories of ideas reflected in this list (cognitive breadth); number of relevant information-seeking questions asked.

In still another task (Figure 2) the student was asked to write an essay about the urgent social problem of poverty. The number of causes of

[2] When we gave this problem it was intended to evoke thinking about a purely hypothetical medical possibility of the future. Eight months later came the first successful transplant of a human heart by Dr. Christian Barnard in South Africa. Thus the future overtook the present, and the productive thinking skills intended for the world of tomorrow had to be pressed into service to deal with the world of today. No doubt this pattern of future developments that suddenly and unexpectedly become present realities is an occurrence that will be repeated often during the lives of these students; hence the necessity of providing them with appropriate thinking skills now.

poverty mentioned and the number of suggestions made about how to end poverty were scored as indices of productive thinking in this task.

As a final example, the student worked on a hypothetical problem in archeology, in which he was asked to discover which one of ten possible persons was buried in a nameless ancient tomb. He was scored on the number of appropriate strategic steps that he could specify for attacking the problem, on correct elimination of suspects who did not fit the facts, and on achievement of final solution of the problem—successful identification of the person who was buried in the tomb. The total set of tasks making up the three test batteries is as follows.

Pretests

Controlling the weather — Student thinks of various consequences of man's future ability to change the weather.

Project for a village — Student puts himself in the shoes of a Peace Corps volunteer who must first acquaint himself with the customs and mores of a tribal village. Then, without offending such customs, he must figure out ways the inhabitants can earn money for their village needs.

Post-tests

Transplanting organs — Student thinks of various consequences of man's future medical ability to transplant bodily organs from one person to another.

"Black House" problem — Student attempts to solve a puzzling mystery problem in which he must make an insightful reorganization of the elements of the problem.

A visit to Karam — Student puts himself in the shoes of a diplomat who is the first outsider in 50 years allowed into a small country. He sees many puzzling things on his short visit. Student attempts to explain what is going on in this country.

Conflict among tribes — Student attempts to generate new and more fruitful ways of looking at an intertribal problem faced by many newly independent African nations.

Bird migration — Student reads an account of the migratory behavior of a hypothetical flock of birds. He is asked to note anything about the behavior of the flock that

	seems puzzling, and to try to account for these puzzling facts.
Poverty essay	Student writes an essay in which he has the opportunity to demonstrate his thinking ability in connection with the problem of poverty.

Follow-up Tests

The missing jewel problem	Student attempts to solve a puzzling mystery problem in which he must make an insightful reorganization of the elements of the problem.
The nameless tomb	Student works on a hypothetical problem in archeology in which he must discover which of ten possible suspects is buried in a nameless ancient tomb.
The lost colony	Student reacts to the challenge of a problem that requires thinking about the puzzling failure of the first attempted English colony in the New World.
Understanding thinking	Student indicates what thinking strategies are useful at various stages of work on a complex problem.
Natural resources essay	Student writes an essay in which he has the opportunity to demonstrate his thinking ability in connection with the problem of conserving natural resources.

Several points about this set of tasks should be underlined. First, it is obvious that the tasks are highly diverse in content. Second, the tasks vary widely along a convergent-divergent dimension of thinking—from those that are fairly well *structured,* permitting only a limited range of acceptable responses (for example, the bird migration problem) to those that are open-ended, permitting much greater scope for creativity in responses (for example, the poverty essay). Third, the tasks are chosen so as to reflect in some degree virtually all the important components of productive thinking.

Composite performance scores

All the Instruction and Control students took the three different batteries of productive thinking tests. The pretest battery was administered one week before the instructional program began; the post-test battery was administered just after the eight-week instructional period had ended; the follow-up battery was given six months after the post-test.

In each of the three batteries, a given student's performance was summarized in a single composite score that reflected his overall productive thinking skill, based on the various measures in that battery. The composite score was compiled in the following manner. For each variable, the scores of all students (both Instruction and Control) were pooled and arranged in a frequency distribution. Any student whose score fell above the median of this distribution was given one point on the variable, while any student scoring at or below the median received no credit on the variable. The composite score was the sum of points earned on all the variables of the test battery. For example, five variables were scored in the pretest, so the maximum composite score possible for that battery was five (indicating that such a student had scored above the median on all five variables) and the lowest possible score was zero. Similarly, 13 variables were scored in the post-test battery, permitting a maximum composite score of 13, while a maximum score of 10 was possible on the 10-variable follow-up battery.

The use of such composite scores as summary indices of overall productive thinking skill adds considerable stability and generality to the following analyses of results.

Results

Table 2   Composite Performance Scores of Instruction and Control Groups on Productive Thinking Test Batteries.

Test Battery	Instruction		Control		t*	p
	Mean	S.D.	Mean	S.D.		
Pretest	2.36	1.47	2.52	1.36	0.39	n.s.
Post-test	7.12	2.78	4.76	2.69	2.69	<.01
Follow-up	5.20	1.77	3.40	1.68	3.15	<.005

* $df = 48$

Table 2 compares the composite productive thinking scores of the Instruction and Control groups on each of the three test batteries. The findings may be summarized as follows:

1. Performances of the Instruction and Control groups were nearly identical on the pretest battery, indicating that they were well matched in productive thinking proficiency before instruction began. Indeed, the small difference that did exist favored the Control group.

2. After the instructional program had been completed, a clear and substantial superiority in thinking was shown by the students who had received instruction.

3. On the follow-up battery, performance of the Instruction group continued to surpass that of the Control group by a significant margin. Thus the gain in thinking skills produced by the eight weeks of instruction was still evident more than six months after instruction had ended.

The most comprehensive measure of thinking performance was obtained by combining each student's scores on the post-test and follow-up test batteries. This measure reflected his overall performance based on 23 different indices of productive thinking, and hence was a measure of considerable scope. The clear superiority of the instructed students on this measure is graphically demonstrated in Figure 3, which shows the distributions of scores for the Control and the Instruction groups.

Note that the entire distribution of scores for the Instruction group of students is shifted more or less uniformly upward as compared with the distribution of the Control group. This implies that the positive effect of training was not limited to only a few of the instructed students but was evident across the board regardless of whether a student was initially low or high in thinking proficiency. The sheer magnitude of this effect can be appreciated by noting the point at which the median of scores for all the

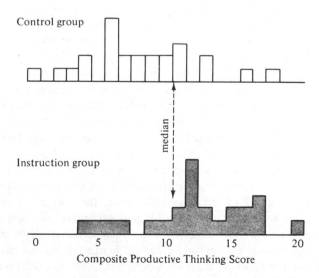

Figure 3   Distributions of 23-item productive thinking composite scores for Instruction and Control groups, showing the median of the combined groups. A significantly higher proportion of Instruction than of Control students scored above this median ($x^2 = 22.09$, p < .001).

students cuts the two distributions. The fact is that 72 percent of the Instruction group fall above this midpoint, while only 24 percent of the Control group do so.

Specific examples of training effect

The preceding results are based on composite performance scores which, although valuable for summary purposes, give no information about the effects of the training on specific tests or specific functions of productive thinking. We will present a few such specific data now.

In the post-test "bird migration" problem, the student was asked to try to explain three puzzling facts about the migratory behavior of a hypothetical flock of birds. Students in the Control group managed to explain an average of 1.08 of these facts, while students in the Instruction group were able to account for an average of 1.90—nearly twice as many. Moreover, if we consider only those students who were able to account for all three puzzling facts, it is found that 38 percent of the Instruction students were able to do so, as compared with only 12 percent of the Control students—a superiority of three-to-one.

Another example of the increased thinking skill of the Instruction group can be seen in performance on the "nameless tomb" problem of the follow-up test battery. In this hypothetical archeology problem, the student's task was to figure out which one of ten possible personages was buried in a nameless ancient tomb. Seven of these suspects could easily be eliminated on the basis of a few simple facts contained in the problem that made it impossible for any of those individuals to be buried there. Of the three remaining suspects, one was rendered the most likely by a clue that was obvious, but the significance of which was apparent only if the student was able to break free of one line of thought and to entertain another main possibility. Throughout the problem, the student was given a great deal of prompting in the form of suggestions, hints, and leading questions; the intent was to present him with a problem in which the strategic plan of attack had already been worked out for him, so that his task would be straightforward and relatively easy. With such careful guidance, the Control students demonstrated a respectable level of performance; for example, 37 percent of them correctly eliminated the seven suspects who could not have been buried in the tomb. However, they were far surpassed by the Instruction students, of whom 69 percent made the correct eliminations. Moreover, while 91 percent of the Instruction students were able to grasp the significance of the final clue and hence solved the problem, only 58 percent of the Control students were able to do so. Differences of this magnitude, obtained some six months after the instructional program had ended, indicate significant and enduring facilitation of the skills required in insightful use of data in problem solving.

A final example can be seen in quite a different type of thinking task,

the "poverty essay" (Figure 2). As we have said, this task was entirely
open-ended, the student being left completely free to write whatever he
wished about this important social problem. His essay was scored on three
variables: (a) the number of *descriptions* of poverty included in the essay
(e.g., "The people don't have any money"; "Their houses are broken
down"); (b) the number of *causes* of poverty mentioned (e.g., "They got
replaced by machines"; "Some of them are black and there's discrimination"); (c) the number of suggestions made about *how poverty might be
ended*. The mean scores of Instruction and Control groups on the first two
of these variables are presented in Table 3.

**Table 3   Performance of Instruction and Control Groups
on Post-test Poverty Essay Task.**

Variables	Instruction		Control		Significance Test	p
	Mean	S.D.	Mean	S.D.		
Number of Descriptions	2.20	2.63	1.68	1.55	$t = 0.82$ *	n.s.
Number of Causes	4.72	3.98	1.50	1.44	$\chi^2 = 9.63$ †	$<.002$

* $df = 45$
† The nonparametric median test was used here because of the large difference in the
variances of Instruction and Control groups.

Note first that the Instruction and Control groups did not differ significantly in the number of purely descriptive statements about poverty
they offered. Such descriptive statements require no productive thinking on
the problem; they represent at best some nominal grasp by the student of
the concept of poverty. Thus, we can infer that the two groups were
roughly equivalent in basic *knowledge* about poverty.

In terms of the amount of *thinking* demonstrated in the essays, however, the two groups differed considerably. One evidence of this is given
by the greater number of causes of poverty mentioned by the Instruction
students. This variable differs from most of the other performance variables in that it is not so much a measure of the student's *ability* to think as
it is an index of his actual *readiness* to do so. The student was not specifically directed or urged to mention causes of poverty in this open-ended
essay; he was entirely free to write whatever he wished. Hence, choosing
to consider causes of poverty is a step toward self-initiated productive
thinking on this problem. In light of this consideration, it is impressive
that students in the Instruction group mentioned an average of nearly five
causes per essay, more than three times the Control students' average of
1.5 (Table 3). An additional step toward creative thinking was taken by
those few students who went on to suggest ways that poverty might be
ended. Of the five students who did so, four were in the Instruction group.

Taken together, these findings indicate that one of the results of the instructional program was to strengthen the student's readiness to think even when not required to do so by the specific task. Such a positive set toward productive use of the mind is, of course, a prime goal of education.

IQ and the effects of instruction

The results presented so far show that the Instruction group as a whole demonstrated substantial and enduring gains in productive thinking skills from having participated in the instructional program. Beyond this, however, it is important to know whether these gains occurred for students throughout a wide range of intellectual ability, or whether the effectiveness of instruction was limited primarily to students of a particular IQ level— for instance, to the gifted. To investigate this question, the Instruction and Control groups were each subdivided: students with IQ's above 115 were placed in the so-called high-IQ subgroup, while all other students were placed in the so-called average-IQ subgroup. The IQ means and ranges of the subgroups, presented in Table 4, indicate that the subgroups were appropriately named.

Table 4   IQ and Composite Productive Thinking Score for Average-IQ and High-IQ Subgroups.

	Instruction			Control		
Subgroup	IQ Mean	IQ Range	Composite Score	IQ Mean	IQ Range	Composite Score
Average-IQ	99.0	(80-110)	10.0	102.8	(86-114)	5.9
High-IQ	129.4	(116-148)	13.6	124.2	(116-140)	10.6

The mean performance score of each subgroup on the 23-item productive thinking composite is also presented in Table 4. Two of the findings are noteworthy:

1. At both high and average intelligence levels, the Instruction students outperformed the Control students by a sizable margin. This finding indicates that students at *both* levels of ability demonstrated significant instructional benefits, and confirms similar results in earlier studies with the program (Covington and Crutchfield, 1965; Olton, et al., 1967).

2. The performance of the high-IQ groups surpassed that of the average-IQ groups, both trained and untrained. Thus there is a positive relationship between IQ and performance on productive thinking tasks. Despite this relationship, the instructional effects were great enough that the performance score of the average-IQ students after training (10.0) was virtually as high as that of the high-IQ students who were not

trained (10.6). In other words, the program raised the level of thinking skill shown by an "average" student to the level typical of a student with an IQ some 25 points higher. Similar gains have been reported in a previous study using an earlier version of these materials (Covington and Crutchfield, 1965).

Gains of this magnitude imply that existing school programs are doing less than they should in teaching students how to think, because if the schools were being more effective in this regard, one would not expect to be able to produce these appreciable gains in thinking ability with a program of such modest proportions. Such gains produced in a relatively short period of time also imply that the instructional program did not achieve its effects by changing the basic cognitive *capacities* of the student. Rather, it seems likely that the program showed the student how to make far more effective *use* of the cognitive capacities he already had. Perhaps this point can be made best by citing the comment of one Instruction student on an end-of-the-study questionnaire. The student wrote: "Now I see that I'm not dumb; I just didn't know how to use my mind."

Change in attitudes

The progressive development of a skill, such as skill in productive thinking, is likely to be associated with positive attitudes toward that skill. On the one hand, the effectiveness of training in the skill may be reinforced by building up positive attitudes about it; on the other hand, the very growth of the successful skill may result in positive attitudes toward its use. An essential part of the process of developing productive thinking skills, therefore, is the promotion of positive attitudes toward productive thinking. Accordingly, *The Productive Thinking Program* includes not only direct instruction and practice in thinking performance but also some carefully interwoven material intended to influence the student's attitudes toward thinking. Considerable stress is placed on building up the student's positive evaluation of productive use of the mind and his confidence in his own abilities and potential as a thinker.

For these reasons an attempt was made in this study to measure some of the student's opinions and beliefs about productive thinking activities and to assess changes occurring in these opinions and beliefs as a result of the instructional program. This was done by means of an objective questionnaire, similar to the *Children's Attitude Inventory for Problem Solving* (Covington, 1966). The questionnaire consisted of 20 statements about productive thinking activities in the school setting, the student being asked to indicate the extent of his agreement or disagreement with each statement on a five-point scale. An overall index of positive attitudes toward productive thinking was obtained by summing the scale values for the 20 items. Sample statements (scored "plus" for agreement): "I am often curious about unexplained things around me and want to try to understand them"; "I think I have the makings of a really creative thinker." Sample statements (scored "plus" for disagreement): "Some students are just naturally poorer thinkers than others and there is nothing they can do about it"; "I often keep my ideas to myself because I think others may laugh at them."

This questionnaire was administered as part of all three test batteries (pretest, post-test, and follow-up) thus permitting an analysis of changes that occurred throughout the nine-month time period encompassed by the complete study. The pretest index score was found to be equivalent for the Control and the Instruction groups. On the post-test and the six-month follow-up, the students who had gone through the instructional program tended to change toward higher scores on the index, that is, tended to express beliefs and opinions more favorable to productive thinking activities and toward themselves as thinkers.

The greatest shift occurred between the pretest and the follow-up test, some nine months later. Of the Instruction students, 68 percent showed an increase in their favorability index over this period as compared with 42 percent of the Control students. However, the variance in individual scores was very large and the obtained differences were only marginally significant.

Much stronger evidence of the favorable impact of the instructional program on the attitudes of the students is given by their answers on a questionnaire evaluating the program, which was filled out at the end of the eight-week instructional period. Table 5 presents the results of this survey made of all 202 fifth-grade and sixth-grade students who went through the thinking program. Clearly, the majority of the students felt that they had improved in thinking skills, had come to enjoy using their minds more than before, and were favorably inclined toward further instruction in productive thinking.

Summary and conclusions

The instructional program described in this study produced substantial and enduring gains in the productive thinking skills of fifth- and sixth-grade students. These gains were evident on a broad variety of educationally relevant thinking tasks that involved many different aspects of productive thinking and varied widely in form and content. Students of a wide range of intellectual ability demonstrated such gains and many also developed somewhat more positive attitudes toward productive thinking as a result of the program.

The fact that these substantial and enduring gains could be produced by a program of modest proportions suggests that existing school programs are doing less than they should in teaching students how to think because, as already observed, if the schools were being more effective in this regard, it is unlikely that such a modest program would have had such im-

Table 5   Number of Students Choosing Each Alternative on an End-of-Instruction Questionnaire.*

1. Do you feel that *your thinking has improved* since you began working with the lessons in productive thinking?

1	14	87	86	11
became poorer	no change	improved slightly	improved quite a lot	improved greatly

2. Do you now *enjoy using your mind* more than you did before you began the lessons in productive thinking?

7	50	55	62	28
less than before	about the same as before	a little bit more than before	quite a bit more than before	very much more than before

3. Do you feel that the lessons and exercises in productive thinking have *helped you in your regular school work?*

3	61	96	27	11
have made me poorer in my regular school work	have not helped my regular school work	have helped slightly in my regular school work	have helped quite a bit in my regular school work	have helped a great deal in my regular school work

4. Do you feel that the lessons in productive thinking have made your *school work more interesting?*

4	95	48	39	13
have made it less interesting	have made it neither more nor less interesting	have made it slightly more interesting	have made it quite a bit more interesting	have made it a great deal more interesting

5. Do you think it would be a good idea for the students who are coming into this same grade next year to be given these lessons in productive thinking?

19	183
NO	YES

6. Would you like to have some new lessons in productive thinking as part of your school work next year?

89	106
NO	YES

* Total number of respondents was 202; a few of the questionnaires were incomplete.

pressive effects. Therefore, if the schools intend to make effective progress toward the newly emphasized goal of teaching the student *how* to think rather than merely teaching him *what* to think, there must be new educational programs designed to provide extensive, systematic instruction in productive thinking skills for all students and at all grade levels.

The results of this study also suggest that considerable increments in thinking proficiency can be produced by showing the student how to make more effective use of the basic cognitive capacities he already possesses, rather than by attempting to acclerate the emergence of basic capacities that normally develop at a later age. Since most current studies of developmental cognition are concerned with the emergence of basic capacities, we believe that far too little attention is being paid to the extent to which important gains in thinking ability might be achieved by providing appropriate instruction in the use of cognitive capacities that are naturally present at each successive stage of development. The results of the present study suggest that this latter aspect of cognitive development is an important area for future research.

REFERENCES

Aschner, Mary Jane, & Bish, C. F. (Eds.) *Productive thinking in education.* Washington, D.C.: National Education Association, 1965.

Covington, M. V. A childhood attitude inventory for problem solving. *Journal of Educational Measurement,* 1966, 3, 234.

Covington, M. V., & Crutchfield, R. S. Facilitation of creative problem solving. *Programmed Instruction,* 1965, 4 (4), 3–5, 10.

Covington, M. V., Crutchfield, R. S., & Davies, Lillian B. *The productive thinking program.* Berkeley, California: Brazelton Printing Co., 1966. 633 pp. (Augmented edition, by Covington, M. V., Crutchfield, R. S., Davies, Lillian B., & Olton, R. M., to be published in 1971 by Charles E. Merrill Publishing Co., Columbus, Ohio.)

Crutchfield, R. S. Creative thinking in children: Its teaching and testing. Brim, H., Crutchfield, R. S., & Holtzman, W. *Intelligence: Perspective 1965.* New York: Harcourt, Brace & World, 1966, 33–64.

Fair, Jean, & Shaftel, Fannie R. *Effective thinking in the social studies.* Washington, D.C.: National Council for the Social Studies (A Department of the National Education Association), 1967.

Olton, R. M., Wardrop, J. L., Covington, M. V., Goodwin, W. L., Crutchfield, R. S., Klausmeier, H. J., & Ronda, T. *The development of productive thinking skills in fifth-grade children.* Technical Report, Research and Development Center for Cognitive Learning. Madison, Wisconsin: University of Wisconsin, 1967.

Torrance, E. P. *Rewarding creative behavior: Experiments in classroom creativity.* Englewood Cliffs, N.J.: Prentice-Hall, 1965.

21 | Training creativity in adolescence: A discussion of strategy[1]

GARY A. DAVIS
University of Wisconsin

Reprinted with permission of the publisher from the article of the same title, in R. E. Grinder (Ed.), Studies in Adolescence II. New York: The Macmillan Company, 1969. Pp. 538–545.

Contemporary psychologists are beginning to do more than identify those traits characteristic of creative adolescents, for while a trait approach to creativity is indeed informative, it fails to suggest precisely how creativity may be enhanced. In the following paper, Davis suggests that creativity profitably may be conceptualized as consisting mainly of three trainable components: (1) appropriate creative *attitudes,* the most critical of which is a favorable attitude toward highly imaginative problem solutions; (2) various cognitive *abilities* which facilitate whatever mental abstracting, combining, perceiving, associating, and filling in gaps, and so on, contribute to the fluent production of original ideas; (3) *techniques* for the conscious and systematic production of new combinations of ideas. Further, by incorporating many concepts and principles from this three-part model, Davis describes a novel program for developing creativity in adolescents.

Psychological studies of the personalities and histories of artistic adolescents and of individuals scoring high or low on "creativity" tests have been successfully used to define numerous characteristics common to creative adolescents (Barron, 1958; Getzels and Jackson, 1962; Hammer, 1961; MacKinnon, 1962; Torrance, 1962). Typically independent, confident, and self-assertive, adolescents often involve themselves in radical, nonconforming, and imaginative situations. Their curiosity, which draws them toward

[1] This report was prepared pursuant to contract OE 5-10-154 with the United States Office of Education, Department of Health, Education, and Welfare, under the provisions of the Cooperative Research Program. Comments and suggestions on the manuscript by Susan E. Houtman and Mary L. Stelly are gratefully acknowledged.

the complex and ambiguous, extends both inward, rendering them intro-spective and fantasy-prone, and outward, making them energetic and per-sistent.

Identification of these traits, however, is not sufficient; adolescents must be trained to be creative in order to approach their education, inter-personal relations, and ultimately their careers from broader, more flexible perspectives. The following discussion, therefore, aims to clarify three major dimensions or parameters of creativity, i.e., attitudes, abilities, and creative-thinking techniques, to emphasize the training strategies underlying each, and to show how these parameters may be integrated into a coherent, plau-sible classroom program useful for developing adolescent creative potential.

Creative attitudes

Attitudes may be defined as learned, emotionally toned predispositions to react consistently, favorably or unfavorably, toward persons, objects, or ideas (Klausmeier and Goodwin, 1966, p. 343). The most important attitudes contributing specifically to creative development are those that predispose individuals to react favorably to new and innovative ideas and that stimu-late them to engage in imaginative behavior (e.g., Parnes, 1966).

In recognizing the importance of these concepts, researchers have devised strategies designed to shape attitudes conducive to spontaneous, creative productivity. Osborn's brainstorming, for example, suggests the necessity of favorable attitudes toward both one's own and others' wild, new ideas (Osborn, 1963). Effective brainstormers must be instructed never to criticize even the most far-fetched problem solutions; rather, they are en-couraged and reinforced for uninhibited idea production. The Covington, Crutchfield, and Davies (1966) *Productive Thinking Program,* which has been shown to improve problem-solving and creativity scores of fifth- and sixth-grade students, reveals the importance of positive attitudes towards open-mindedness, perseverance, and self-confidence in problem solving. Covington, et. al., repeatedly remind students that their "ideas can be as good as other people's," and that they should not "jump to conclusions" or "give up too easily." Also successfully used to improve creativity, the Myers and Torrance (1964, 1965a, 1965b, 1966a, 1966b) *Idea Books* seek to foster favorable attitudes toward novel combinations of ideas by reinforcing imaginative responses to such nonsense questions as "Does the sun sound tired today?"

Creative abilities

Despite the intrinsic complexity of the problem, psychologists have sought to distinguish various relatively unlearned mental abilities (Thur-stone, 1938). One of the most plausible analyses of abilities that may con-tribute specifically to creative behavior is that of Guilford (1962), who identified the abilities of *fluency,* the total number of ideas which can be produced in a given period of time, *flexibility,* the number of distinctly different categories of solutions to a problem, and *originality,* the uniqueness of the solutions. When asked to think of unusual uses for a brick, for example, more creative individuals not only list larger numbers of unusual brick uses, but their ideas tend to be of different types, e.g., make a doorstop, drown a cat, build a barbecue, hold test tubes. In addition to specifying these creative abilities, Guilford has suggested also that they may in fact be strengthened by giving students exercises similar to the tests measuring the particular abilities. For example, he assumed that if the number of responses to such tests as "List things which are solid, white, and edible" or "Name synonyms for the word *dark"* is a good indicator of the *fluency* ability, then the use of these tests as exercises might strengthen this ability.

Consistent with Guilford's suggestion of increasing abilities through exercise, Myers and Torrance attempt to both identify and strengthen a broad spectrum of simple and complex creative abilities. Children or adolescents, for example, are given exercises in remembering, free-associating, discerning problems, perceiving relationships, imagining and elaborating on wild ideas, predicting or making up consequences of unusual events, filling in information gaps, pretending, and being more aware of sights and sounds. They also are trained to use descriptive adjectives, to find unusual uses for common objects, and to make up story plots, puzzles, punch lines, mysteries, and even more exercises.

Creative thinking techniques

Creative-thinking techniques are conscious and deliberate procedures for producing new combinations of ideas. A major contribution of existing, professional level creativity programs has been to suggest techniques that may be readily adopted for classroom use. Osborn's brainstorming, operating on the principle of deferred judgment, is the best known. It encourages students to produce freely a large number of wild ideas, since the greater the number, the greater the likelihood of finding useful ones. In addition to contributing ideas of their own, students are encouraged to suggest how two or more ideas may be combined into still others.

While brainstorming may be effective, it is a relatively broad, unstructured approach to group or individual problem solving which mainly provides an atmosphere conducive to unrestrained imagination. There are, however, a number of more specific creative-thinking techniques that teach students precisely how to produce new and potentially valuable combinations of ideas. Let us consider, in order, the methods of (1) attribute listing, (2) morphological synthesis, (3) checklisting, and (4) synectics.

(1) The *attribute-listing* technique (Crawford, 1954; see also Davis,

Manske, and Train, 1967) is a simple and effective method for generating creative ideas to improve or change virtually anything. Using this method, teachers might ask students to itemize important attributes (or parts) of a product and then consider each attribute as a source of potential change or improvement. For example, with an object as simple as classroom chalk, students might learn to identify the attributes of size, shape, color, and material. Then, by considering changes for each of these individual attributes, ideas for a large variety of chalk may be quickly produced. While the usefulness of the attribute-listing procedure is limited to problems whose important attributes are identifiable, its scope is still wide: "Objects" in art, literature, science, business, and industry, for example, can be improved with this method. New ideas for writing short stories may be found by identifying and systematically changing such important attributes as the *setting, characters,* and *plot.* Or, in studying industry, students may learn to identify and improve the attributes of material, cost, market, and production processes. Attribute listing both sensitizes students to various properties of objects and equips them with a simple yet very productive means of innovation.

(2) The *morphological-synthesis* technique (Allen, 1966; Davis, Roweton, Train, Warren, and Houtman, 1969), which is fairly similar to that of attribute listing, may be used to produce more idea combinations than any other. Students first identify two or more important characteristics or dimensions (e.g., color, shape) of a problem and list specific values (e.g., red, blue, green; square, round, triangular) for each. They then examine all possible combinations, utilizing one value of each characteristic. For example, if students are asked to "invent" a new line of pop-up toasters, all combinations of 15 shapes, 20 different colors and color patterns, and 5 sizes would instantly produce 1500 possible products. It is possible, however, that a rigid application of the morphological analysis procedure conceivably might prevent a thinker from approaching a problem from different, more imaginative perspectives. For example, students intent on examining the 1500 combinations of ideas for pop-up toasters may fail to detect entirely new means of toasting bread. But the morphological-synthesis technique invariably produces an enormous quantity of idea combinations in a very short time and thus guarantees the production of idea combinations never before considered, some of which may prove to be surprisingly valuable.

(3) With the *checklist* procedure, students consider each item on a prepared list as a possible source of innovation in respect to a given problem (Osborn, 1963; Davis, Roweton, Train, Warren, and Houtman, 1969). In the classroom, for example, they may be taught to consult a history book as a "checklist" of ideas for writing themes or short stories. Faced with the problem of selecting a career, they might consult the Yellow Pages, a checklist containing thousands of vocational suggestions. Like-

wise, a department store catalogue would provide ideas for solving a gift-giving problem.

A recently developed checklist (Davis, *et. al,* 1969), intended to stimulate ideas for changing a product, includes just seven items: (1) add and/or subtract something; (2) change color; (3) vary materials; (4) rearrange parts; (5) vary shape; (6) change size; (7) modify design or style. Compared with the performance of control subjects, college students using this checklist produced a significantly larger number of creative ideas for changing or improving a *thumbtack* and a *kitchen sink.* For example, students improved a kitchen sink by adding a soap or hand lotion dispenser, by thinking of such unusual sink colors as orange or silver, by constructing the sink of such materials as nylon, plastic, or copper, by making it extra large or small in size, or by designing it in an Oriental or Scandinavian mode. The checklist essentially provided students with general categories of problem solutions which stimulated a large number of specific ideas.

One might argue that this technique could make students dependent on checklists, thus preventing them from "thinking for themselves." However, idea checklists mainly serve to stimulate original thinking. Thus, they are intended to supplement, not to replace, more intuitive forms of creative behavior.

(4) The *synectic* method (Gordon, 1961; Prince, 1968) mainly emphasizes the use of metaphors and similes, especially those drawn from nature. After posing a problem, teachers encourage students to ask how animals, insects, or even plants have solved similar problems. Solutions for a parking problem, for example, may be found by considering how bees or ants "store things." Proposing *ideal* but apparently ridiculous problem solutions, such as having insects work on command to solve a transportation problem, is another synectic method for stimulating new viewpoints on a problem. "Playing with" or free-associating word meanings may lead to still more new ideas. For example, speculating on the meaning of the word "opening" (cutting, prying, unfolding, etc.) may suggest new designs for a can opener. Ideas stimulated by using the synectic methods may seem "silly" and inappropriate for solving serious problems. However, it is exactly the wild, far-fetched, perhaps "silly" ideas which are sought, since these often lead to the most creative and workable problem solutions. For instance, when faced with the problem of inventing a vapor proof closure for space suits, one Synectic group imagined insects running up and down the closure manipulating little latches—a far-fetched idea which led to a workable air-tight zipper (Gordon, 1961, pp. 48–51).

The above parameters of creativity—attitudes, abilities, and creative-thinking techniques—contribute to our understanding of creativity, and the strategies for training each possess some proven merit for fostering creative potential. Creative attitudes, mainly a prerequisite to creative behavior, may be altered in a more flexible, imaginative direction. Innate creative abilities, likewise, may be strengthened through exercise. Finally, relying less on "intuitive" creativity, instructors may teach techniques for producing new combinations of ideas.

Although these strategies have been employed in many existing college and industrial level creative-thinking courses (Edwards, 1968), an integrated attempt to incorporate them into a coherent and interesting program has been lacking. Such an effort, however, aimed at developing creative potential in adolescents, is presented below.

A working classroom strategy
for training creative thinking in adolescents

Thinking Creatively: A Guide to Training Imagination (Davis and Houtman, 1968) represents an effort to consolidate the various strategies for stimulating creativity in a meaningful, yet deliberately free and even humorous fashion. The program is in the form of dialogue among four characters. Mr. I is a backyard scientist-inventor who tries to teach the other three characters creative attitudes and various problem-solving techniques. He often engages in activities consistent with a permissive, creative atmosphere, such as regularly making a carrot sandwich, pumpkin cake, or some other surprising delight. Dudley Bond, a distant relative of a very famous secret spy, is an eager young male character. While a bit awkward at times, Dudley displays a fine sense of humor and often enjoys the fascination and challenge of finding ideas for solving problems. Maybelle is Dudley's friend who needs help in learning to find ideas. Last, but hardly least, is Max, a professional bear who, being the clown of the program, rarely understands anything very clearly. He often displays his uncreative mean streak and freely criticizes some of the "nutty" ideas, thus allowing the others frequent opportunity to repeat the important creative attitudes. Throughout the program, the four friends attack numerous simple and complex problems. Mr. I explains the creative problem-solving procedures and attitudes likely to aid in solving a given problem, and Dudley, Maybelle, and sometimes Max use the principles to produce specific problem solutions.

The program is based on several assumptions. First, supposing that most adolescents are largely unaware of or unconcerned with creative innovation, the importance of new ideas in all aspects of our fast-changing society is emphasized. Perhaps more directly relevant to students is the discovery that their capacity to produce new ideas will tremendously aid their own future occupations, whether they are in business, the arts, or professional sports.

The program assumes that appropriate attitudes are essential for creative productivity. Thus, by reading of the favorable problem-solving attitudes of the story characters, students learn to value unusual, new ideas in their own problem solving and to be receptive to those of others. They are taught an attitude of "constructive discontent"—the notion that virtually anything can be changed for the better. The story characters, for example, demonstrate this principle by finding improvements for a dull pocketknife, a wad of paper, a lost key, and a broken pencil, all of which Dudley happened to find in his pockets. Above all, adolescents learn that they themselves are capable of becoming more creative individuals. After having Mr. I continually remind them that they can become better "idea finders," students do exercises which allow them to see their developing creative capabilities.

A further assumption is that students' creative potential would be greatly enhanced if they understood creative-thinking procedures used by others to produce new combinations of ideas. Therefore, Mr. I, the scientist-inventor, teaches the other three characters a repertoire of techniques which closely parallel those described above. With the *part-changing* method, another name for the *attribute-listing* procedure, students learn to identify and improve the main parts or qualities of objects. With the *checkerboard* or *morphological-synthesis* method, they list specific ideas for changing one part along one axis of a two-dimensional diagram, list specific ideas for another part along the other axis, and then examine all possible idea combinations for potentially valuable problem solutions. Using the *checklist* procedure, students find they can be more efficient in producing a large number of potentially good ideas. The *synectic* methods are the source of some idea-finding techniques which focus on the use of analogies. Students learn to find problem solutions by studying how other people, animals, insects, and plants have solved similar problems, by "playing with" or free-associating word meanings, and by looking for perfect or ideal problem solutions—such as having the problem solve itself.

As a final main assumption, the training program recognizes that strong pressures exist which inhibit a free flow of ideas that might be judged nonconforming or perhaps "silly." However, judging from transcripts of comical and enjoyable brainstorming and synectic group sessions, there is reason to assume that a good sense of humor is very important for an uninhibited imagination. Therefore, to create an atmosphere conducive to relaxed spontaneity, in which the wildest ideas may be freely suggested, the program deliberately uses *humor*. The story characters readily propose "funny" problem solutions and, at the same time, engage in slapstick comedy.

Of course, there may be unforeseen difficulties with the present interpretation of creativity and its training. It would be unfortunate, for example, if the "intuitive" creativity of able students were adversely affected by teaching specific idea-generating techniques. Also, the humor in the program conceivably may not function as intended; for example, the students may be excessively entertained and thus distracted from the "serious" program content. Validation studies currently underway will answer these and other questions and therefore provide a suitable basis for modification.

Despite these possible shortcomings, the program may be used effectively. One major asset is its versatility. It might serve as a primary text for a creative-thinking course or as material for an independent-study project in creativity, thereby becoming a new subject area in the school curricula. Alternatively, it may be incorporated into any of several traditional subject-matter areas, especially those clearly dealing with new ideas. Any writing, art, or industrial arts class requires ideas for its literary, artistic, or commercial products, while science and history courses frequently focus on innovation in society.

Since it is largely self-explanatory, students and teachers may read the program together or students may study it at home without assistance. In either setting, they may work on problems presented at the end of most chapters. These simultaneously provide practice with the creative-thinking techniques and exercise in some important creative abilities.

Students in a wide range of ages, socioeconomic levels, and abilities may benefit from the program. Younger, lower economic level, and less able students seem to enjoy particularly the "unacademic" humor; older, higher economic level, and more capable students may like having their abilities challenged and substantiated. For all students, the concepts, exercises, reading level, drawings, and humor are intended to be meaningful and interesting.

In sum, *Thinking Creatively: A Guide to Training Imagination* represents a new effort to combine the main components of the various strategies for stimulating creativity into a package which is both interesting and informative for adolescents. It attempts to increase students' awareness of and appreciation for novel ideas, to teach techniques for producing new idea combinations, to provide exercise for some creative abilities, and, through humor, to create a free atmosphere encouraging spontaneity and imagination.*

* *Author's Note*—Since this article was prepared, a pilot test with upper–middle-class seventh-grade students showed that 23 subjects using the program produced 65 percent more ideas on three divergent thinking tasks (ideas which were rated as significantly more "creative") than 32 control subjects. An attitude survey indicated that the experimental students were significantly more confident of their creative ability, more appreciative of unusual ideas, and more aware of the importance of creative innovation in society. A field test with 197 average and disadvantaged sixth- and eighth-grade students showed less striking, but still measurable, improvement in divergent thinking scores and in creative attitudes as a result of training with the program.

REFERENCES

Allen, M. A. *Psycho-dynamic synthesis.* West Nyack, N.Y.: Parker, 1966.

Barron, F. The psychology of imagination. *Scientific American,* 1958, 199, 151–166.

Covington, M. V., Crutchfield, R. S., & Davies, L. B. *The productive thinking program.* Berkeley: Brazelton Printing Co., 1966.

Crawford, R. P. *The techniques of creative thinking.* New York: Hawthorn, 1954.

Davis, G. A., Manske, M. E., & Train, A. J. Training creative thinking. Occasional Paper No. 6, Wisconsin Research and Development Center for Cognitive Learning, University of Wisconsin, 1967.

Davis, G. A., & Houtman, S. E. *Thinking creatively: A guide to training imagination.* Wisconsin Research and Development Center for Cognitive Learning, University of Wisconsin, 1968.

Davis, G. A., Roweton, W. E., Train, A. J., Warren T. F., & Houtman, S. E. Laboratory studies of creative thinking techniques: The checklist and morphological synthesis methods. Technical Report No. 94, Wisconsin Research and Development Center for Cognitive Learning, University of Wisconsin, 1969.

Edwards, M. O. A survey of problem solving courses. *Journal of Creative Behavior,* 1968, 2, 33–51.

Getzels, J. W., & Jackson, P. W. *Creativity and intelligence.* New York: Wiley, 1962.

Gordon, W. J. J. *Synectics.* New York: Harper & Row, 1961.

Guilford, J. P. Creativity: Its measurement and development. In S. J. Parnes & H. F. Harding (Eds.), *A source book for creative thinking.* New York: Scribner, 1962. Pp. 151–168.

Hammer, E. F. *Creativity.* New York: Random House, 1961.

Klausmeier, H. J., & Goodwin, W. *Learning and human abilities.* New York: Harper & Row, 1966.

MacKinnon, D. W. The nature and nurture of creative talent. *American Psychologist,* 1962, 17, 484–495.

Myers, R. E., & Torrance, E. P. *Invitations to thinking and doing.* Boston: Ginn, 1964.

Myers, R. E., & Torrance, E. P. *Invitations to speaking and writing creatively.* Boston: Ginn, 1965. (a)

Myers, R. E., & Torrance, E. P. *Can you imagine?* Boston: Ginn, 1965. (b)

Myers, R. E., & Torrance, E. P. *Plots, puzzles, and plays.* Boston: Ginn, 1966. (a)

Myers, R. E., & Torrance, E. P. *For those who wonder.* Boston: Ginn, 1966. (b)

Osborn, A. F. *Applied imagination* (3d ed.). New York: Scribner, 1963.

Parnes, S. J. *Workbook for creative problem solving institutes and courses.* Buffalo: Creative Education Foundation, 1966.

Prince, G. M. The operational mechanisms of synectics. *Journal of Creative Behavior,* 1968, 2, 1–13.

Thurstone, L. L. Primary mental abilities. *Psychometric Monographs,* 1938, No. 1.

Torrance, E. P. *Guiding creative talent.* Englewood Cliffs, N.J.: Prentice-Hall, 1962.

22 | Can creativity be increased?

SIDNEY J. PARNES
Creative Education Foundation

Reprinted and abridged with the permission of the author from two articles, "Can Creativity Be Increased?" and "The Creative Problem Solving Course and Institute at the University of Buffalo," both in S. J. Parnes and H. F. Harding (Eds.), A Source Book for Creative Thinking. *New York: Scribner, 1962. Pp. 185–191, 307–323. A current explanation of Parnes' program is provided in his excellent* Creative Behavior Guidebook *and* Creative Behavior Workbook (*Scribner, 1967*).

The prototype for many university and professional creative thinking courses is Parnes' course at the Buffalo State University College (originated in 1949 at the University of Buffalo, now the State University of New York at Buffalo). This selection, abridged from a fuller treatment in Parnes and Harding (1962, see credit), describes both the deferred-judgment based content of the course and the effects of the training upon student capabilities. As with students in similar programs, Parnes' students improved not only in their awareness of problems and their idea-finding potential, but they also became more receptive to the "wild" ideas of others and more confident of their own initiative and leadership potential—profoundly important benefits.

More and more educators have been debating the question of whether creative thinking can be effectively taught—whether imaginative ability in problem solving can be deliberately developed through instruction and practice. Scientific research has now helped to answer this question.

Before-and-after examination had previously indicated that courses in creative problem solving enabled students to improve their idea-production ability by about 75 percent on the average. But such findings were far from conclusive because rigid experimental methods had not been followed, and the means of measurement were far from scientific.

Scientific evidence

During the past four years, the Creative Education Foundation has underwritten an extensive scientific investigation at the University of Buffalo, under the direction of University psychologists and the author. The series of studies involved over 350 students.

This research was made possible by the fact that our university had available a large number of students taking the course which was to be evaluated.

Background of course

The first class in creative problem solving was inaugurated in our evening Millard Fillmore College 12 years ago, under the direction of Dean Robert F. Berner. The syllabus was based on the principles and procedures set forth in *Your Creative Power,* written by Alex F. Osborn and published by Scribner. Since then, over 1,200 day students and evening students have completed such courses. In addition, another 1,600 executives from business, government, and education have completed the condensed equivalent of the course at our university.

Description of course

In the creative-problem-solving course at the University of Buffalo students are taught the concepts in Alex F. Osborn's textbook, *Applied Imagination.* The text emphasizes the importance of imagination in all walks of life, the universality of imaginative talent, and the use of creativity in all stages of problem solving, from orientation to evaluation.

Perceptual, emotional, and cultural blocks to creative thinking are demonstrated and discussed in the course. Under perceptual blocks are covered such matters as the difficulty in isolating problems, difficulty from narrowing the problem too much, inability to define or isolate attributes, failure to use all the senses in observing. Under cultural and emotional blocks are emphasized the effects of: conformity; overemphasis on competition or cooperation; excessive faith in reason or logic; fear of mistakes, failure, or looking foolish; self-satisfaction; perfectionism; negative outlooks; reliance on authority.

Early in the course students are taught the deferred judgment principle (artificially separating creative from judicial thinking at various stages of problem solving) as applied both to individual ideation as well as to group ideation. The principle of deferred judgment allows the student more freedom for applying the other techniques that are stressed. In other words, students are taught to ideate first, judge afterwards. This forced separation of the creative and judicial functions is emphasized throughout the course.

Within the "free wheeling" atmosphere that the principle of deferred judgment provides, students are given practice in attribute listing (learning to look at problems from a variety of viewpoints). For example, in considering other uses for an object, such as a piece of paper, students are taught to look at each attribute of the paper, such as its whiteness, its four corners, its straight edges, etc. Each of these attributes then suggests a number of possible uses.

Checklist procedures are encouraged, such as Osborn's checklist of idea-spurring questions. In this procedure students are taught to analyze a problem from the standpoint of a number of questions, such as: How can we simplify? What combinations can be utilized? What adaptations can be made?

Forced relationship techniques are utilized in the course. For example, a list of ideas is produced as tentative solutions to a problem. Each of these ideas is then artificially related to each other idea on the list in order to force new combinations. Sometimes a somewhat ridiculous idea is taken as a starting point. By associating the idea with the actual problem a series of associations is produced which leads in some novel direction towards solving the problem. For example, an idea for selling more flowers by utilizing vending machines was rejected as a poor idea. However, by forced association of the thought of "vending machines" with the problem of "selling more flowers," a useful solution was reached as follows: approach companies who provide vending machines for employees, in order to persuade these companies to utilize the profits from the machines for purchasing flowers for employees on birthdays, anniversaries, etc.

Throughout the course the following matters are stressed: the importance of taking notes (keeping a record of ideas that come to one at all times, rather than just when one is working on a problem), setting deadlines and quotas for production of ideas, and setting aside certain times and places for deliberate idea production. Much opportunity is given in the course for deliberate practice in problem solving on a variety of problems, including many of those brought in from the personal lives of the students.

Students are taught to sense problems in their studies, work, and personal lives, and to properly define these problems for creative attack. The separation of creative and judicial functions is then practiced in all stages of solving these problems. For example, during the analysis step, students are taught to list every conceivable fact that would relate to the problem. After they have exhausted this "freewheeling" effort, they then apply judgment to culling the most important facts related to the problem. Students next create the longest possible list of questions and sources of additional data that could be of use in solving the problem. Then they go back to the judicial process of selecting the most important questions and sources of data. This procedure continues throughout the final stages of evaluation and presentation of ideas. In evaluation, for example, students are taught to develop the longest possible list of criteria by which to evaluate their tentative solutions. Then they apply judgment in terms of selecting the most useful criteria for this purpose. Thus the principle of deferred judgment is emphasized in both individual and group thinking in all the aspects of the course.

Informal procedures are utilized throughout the course. Chairs are arranged in a semicircle in order to encourage the greatest amount of group participation and discussion. Small groups are organized in many sessions in order to provide practice in team and group collaboration for production of ideas. Students are given opportunities to serve as leaders of these small groups on various aspects of their own problems, as well as in assigned practice problems.

Major findings

Analyses of the results of this phase of the research include these major findings:

1. The creative-problem-solving students showed substantial gains in quantity of ideas on two tests of idea quantity repeated at the end of the course. Students in the control group showed relatively insignificant gains on these tests at the end of the semester.

2. On three tests of idea quality, the creative-problem-solving students showed clear superiority over the students in the control group. On a fourth test in this area, the creative-problem-solving students showed improvement greater than that shown by the control students, but not sufficiently greater to be regarded as significant. The fifth measure of quality showed no superiority for the creative-problem-solving students.

3. Three tests were designed to measure personality traits designated by psychologists as "dominance," "self-control," and "need to achieve." The creative-problem-solving students gained substantially in dominance as a result of the course, but showed no significant changes in self-control or need to achieve. The dominance scale used is regarded by psychologists as measuring such characteristics as confidence, self-reliance, persuasiveness, initiative, and leadership potential (Gough, 1957). Other researchers previously had determined that dominance is a personality trait associated with creative persons.

It is significant that dominance was the single personality trait in which the creative-problem-solving students showed an increase. This is the particular trait which the course methods were designed explicitly to develop.

Most of the tests used to measure improvement in quantity and quality of ideas emphasized a practical type of creativity. Psychologists describe these tests as measuring the factors of originality, sensitivity to problems, spontaneous flexibility, and ideational fluency. It was on these tests that the students who took the course registered substantial gains.

Two of the tests emphasized a more literary type of creativity. Students were required to create clever story titles and original plots. On neither of these tests were the gains registered by the students who took the course large enough to indicate superiority over the control students. The test requiring clever story titles, however, showed the greater gain by the course students. A later experiment with this same test showed significant evidence of carry-over effects of the course to this more literary type of creativity.

Other findings

In general, the creative-problem-solving courses were found to be equally helpful to students of low and high initial creative ability, and equally helpful to those with low and high intelligence levels. This is in line with Dr. Guilford's conclusion that although heredity may place limitations on the skills involved in creativity, these skills can be extended within those limitations through education.

Older students (aged 23 to 51) in our evening classes, in general, gained as much from the course as did the younger students (aged 17 to 22) in our day classes. Likewise, males as compared with females demonstrated equivalent gains.

Persistence of improvement

There is also evidence from our research that when creativity has been developed by education it remains in its improved state. Matched experimental and control subjects were compared on six creative ability tests. Experimental subjects were ones who had completed the Creative Problem Solving course an average of 18 months before the experiment. Control subjects were students *registered,* but uninstructed, in the Creative Problem Solving course. None of the students had ever before taken the creative thinking tests.

Results indicated that the course alumni outperformed two separate groups of control subjects on all six measures, which included two quantity and four quality tests. All differences proved to be statistically significant in the comparisons with one control group; all but two were significant with the second control group.

A popular misconception exists that the deferred judgment principle can be utilized only in group ideation. The fallacy of this impression is demonstrated by the fact that all measurements in the current scientific investigations at the University of Buffalo were made on the basis of individual thinking, not on group collaboration.

Quantity breeds quality

Valuable use is being made of part of the countless data which are available as a result of the electronic machine processing of the information obtained in the first research projects. For example, further analyses have been made to discover proportions of *good* ideas in the first half of a subject's total idea output versus the last half. Findings of one study have demonstrated 78 percent *more* good ideas among the last half than among the first. Qualitative scoring was again based on uniqueness and usefulness. A subsequent experiment indicated a trend towards *increasingly* greater proportions of good ideas as a subject's total quantity increased. The results of both experiments were found to be statistically significant.

The above findings support Osborn's theory that in idea production, quantity leads to quality. The results also seem to be in accordance with Gordon's (1956) explanation of "deferment" in the creative process. He describes deferment as "the capacity to discard the glittering immediate in favor of a shadowy but possibly richer future." The *noncreative* problem-solver gets an idea, sees it as a possible solution to his problem, and settles for it without further ado. The *creative* problem-solver is not satisfied with his first idea. Like the person who invests money to obtain greater rewards later, the creative person forgoes the immediate reward of applying his first idea, in expectation of a better solution (greater reward) ultimately. A further hypothesis suggested by Osborn's and Gordon's theories is that the *best* idea will come late in the total production period. The author is currently preparing experiments to test this particular hypothesis.

Conclusion

The study of creativity is far too immature to make certain exactly what happens in a person who studies and practices the principles of creative thinking. We feel it is a combination of attitude and ability developments. But recent research does seem to warrant the postulate that the gap between an individual's innate creative talent and his lesser actual creative output can be narrowed by deliberate education in creative thinking.

It is true that the accuracy of our measuring sticks is subject to further improvement. Valid tests of creative ability, such as used in the evaluation of our courses, are only recent in their development. But the evidence of the current research does point to a definite contradiction of the age-old notion that creativity cannot be developed.

At a time of mounting national concern over the high degree of creativity so essential in the fields of science and technology—and hardly less essential in government, business, and other areas—education in creative thinking may do much to unlock the door to a vast treasure-house of latent ability.

REFERENCES

Gordon, W. J. J. Operational approach to creativity. *Harvard Business Review,* 1956, 34(6), 41–51.

Gough, H. G. Manual for the California Psychological Inventory. Palo Alto, Calif.: Consulting Psychologists Press, 1957.

23 Examples and rationales of test tasks for assessing creative abilities[1]

E. PAUL TORRANCE
University of Georgia

Reprinted with permission of the author and publisher from the article of the same title, Journal of Creative Behavior, *1968, 2, 165–178.*

Researchers, teachers, and perhaps others in education or business often are faced with the very difficult task of measuring creativity. Among professionals, such criteria as the number of art or poetry awards, published pages of poetry, number of patent applications or scientific articles, or even creativity ratings by colleagues, seem intuitively valid indicators of creative ability. Unfortunately, such ideal measures are rarely available for the teacher or researcher who, in perhaps minutes, must estimate an individual's capacity for creative performance. To meet this need, E. Paul Torrance has developed several test batteries, of which the *Torrance Tests of Creative Thinking* are probably the best known and most carefully researched, that may be used with preschool to adult aged groups. In this article, Torrance describes the types of items comprising his various tests, explaining the particular abilities these items try to measure. Additionally, Torrance mentions briefly some nontest indicators of creativity, such as checklists of creative achievements, biographical inventories, and motivation inventories.

The constellation

The term "creative thinking abilities," as I use it, refers to that constellation of generalized mental abilities that is commonly presumed to be brought into play in creative achievements. Many educators and psychologists would prefer to call these abilities "divergent thinking," "productive thinking," or "imagination." Some scholars prefer to use the term "crea-

[1] This article is a revision of a paper originally prepared for the International Workshop on Possibilities and Limitations of Educational Testing, Pädagogisches Zentrum, Berlin, Germany, May 16–24, 1967.

tive" only to refer to a rare, particularized, and substantive capacity; others object to the use of "creative" on the grounds that "a generalized constellation of intellectual abilities, personality variables, and problem-solving traits" does not constitute the essence of creativity. However, a high degree of the abilities measured by the test tasks I shall describe increases the chances that the possessor will behave creatively. And certainly I would never argue that possession of these abilities guarantees that an individual will behave creatively, any more than a high degree of measured intelligence guarantees intelligent behavior.

Burnham's theory

There is considerable historical precedent for thinking of general creative abilities. Burnham, in 1892, pointed out that it had become customary to distinguish between reproductive imagination and creative, productive imagination, that the mental abilities involved in remembering and reproducing information are different from those brought into play in recombining original impressions to produce new wholes. He saw creative imagination as limited by reproductive imagination but as varying in degree rather than in kind; and, according to him, it was the reproductive imagination or memory that is particularized. Burnham also maintained that "all children, unless they be idiots, have productive, creative imagination in some measure."

Spearman's concept

Scientific investigators during the early part of the twentieth century generally championed the concept of a general, nonparticularized, content-free mental creativity. Spearman (1930) asserted that "the power of the human mind to create new content—by transferring relations and thereby generating new correlates—extends its sphere not only to representation of ideas, but also to fully sensuous presentations, such as are given in ordinary seeing, hearing, touching, and the like of every one of us."

Simpson's definition

In the rationale for his test of creative imagination, Simpson (1922) defined creative ability as the initiative that one manifests by his power to break away from the usual sequence of thought. Concerned with identification of the searching, combining, synthetic type of mind, he argued that tests of creative thinking ability should be added to traditional tests of intelligence, which, he maintained, call for reproductive kinds of abilities and do not evaluate "a vital creative energy."

By labeling such abilities as sensitivity to deficiencies, fluency, flexibility, originality, elaboration, and redefinition as "creative," I have run the risk of being accused of equating creativity with all thinking. Yet, since thinking is a complex mental process, it does not seem at all strange to me that these abilities might at some time enter to some degree into any type of thinking. On the other hand, these abilities are more predominant or critical in creative thinking than in other types of problem solving.

Developing tests

Over a period of about ten years, my associates and I (Torrance, 1965a; Torrance, 1965b) have been developing several batteries of test tasks for use in all cultures and from kindergarten through graduate school. We have tried deliberately to construct items that are models of the creative thinking process, each involving different kinds of thinking and each contributing something unique to the batteries under development. These tests represent a fairly sharp departure from the factor type tests developed by Guilford and his associates (Guilford, Merrifield, and Cox, 1961; Merrifield, Guilford, and Gershon, 1963); and they differ, too, from the battery developed by Wallach and Kogan (1965), which contains measures representing creative tendencies that are similar in nature. I have tried, however, to retain in the test instructions and format some of the invitation to play or regress cultivated by Wallach and Kogan.

These batteries, or test items from them, have been used in over three hundred investigations by graduate students and mature investigators. (Both individual and group methods of administration have been used.) Examples given in this article are largely limited to items from a "Demonstrator Form," developed to communicate the nature of the published tests (available in two alternate batteries) without compromising or invalidating them.

Ask-and-guess

One of the clearest and most straightforward models of the creative thinking process is found in the Ask-and-Guess Test, of which there are several different forms. In all forms, subjects are shown a picture and given the following series of instructions:

Asking questions

The next three tasks will give you a chance to see how good you are at asking questions to find out things that you do not know and in making guesses about possible causes and consequences of events. Look at the picture. What is happening? What can you tell for sure? What do you need to know to understand what is happening, what caused it to happen, and what will be the result?

Young children are asked to dictate their responses to an adult, and older children and adults are asked to write theirs. In the written version, the following instructions are given for the first of the three tasks:

> On this page, write out all of the questions you can think of about the picture on the page before this one. Ask all of the questions you would need to ask to know for sure what is happening. Do not ask questions that can be answered just by looking at the drawing.

The reader who would like to test himself can get a sheet of paper and respond to the foregoing instructions with the stimulus picture, Figure 1. The time limit for the regular test is five minutes but for this demonstrator form it is three minutes. At the end of this article there is a list of the *common* responses carrying a score of zero.

Guessing causes

After five minutes, subjects are given the following instructions for the second task (Guessing Causes):

> In the spaces below, list as many possible causes as you can of the action shown in the picture. You may use things that might have happened just before the event in the picture or something that happened a long time ago and made the event happen. Make as many guesses as you can. Do not be afraid to guess.

Guessing consequences

After another five minutes, the following instructions are given for the third task (Guessing Consequences):

> In the spaces below, list as many possibilities as you can of what might happen as a result of what is taking place in the picture. You may use things that might happen right afterwards or things that might happen as a result long afterwards in the future. Make as many guesses as you can. Do not be afraid to guess.

The first task is designed to reveal the subject's ability to sense what he cannot find out from looking at the picture and to ask questions that will enable him to fill in the gaps in his knowledge. The second and third tasks are designed to reveal the subject's ability to formulate hypotheses concerning cause and effect. The number of relevant responses produced

Figure 1.

by a subject yields one measure of ideational fluency. The number of shifts in thinking or number of different categories of questions, causes, or consequences gives one measure of flexibility. The statistical infrequency of these questions, causes, or consequences or the extent to which the response represents a mental leap or departure from the obvious and commonplace gives one measure of originality. The detail and specificity incorporated into the questions and hypotheses provide one measure of ability to elaborate.

In another task, subjects are asked to produce unusual or provocative questions about common objects such as ice, grass, apples, or mountains. Subjects are encouraged to ask questions that lead to a variety of different answers and that might arouse interest and curiosity in others concerning the object.

Product improvement task

The Product Improvement Task calls for the production of clever, interesting and unusual ways of changing a toy stuffed animal (for example, a toy dog like the one in Figure 2) so that it will be more interesting and more fun for children to play with. If you would like to test yourself and see what kind of thinking is involved, try to think of ways of improving the stuffed toy dog. Limit yourself to two and one-half minutes. (In the actual test, ten minutes is allowed for this task.)

You will find a list of the commonplace or zero originality responses listed at the end of this article.

Unusual uses task

The Unusual Uses Task calls for interesting and unusual uses of common objects such as junk autos. To understand the kind of thinking that is involved, the reader might spend two and one-half minutes trying to see

Figure 2.

how many unusual uses of junk autos he can produce. At the end of the article is a list of the common, unoriginal responses that are scored zero for originality.

"Just suppose"

The Just Suppose task presents the subject with an improbable situation and asks him to think of all of the things that might occur if that improbability really happened. In other words, the subject must "pretend" that it has happened in order to think of its possible consequences. For example, "Just suppose it was raining and all the drops stood still in the air and wouldn't move—and they were solid." Each "Just Suppose" is accompanied by an interesting drawing depicting the improbable situation. The reader might try this one, also, limiting himself to two and one-half minutes. Again, some common, unoriginal responses are listed at the end of this article.

Imaginative stories

The Imaginative Stories Test calls for writing imaginative stories about animals and people having some divergent characteristic. Subjects are asked to select one from a set of ten titles such as:

The Flying Monkey
The Lion That Won't Roar
The Man Who Cries
The Woman Who Can But Won't Talk

Sounds and images

The Sounds and Images Test asks the subject to produce imaginative and original images suggested by each of a series of four sound effects, ranging from a familiar and well-organized sound effect to one consisting of six rather strange and relatively unrelated sounds. The four-sound series is presented three times, and each time the subject is asked to stretch his imagination further.

Mother Goose

My newest preschool battery consists of five problems based on the world-famous Mother Goose rhymes. The four- and five-year-old children are supplied with booklets containing drawings of the five situations and encouraged to color them while they discuss the problems with the examiner. The children's booklets are used only to make the children psychologically comfortable and are retained by them. An examiner's booklet contains a set of standardized encouraging questions to be used to help the child stretch his thinking. The following is an example of a problem the reader might experiment with, using a time limit of two and one-half minutes:

> If Boy Blue lost his horn, what are all of the ways that he might use to get the cows out of the corn?

Each of the tasks is based on a rationale developed from some research finding concerning the nature of the creative process, the creative personality, or the conditions necessary for creative achievement. The tasks are designed to involve as many different aspects of verbal creative functioning as possible. Most of the tasks are evaluated for fluency (number of different relevant ideas), flexibility (number of shifts in thinking or different categories of response), originality (number of statistically infrequent responses that show creative intellectual energy), and elaboration (number of different ideas used in working out the details of an idea). These are not factorially pure measures and there is some overlap among them, but it has been found that each makes a useful contribution to an understanding of a child's thinking.

Figural battery

Although a variety of figural test tasks have been developed, the standardized batteries consist of three tasks, each designed to tap a somewhat different aspect of creative functioning.

Picture construction

The Picture Construction Test is accompanied by the following instructions:

> At the bottom of this page is a piece of colored paper in the form of a curved shape. Think of a picture of an object in which this form would be an important part. Then lift up the piece of colored paper and stick it wherever you want it on the next page, just like you would a postage stamp. Then add lines with pencil or crayon to make your picture.
>
> Try to think of a picture that no one else will think of. Keep adding new ideas to your first idea to make it tell as interesting and as exciting a story as you can.
>
> When you have completed your picture, think up a name or title for it and write it at the bottom of the page in the space provided. Make your title as clever and unusual as possible. Use it to help tell your story.

This, as well as the other two figural tasks, can be administered at all educational levels from kindergarten to graduate school and to various occupational groups. It is a task to which kindergartners can respond in groups and one which provides sufficient encouragement to regression to be useful with graduate students and other adults. In each battery a different shape (such as a tear drop or jelly bean) is used as the stimulus object.

Figure completion

The stimulus material for the Figure Completion Test consists of ten incomplete figures and is accompanied by the following instructions:

> By adding lines to figures on this and the next page, you can sketch some interesting objects or pictures. Again, try to think of some picture or object that no one else will think of. Try to make it tell as complete and as interesting a story as you can by adding to and building up your first idea. Make up a title for each of your drawings and write it at the bottom of each block next to the number of the figure.

The reader might test himself with the two figures shown in Figure 3 and then turn to the end of the article to see if he is able to get away from the common, obvious, unoriginal ideas.

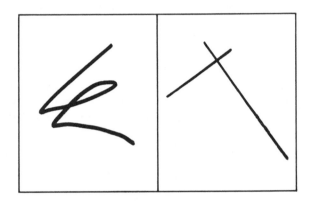

Figure 3.

Repeated closed figures

The Repeated Closed Figures Test consists of two or three pages of closed figures such as triangles. The instructions for this version of the test are as follows:

> In ten minutes see how many objects or pictures you can make from the triangles. . . . The triangles should be the main part of whatever you make. With pencil or crayon add lines to the triangles to complete your picture. You can place marks inside them, on them, and outside them—whatever you want to do in order to make your picture. Try to think of things that no one else will think of. Make as many different pictures or objects as you can and put as many ideas as you can in each one. Make them tell as complete and as interesting a story as you can.

As with the other two figural tests, ten minutes is allowed for this task, but in the demonstrator version only two and one-half minutes is given. The common, unoriginal responses are listed at the end of this article.

What the tests do

This triad of test tasks (Picture Completion, Figure Completion, Repeated Closed Figures) in a sense represents three different creative tendencies. The Figure Completion task calls into play the tendency toward structuring and integrating. The incomplete figures create tension in the beholder, who must control this tension long enough to make the mental leap necessary to get away from the obvious and commonplace. Failure to delay gratification usually results in the premature closure of the incomplete figures and an obvious or commonplace response. The invitation to "make the drawing tell a story" is designed to motivate elaboration and the further filling in of gaps. The Triangles Test, as well as other closed figures tasks, brings into play the tendency toward disruption of structure in order to create something new. The repetition of a single stimulus requires an ability to return to the same stimulus again and again and perceive it in a different way. The Picture Construction Test sets in motion the tendency toward finding a purpose for something that has no definite purpose and to elaborate it in such a way that the purpose is achieved.

Discoveries and their applications may take place in two major ways: (1) there may be deliberate attempts to discover a creative solution to a problem or (2) some discovery may occur and the discoverer sets out to see what problems the discovery will solve. Theoretically, the Picture Construction Test symbolizes the latter.

These tasks tend to discriminate between the good elaborators and the productive original thinkers. Some subjects produce a large number of very original ideas but fail to elaborate any of them very well; some produce very few ideas of any kind but make them very elaborate or "fancy"; still others produce a large number of very commonplace ideas with little elaboration.

General findings

With children

Thus, an attempt has been made deliberately to base the test stimuli, the test tasks, instructions, and scoring procedures on the best that we know from research about creativity. The same test tasks, in most instances, have been administered at all educational levels. This has made it possible to determine whether or not children and young people identified as "creative" behave in ways similar to those in which eminent creative people of the past behaved when they were children and young people. It also enables us to determine whether or not adults identified today as relatively creative on the basis of outside criteria behave in ways that can be called "creative" on the basis of test scores. In general, the evidence has been quite positive in spite of the complexities introduced by problems of motivation, unfavorable conditions, and the difficulties of conducting well-controlled studies.

In observational studies we found that children scoring high on tests of creative thinking initiated a larger number of ideas, produced more original ideas, and gave more explanations of the workings of unfamiliar science toys than did their less creative peers. When matched for intelligence, sex, race, and teacher, the most creative children in forty-six classrooms from grades one through six more frequently than their controls had reputations for having wild and fantastic ideas, produced drawings and other products judged to be original, and produced work characterized by humor, playfulness, relative lack of rigidity, and relaxation.

Weisberg and Springer (1961) studied a sample of gifted (high IQ) fourth-grade pupils. In comparison with those who made the lower test scores, those who made the higher scores were rated significantly higher on strength of self-image, ease of early recall of life experience, humor, availability of Oedipal anxiety, and even ego development. On the Rorschach Ink Blots, they showed a tendency toward unconventional responses, unreal percepts, and fanciful and imaginative treatment of the blots. Their performance was described as being both more sensitive and more independent than that of their less creative peers.

Among sixth-grade children, Fleming and Weintraub (1962) found significant negative relationships between the measures of originality, fluency, and flexibility and the measures of rigidity.

With adults

Encouraging evidences of concurrent validity for the Torrance tests of creative thinking have also been derived from studies with adults, using the same test tasks that are administered to children. The author in his own graduate classes has found rather consistently that those who achieve high scores on the tests of creative thinking develop original ideas in the content area of the course and make more creative applications of knowledge than do their less creative peers.

Torrance and Hansen (1965) found that the more creative business education teachers asked more provocative questions, more self-involving questions, and more divergent ones than did their less creative peers. Hansen found a number of other significant differences between her high and low creative teachers, showing that the more creative teachers, as identified by the tests, behaved more creatively in the classroom as judged by detailed classroom observations.

Sommers (1961) found that students carefully identified by college industrial arts instructors as creative scored significantly higher on the tests of creative thinking than did their less creative peers.

Wallace (1964) found that saleswomen ranking in the upper third on sales in a large department store scored significantly higher on tests of creative thinking than did their peers ranking in the lower third. He also found that the more creative women had tended to gravitate to those departments judged by personnel managers as requiring more creativity. Wallace (1964) also found that measures of originality and fluency differentiated the several echelons of personnel in a large national sales organization. [For additional observations on sales personnel, see Chapter 11 by Cloyd Steinmetz.]

Nontest indicators

My associates and I have not limited our concern to the kind of ability measures that have been described thus far in this article. We have given considerable attention to checklists of creative activities that children in particular do on their own, checklists of creative achievements, biographical or life experience inventories, an inventory of personal-social motivations, and a variety of other nonaptitude measures. Even though test performances may make teachers and clinicians aware of potentialities that would otherwise be missed, they do not have to be dependent upon tests for identifying creative potential among children. Nontest indicators may be obtained both in regular classroom activities and by creating classroom situations especially designed to evoke creative behavior. Certainly there seems to be a great deal of evidence to support the belief that creative individuals—so valuable when well placed in life situations—are being overlooked and even undermined psychologically for lack of widespread use of whatever detection instruments, structured or unstructured, are available.

List of common, unoriginal responses to demonstrator form (zero credit for originality)

1. *Ask Questions*
   How can it run connected only to wooden drawers?
   Why is it plugged into chest/table?
   Why is the fan blowing?
   Why is it on the chest of drawers?
   Who is he (man)?
   Is he a teacher?
   Whom is he speaking/talking to?
   What is he pointing at?
   What is he talking about?
   Why is he pointing to the fan?
   What/what kind of machine is it?
   What are the levers/buttons, etc.?
   What do the lines represent?
   What is in the drawers?

2. *Product Improvement* (*Toy Dog*)
   Bark, make it
   Bell, add on neck, feet, etc.
   Bow, add
   Color, add or change
   Cuddly, make it
   Ears, bigger, longer
   Eyes, bigger, move, wink, sparkle, glow, etc.
   Face, give expression, personality
   Fluffy, more like real fur
   Fuzzy, make
   Larger, longer, taller, etc.; legs longer
   Mouth, bigger
   Movable parts at joints
   Music box inside
   Noise, have him make
   Nose, bigger
   Paws, add, make bigger, etc.
   Realistic, make
   Ribbon, add brighter color, bigger bow, etc.
   Smile, make
   Softer
   Tail, curl up, make longer
   Tongue, longer
3. *Unusual Uses* (*Junk Autos*)
   Art, abstract, modern sculpture, pop art
   Autos, make one from several
   Autos, play on playground
   Chairs
   Demolition derby
   Demonstration, warning for drivers
   Educational uses, rebuild to learn, give to teenagers to learn about cars
   Flower planter
   Playground, pretend cars
   Racing
   Repair to sell
   Scrap iron, metal, etc.
   Spare parts, see for use on other cars
   Swing, tires used for
   Tension reducer, smash with hammer
   Tires, recap and sell
   Toy on playground
4. *Just Suppose* (*Rain Still and Solid*)
   No water

No grass, no leaves on trees, no flowers, no plant life
People would be bumping into them
Earth would be parched
No fish to catch
Sunshiny, no clouds in sky
No travelling
Airplanes could not fly
Couldn't take a bath
No boating, swimming, etc.
No floods
No need for raincoats
Animals would die
No rivers, creeks, etc.

5. *Incomplete Figures*
Figure 3, left:
Abstract figure
Bird(s)
Human (man, woman, child)
Figure 3, right:
Abstract figure
Horse head or horse body
House
Kite

6. *Repeated Triangles*
Amorphous, indistinct figure
Cottage, house, etc.
Design
Human face
Human figure (man, woman, child)
Star (six-point)
Tent, tepee
Tree
Triangle

REFERENCES

Burnham, W. H. Individual differences in the imagination of children. *Pedagogical Seminars,* 1892, 2, 204–255.

Fleming, E. S., & Weintraub, S. Attitudinal rigidity as a measure of creativity in gifted children. *Journal of Educational Psychology,* 1962, 53, 81–85.

Guilford, J. P., Merrifield, P. R., & Cox, A. B. *Creative thinking in children at the junior high level.* Los Angeles: Psychological Laboratories, University of Southern California, 1961.

Merrifield, P. R., Guilford, J. P., & Gershon, A. The differentiation of divergent-production abilities at the sixth-grade level. Los Angeles: Psychological Laboratories, University of Southern California, 1963.

Simpson, R. M. Creative imagination. *American Journal of Psychology*, 1922, 33, 234–243.

Sommers, W. S. The influence of selected teaching methods on the development of creative thinking. Unpublished doctoral dissertation, University of Minnesota, 1961.

Spearman, C. E. *Creative mind*. New York: Cambridge, 1930.

Torrance, E. P. *Rewarding creative behavior*. Englewood Cliffs, N.J.: Prentice-Hall, 1965. (a)

Torrance, E. P. Different ways of learning for different children. In E. P. Torrance & R. D. Strom (Eds.), *Mental health and achievement*. New York: Wiley, 1965. Pp. 253–261. (b)

Torrance, E. P., & Hansen, E. The question-asking behavior of highly creative and less creative basic business teachers identified by a paper-and-pencil test. *Psychological Reports*, 1965, 17, 815–818.

Wallace, H. R. Creative thinking: A factor in the performance of industrial salesmen. Unpublished doctoral dissertation, University of Minnesota, 1964.

Wallach, M. A., & Kogan, N. *Modes of thinking in young children*. New York: Holt, Rinehart and Winston, 1965.

Weisberg, P. S., & Springer, K. J. Environmental factors in creative function. *Archives of General Psychiatry*, 1961, 5, 554–564.

The reader interested in nontest measures of creativity might wish to consider some of the following:

Alpha Biographical Inventory, available from the Institute for Behavioral Research, Box 298, Greensboro, North Carolina. This questionnaire is composed of three hundred biographical items which attempt to predict creative scientific talent in high school students.

Childhood Attitude Inventory for Problem Solving, developed by Richard S. Crutchfield and Martin V. Covington, Department of Psychology, University of California, Berkeley, California. This survey is intended to detect attitudes towards one's own problem-solving ability, the possibility of improving problem-solving skills, appreciation for novel ideas, and other attitudes related to creative performance.

Similes Preference Inventory of Salvatore R. Maddi, Department of Psychology, University of Chicago. Fifty-four items focus on determining "tendency toward variety." (The inventory is reproduced in S. R. Maddi and P. A. Pearson. "The Similes Preference Inventory: Development of a Structured Measure of the Tendency toward Variety." *Journal of Consulting Psychology,* 1966, 30, 301–308.)

Thinking Interest Inventory, developed by Philip R. Merrifield, Department of Educational Psychology, New York University. The items are considered by the author to be measures of motivation or attitude, rather than thinking ability.

Index

A

Abilities, creative, 262–263
Abnormality, 211–212
Abstraction, 62
A.C. Sparkplug Division of General Motors, 83
Adolescents, creativity training for, 261–269

Aeronautical Systems Division (ASD), U.S. Air Force, 44
Age, creativity and, 32
Air Force Cambridge Research Center, 48
Air Reduction Inc., 13
Alcoa, 83
Alexander, Tom, 1–13
Alexander, William R., 5